T0052090

THE RISE

CREATIVITY, THE GIFT OF FAILURE,
AND THE SEARCH FOR MASTERY

SARAH LEWIS

Simon & Schuster Paperbacks

NEW YORK   LONDON   TORONTO   SYDNEY   NEW DELHI

For the prototype for principled, passionate pursuit,
Shadrach Emmanuel Lee, my parents, and the three graces

Simon & Schuster Paperbacks
A Division of Simon & Schuster, Inc.
1230 Avenue of the Americas
New York, NY 10020

Copyright © 2014 by Sarah Lewis

Gail Mazur, "Michelangelo: To Giovanni da Pistoia When the
Author Was Painting the Vault of the Sistine Chapel," in *Zeppo's First Wife:
New and Selected Poems*, p. 116-17. © 2005 by The University
of Chicago. All rights reserved.

Tracy K. Smith, "Us & Co." from *Life on Mars*. Copyright © 2011
by Tracy K. Smith. Reprinted with the permission of The Permissions
Company, Inc., on behalf of Graywolf Press, www.graywolfpress.org.

All rights reserved, including the right to reproduce this book
or portions thereof in any form whatsoever. For information address
Simon & Schuster Paperbacks Subsidiary Rights Department,
1230 Avenue of the Americas, New York, NY 10020

First Simon & Schuster trade paperback edition March 2015

SIMON & SCHUSTER PAPERBACKS and colophon are registered trademarks
of Simon & Schuster, Inc.

For information about special discounts for bulk purchases, please contact
Simon & Schuster Special Sales at 1-866-506-1949
or business@simonandschuster.com.

The Simon & Schuster Speakers Bureau can bring authors to your
live event. For more information or to book an event contact the
Simon & Schuster Speakers Bureau at 1-866-248-3049
or visit our website at www.simonspeakers.com.

Manufactured in the United States of America

10

The Library of Congress has cataloged the hardcover edition as follows:
Lewis, Sarah.
The rise : creativity, the gift of failure, and the search for mastery / Sarah Lewis.—
p. cm
1. Creative ability. 2. Failure (Psychology) 3. Expertise. I. Title
BF408.L625 2014
153.3'—dc23

ISBN 978-1-4516-2923-1
ISBN 978-1-4516-2924-8 (pbk)
ISBN 978-1-4516-2925-5(ebook)

Praise for *The Rise*

"Lewis's voice is so lyrical and engaging that her book, *The Rise*, can be read in one sitting, which is so much the better since its argument is multilayered and needs to be taken whole."

—*The New York Times*

"*The Rise* points us toward the dazzling afterlife of the dead end, shining light on numerous other counterintuitive paths to mastery. It delineates the impetus that can be prized from failure, the genius lurking in amateurism, the scientific insights hidden within artistic process. Sarah Lewis meditates on the ways we can will ourselves across the chasms of self-doubt that separate us from astonishing innovation and insight."

—Andrew Solomon, author of *Far from the Tree*

"Success and failure are often seen as polar opposites, one the peak and the other the abyss. In *The Rise*, Sarah Lewis reexamines our views of both and offers news paths and paradigms. Like Malcolm Gladwell, she brilliantly takes complex ideas and makes them easy to follow, making it possible for us to see the world in a brand new way."

—Edwidge Danticat, author of *Create Dangerously*

"Without a whiff of self-help preachiness, *The Rise* will make you reconsider your own foibles and flops, if only by showing how minor they are compared with the epic setbacks she details. From Martin Luther King Jr.'s struggle to overcome a distracting verbal tic to the phenomenon of elite women archers who go from regularly nailing the bull's-eye to suddenly not even making the target, the book gives the old chestnut 'If at first you don't succeeed . . .' a jolt of adrenaline."

—*Elle*

"Sarah Lewis has assembled a rich trove of reflections not just on creativity but on the too-often ignored role that failure and surrender play in almost any ambitious undertaking. That counterintuitive point of attack makes *The Rise* a welcome departure from standard accounts of artistry and innovation."

—Lewis Hyde, author of *The Gift*

"*The Rise* is a tour de force—uplifting, smart, and important."

—Ellen Langer, professor of psychology, Harvard University, author of *Counterclockwise*

"In this scholarly yet accessible text, art curator and cultural critic Lewis seeks to redefine the place of failure in the creative process. Beginning with the metaphor of the archer's arrow that cannot travel in a direct line but must rise and fall before it hits its target, Lewis deftly weaves together theories on failure from hundreds of sources."

—*Booklist*

"A work of rare insight and sensitivity, brilliantly researched and beautifully written, *The Rise* shows you how to stay open and be fearless. Sarah Lewis takes you to unexpected places, to spheres that just may become fabulous. There is no other book like it in the world."

—Nell Painter, Edwards Professor of American History at Princeton University

"*The Rise* marks the arrival of Sarah Lewis. With wit, heart, and remarkable research, Lewis elegantly demonstrates why excruciating, even humiliating failure is essential for success and mastery. *The Rise* is rich with lessons for all of us."

—Darren Walker, president of the Ford Foundation

"A well-written book that examines creativity, failure, and success. Recommended for anyone who wants to comprehend the value of innovation and discovery, as well as undergraduate and graduate students, scholars, and researchers of psychology, sociology, and the visual and performing arts."

—*Library Journal*

"Creativity is not a process, as so many books would like us to believe. It is a human condition waiting to be unearthed, as Sarah Lewis so beautifully shows us through her sharing of connected stories and personal insights in *The Rise*."

—Ivy Ross, CMO of Art.com

"Sarah Lewis is one the most talented writers and curators of her generation. *The Rise* should be read not just by every artist, but by every person hoping to unearth his or her own capacity for discovery and creativity. She provides an important and positive voice for the arts in a turbulent time."

—Agnes Gund, president emerita, The Museum of Modern Art

"Creativity, like genius, is inexplicable, but Lewis' synthesis of history, biography and psychological research offers a thoughtful response to the question of how new ideas happen."

—*Kirkus Reviews*

"I was raised to be terrified of making mistakes, as though there was a smooth way forward without them. There is no other way forward; either you stumble through error, failure, risk and uncertainty on the available paths or you're stuck. Sarah Lewis's *The Rise* makes a beautiful case both for the necessity of risk and failure and experimentation, and for how the road to success is paved with such things, and along the way she tells us about arctic exploration, a future Supreme Court lawyer's captivation with Louis Armstrong's music, something surprising about Hollywood, Frederick Douglass's emphasis on beauty, and a host of other captivating stories to prove her points.

'My life is full of mistakes. They're like pebbles that make a good road,' said the great ceramicist Beatrice Wood; this is a map of such roads and a collection of the most beautiful of those stones."

—Rebecca Solnit, author of *The Faraway Nearby*

"Independence from everything other than life itself is what makes any writer significant to the serious reader. Sarah Lewis is sensitive to deep meanings that are not common but always, due to her vibrant prose, seem exquisitely natural. Too much about her independence from the expected cannot be said."

—Stanley Crouch, author of *Kansas City Lightning*

"Lewis's erudition in art and history is matched by her sympathy to the iterative failures of great art, making inspiring readers for those in the process of creation."

—*Publishers Weekly*

"Lewis, driven by her lifelong 'magpie curiosity about how we become,' crafts her argument slowly, meticulously, stepping away from it like a sculptor gaining perspective on her sculpture and examining it through other eyes, other experiences, other particularities, which she weaves together into an intricate tapestry of "magpielike borrowings" filtered through the sieve of her own point of view. *The Rise* is a dimensional read in its entirety—highly recommended."

—Maria Popova, *Brain Pickings*

"[I]t is refreshing to encounter Sarah Lewis's unabashed reflections on the origins of personal achievement [. . .] Not a self-help manual in any conventional sense, *The Rise* probes strategies that have inspired artistry and innovation."

—*The Wall Street Journal*

We never know how high we are
Till we are called to rise . . .

—EMILY DICKINSON

My barn having burned down
I can now see the moon.

—MIZUTA MASAHIDE

Men are greedy to publish the success of [their] efforts, but meanly shy as to publishing the failures of men. Men are ruined by this one sided practice of concealment of blunders and failures.

—ABRAHAM LINCOLN[1]

. . . We may encounter many defeats, but we must not be defeated. That sounds goody two-shoes, I know, but I believe that a diamond is the result of extreme pressure and time. Less time is crystal. Less than that is coal. Less than that is fossilized leaves. Less than that it's just plain dirt. In all my work, in the movies I write, the lyrics, the poetry, the prose, the essays, I am saying that we may encounter many defeats—maybe it's imperative that we encounter the defeats—but we are much stronger than we appear to be and maybe much better than we allow ourselves to be.

—MAYA ANGELOU

CONTENTS

LIST OF ILLUSTRATIONS

145 *Levitating Frog.* © High Field Magnet Laboratory, Radboud University Nijmegen.

177 Samuel F. B. Morse, First Telegraph Instrument, 1837. Division of Work and Industry, National Museum of American History, Smithsonian Institution.

178 Samuel F. B. Morse, *Gallery of the Louvre*, 1831-33. Oil on canvas, 73¾ x 108 in. Daniel J. Terra Collection, 1992.51. Terra Foundation for American Art, Chicago / Art Resource, NY.

188 John Baldessari, *Solving Each Problem As It Arises*, 1966–68. Acrylic on canvas 172.1 x 143.5 cm (67¾ x 56½ in.). Yale University Art Gallery. Janet and Simeon Braguin Fund, 2001.3.1

191 Samuel F. B. Morse, *The House of Representatives*, 1822-1823. Oil on canvas. 86 ⅞ x 130 ⅝ in. Corcoran Gallery of Art, Washington D.C. Museum purchase, Gallery Fund.

THE RIDDLE

ARCHER'S PARADOX

The women of the Columbia University archery team stepped out of their van on a cold spring afternoon with a relaxed focus; one held a half-eaten ice cream cone in her right hand and a fistful of arrows with yellow fletching in her left; another sported a mesh guard over her shirt, on top of her breast as protection from the tension line of the bow. Baker Athletics Complex, the university's sporting fields at the northern tip of Manhattan, seemed to have a set of carefree warriors on its grounds.

A man who maintains the property never thought they would arrive. Maybe he was new, because I asked where the archery team would practice and he looked at me quizzically. He didn't believe that archery was a real Columbia team sport. It was understandable. I had arrived early and the targets were not yet up. Releasing arrows at up to 150 miles per hour aimed at targets seventy-five yards away means safety issues for all around, so the archery team doesn't practice next to any other. Mastery of this high-precision sport stays largely out of sight.

Coach Derek Davis drove up with the archers and greeted me with his elbow leaning against the gray van's driver's side window. His silvery-white dreadlocks hung past his shoulders, covered under a blue patterned bandana that matched his Columbia University archery sweatshirt. He struck me as a composite fit to match this clan: gregarious and at ease, yet focused. On the phone a few days earlier, he had told me that he first picked up the sport as a casual hobby at his wife's insistence in the late 1980s ("It was safer than pool and didn't involve alcohol"). He has led the varsity and intramural club teams since 2005 as one-part biomechanical expert, one-part yogi—a university sage fit for ancient warfare turned sport.

The young women smiled and sized me up a little, then passed as I stood beside the chain-link fence entrance to their designated turf. One threw away her melting cone and joined the others who were unpacking the gear from the van's trunk. They spoke not with words, but by exchanging numbers, their ideal scores or degrees to position themselves to hit their targets.

The women were preparing for an upcoming Nationals competition.[1] (There are no men on this varsity team, only at the intramural level of play.) I watched as they carefully set down their compound and recurve bows—like those used at the Olympics, with tips that bend away from the archer—then drew and let loose arrows that curved and fell out of sight as they hit the round target face. Davis didn't hover, but stood a good distance behind them, perhaps assessing who might need support. Spread out, farther off at the edge of the turf, were toolkits filled with spools, pliers, wrenches, hammers, and nails.

Two archers lined up to shoot. Only one wanted to know her score. Davis was looking with his binoculars downrange, the length of nearly two tennis courts from their location, as one archer let her first arrow fly. I could just hear the sound of a whip cracking the air.

"Seven at six o'clock."

"Nine at two o'clock."

Her shots weren't grouping yet.

"Ten, high."

"Ten, way high."

After the next arrow sailed, there was no sound.

"No. Don't look at that one!" she said, shifting her feet, dropping her bow. "I don't even think it hit the target."

"Yeah," Davis confirmed, "I don't even see it."

As I stood behind her, trying to place myself in her position, I couldn't imagine how even one had hit the target. Every archer calculates the arc of a rise (the drop and horizontal shifts of an arrow's path), a trajectory only they can predict. Before even accounting for wind speeds, there is always some degree of displacement that happens when the arrow leaves the bow at a skew angle from the target so that the fletching doesn't hit the string upon release. This is how the arrow is crafted. If you are right-handed in archery, you'll aim slightly to the left to hit the bull's-eye. This skill means focusing on your mark, the likely shape of an arrow's arched flight, and the many variables that can knock it off all at once. The most precise archers call this process of dual focus *split vision*.

It also requires constant reinvention—seeing yourself as the person who can hit a ten when you just hit a nine, as an archer who just hit a seven, but can also hit an eight. Archery is one of the sports that gives instantaneous, precise feedback. It puts athletes into rank order of how they measure up against their seconds-younger selves. Archers constantly deal with the "near win": not quite hitting the mark, but seconds later, proving that they can.

If an archer's aim is off by less than half a degree, she won't hit her target. "Just moving your hand by one millimeter changes everything, especially when you're at the further distances," said Sarah Chai, a recent Columbia graduate and former cocaptain of the varsity archery team.[2] From the standard seventy-five-yard distance from the target, the ten-ring, the bull's-eye, looks as small as a matchstick tip held out at arm's length. Hitting the eight-ring means piercing a circle the size of the hole in a bagel from 225 feet away. And that's while holding fifty pounds of draw weight for each shot.

It's a taxing pursuit. Well into a three-hour practice, two of the women were lying down, their backs on the turf behind the shooting line, staring up at the sky. Three hours per day of meditative focus, trying to find what T. S. Eliot would call "the still point of the turning world," requires a unique, sustained intensity.[3] Living on a landscape where an infinitesimal difference in degree leads to a massive difference in outcome is what makes an archer an archer. It means learning to have the kind of precision that we find in the natural world—like that of a bee's honeycomb or the perfect hexagonal shape of the rock formations on Ireland's Giant's Causeway. When archers start getting good, with scores consistently above 1350 (out of 1440), they taper down, shoot less, and attend to their concentration, breathing techniques, meditation, and visualization. One teammate, overwhelmed with exams, still made it up to Baker's fields because the focus she gets from archery calms her about everything. "When I was studying abroad, I was going crazy without having it," she said. Without the regimen, she felt irritated all the time.

I stayed at the archery practice for three hours. Someone watching me might have wondered why. For all the thrill of discovering a new sport, it was, admittedly, interminable. I hadn't brought binoculars, and it is hard to concentrate for three hours on what is right in front of you but not easily seen. It was also a cold day, but I stayed to witness what I was starting to feel I might never glimpse: "gold fever," or "target panic," as it's called—what happens when an archer gets good, even too good, compared to her expectations, and starts wanting the gold without thinking about process. In extreme cases, it means that one day she is hitting the bull's-eye, the next day her arrows could end up in the parking lot. No one is clear about whether it's choking, a kind of performance anxiety, or some form of dystonia.[4] But what we do know is that the only way to recover fully from it is to start anew, to relearn the motions and to focus on the essentials—breathing, stance, position, release, and posture. None of the archers I saw seemed to have target panic. Few are willing to admit it even if they do.

Yet something else about archery gripped me enough to keep me there. The reason occurred to me as I left practice, walking down Broadway. I stumbled upon a national historic landmark, a restored eighteenth-century Dutch colonial farmhouse owned by the Dyckman family. It once stood on acreage that spanned the width of Manhattan from the Hudson to the East River, but is currently nestled on the busy avenue behind shrubs and foliage, raised and hidden nearly out of sight. The incongruity of the farmhouse on Broadway intrigued me and I went in for a tour. It was, in fact, my second such visit of the day. Watching an archery team in this modern age had been like seeing a similarly ancient relic, a vestige of a past way of work that we rarely spot in action—not a contest, where there is a victor, but the pursuit of mastery.

The mastery I witnessed on the archery field was not glamorous. There was nobility in it all, but no promise of adulation. There is little that is vocational about American culture anymore, so it is rare to see what doggedness looks like with this level of exactitude, what it takes to align your body for three hours to accurately account for wind speeds and hit a target—to pursue excellence in obscurity. It was an unending day in and day out attempt to hit the gold that few will ever behold. Perhaps I noticed it more than I would with the practice required for a more familiar, popular sport such as basketball or football, one with more chance of glory or fame. To spend so many hours with a bow and arrow is a kind of marginality combined with a seriousness of purpose rarely seen.

There was another reason. As each arrow left for its target, the archers were caught between success (hitting the ten) and mastery (knowing it means nothing if you can't do it again and again). If I had to hazard a guess, I would say that this tension between the two, the momentary nature of success and the unending process required for mastery, is part of what creates target panic or gold fever in the first place.

Mastery requires endurance. *Mastery*, a word we don't use often, is not the equivalent of what we might consider its cognate—*perfectionism*—an inhuman aim motivated by a concern with how others view us. Mastery is also not the same as success—an event-based victory based on a peak point, a punctuated moment in time. Mastery is not merely a commitment to a goal, but to a curved-line, constant pursuit.

From a certain height, we can see it: Many of our most iconic endeavors—from recent Nobel Prize–winning discoveries to entrepreneurial invention, classic works of literature, dance, and visual arts—were in fact not achievements, but conversions, corrections after an arrow's past flight. I have long had a magpie curiosity about how we become. As an only child who lived in my imagination, I would delve into the life stories of my elders; my contemporaries; historic innovators, creators, and inventors; and those working at the peak of their powers today—people whose lives are like mine, but at the same time vastly different from my own. I couldn't escape one observation: Many of the things most would avoid, these individuals had turned into an irreplaceable advantage. I still remember the shudder when I sensed a knowing as sure as fact—that I might only truly become my fullest self if I explored and stayed open to moving through daunting terrain.

I had been thinking of this for much of my life, though it only occurred to me when I was midway through writing this book. It happened when I went to Cambridge and walked into a down-sloped room on Harvard's campus as Bill Fitzsimmons, the longstanding Dean of Admissions, told us, an audience of alumni, that he had been expelled from high school for truancy. He had fallen in with the wrong crowd and started skipping school. He had to work to apply to another high school in the neighboring town. It gave him a sort of resilience, he said, and something he thinks is critical for life itself. "I remember your application," the dean said to me when I went to greet him after the panel. He said it again as if he were sure, as he looked at my nametag with my Harvard college alumni year. He grinned, and pursed his lips as if suppressing a thought.

Perhaps he didn't want to disclose what he had recalled and I had forgotten, a memory long-suppressed: I had written my college application essay about the importance and the advantage of failures—my own—as I perceived them at age eighteen, and in general as a matter of course. I stood there and remembered how I had hidden the essay from my parents and even my college advisor, knowing full well that it was classified as "high risk." I revealed it at the last minute so that if there were any objections, the lack of any substitute essay would force their hand and let me send it in. I wanted to explore in writing what I was beginning to sense about life—that discoveries, innovations, and creative endeavors often, perhaps even only, come from uncommon ground.

In hindsight, I realize that I was focused on improbable rises because I was beginning to live with the gift of what it means to be underestimated. What happens when the world often assumes, before you've even uttered a word, that you could be a failure—based on not fitting a given expectation of the human package in which some expect to find excellence—and how have people turned that into an advantage to meet their aspirations, their dreams?

It was a belief that had crystalized when I would visit my maternal grandparents, who lived in rural Virginia, in a wooden house that was just about ready to sink into the earth. All that was holding it together, it seemed, was their will and a handyman's attempt. Life for my late grandfather, Shadrach, and grandmother, Blanche, when I was at their house centered around three rooms—the kitchen, filled with all sorts of food I prayed they didn't eat; the dining room; and the living room, where we did all the things you're supposed to do in the dining room. Uniting them all was a pass-through chamber where my grandfather would paint his multihued world of characters, both human and divine. He was a janitor by night, a jazz musician always, and a sign painter on the weekends. But at that dining-room table, he would show what he had conjured. The dining room was a place for showing dreams, and his dreams were shaped by hardship. The reality of what he didn't want helped him more clearly conjure what he did, and it aided who he would become. Above all, I would not have written this book without his example.

As I stood there in that room in Cambridge, I realized that, fifteen years later, I was still thinking about the unheralded yet vital ways that we re-create our future selves.

We have heard the stories: Duke Ellington would say, "I merely took the energy it takes to pout and wrote some blues."[5] Tennessee Williams felt that "apparent failure" motivated him. He said it "sends me back to my typewriter that very night, before the reviews are out. I am more compelled to get back to work than if I had a success." Many have heard that Thomas Edison told his assistant, incredulous at the inventor's perseverance through jillions of aborted attempts to create an incandescent light bulb, "I have not failed, I've just found 10,000 ways that won't work."[6] "Only one look is enough. Hardly one copy would sell here. Hardly one. Hardly one. Many thanks . . ." read part of the rejection letter that Gertrude Stein received from a publisher in 1912.[7] Sorting through dross, artists, entrepreneurs, and innovators have learned to transform askew strivings. The telegraph, the device that underlies the communications revolution, was invented by a painter, Samuel F. B. Morse, who turned the stretcher bars from what he felt was a failed picture into the first telegraph device. The 1930s RKO screen-test response "Can't sing. Can't act. Balding. Can dance a little" was in reference to Fred Astaire. We hear more stories from commencement speakers—from J. K. Rowling to Steve Jobs to Oprah Winfrey—who move past bromides to tell the audience of the uncommon means through which they came to live to the heights of their capacity. Yet the anecdotes of advantages gleaned from moments of potential failure are often considered cliché or insights applicable to some, not lived out by all.

This book is about the advantages that come from the improbable ground of creative endeavor. Brilliant inventions and human feats that have come from labor—an endeavor that offers the world a gift from the maker's soul—involve a path aided by the possibility of setbacks and the inestimable gains that experience can provide. Some could say that what we call "work" often does not. "Work is what we do by the hour," author Lewis Hyde argues, but labor "sets its own pace. We may get paid for it, but it's harder to quantify. . . . Writing a poem, raising a child, developing a new calculus, resolving a neurosis, invention in all forms—these are labors."[8]

A division line often positions creativity, innovation, and discoveries as a separate, even elite, category of human endeavor: chosen, lived out by a few. Yet our stories challenge this separation. If we each have the capacity to convert the excruciating into an advantage, it is because this creative process is crucial for pathmaking of all kinds.

What we gain by looking at mastery, invention, and achievement is the value of otherwise ignored ideas—the power of surrender, the propulsion of the "near win," the critical role of play in achieving innovation, and the importance of grit and creative practice.

This book rarely uses the word *failure*, though it is at the heart of its subject. The word *failure* is imperfect. Once we begin to transform it, it ceases to be that any longer. The term is always slipping off the edges of our vision, not simply because it's hard to see without wincing, but because once we are ready to talk about it, we often call the event something else—a learning experience, a trial, a reinvention—no longer the static concept of failure. (The word was, after all, not designed for us, but to assess creditworthiness in the nineteenth century, a term for bankruptcy, a seeming dead end forced to fit human worth.)[9] Perhaps a nineteenth-century synonym comes closer—*blankness*—a poetic term for the wiping clean that this experience can provide. It hints, too, at the limitlessness that often comes next.[10] Trying to find a precise word to describe the dynamic is fleeting, like attempting to locate francium, an alkali metal, measured but never isolated in any weighted quantity or seen in a way that the eye can detect—one of the most unstable, enigmatic elements on the Earth.[11] No one knows what it looks like in an appreciable form, but there it is, scattered throughout ores in the Earth's crust. Many of us have a similar sense that these implausible rises must be possible, but the stories tend to stay strewn throughout our lives, never coalescing into a single dynamic concept. As it is with an archer's target panic—an experience widely felt, but not often glimpsed—the phenomenon remains hidden, and little discussed. Partial ideas do exist—resilience, reinvention, and grit—but there's no one word to describe the passing yet vital, constant truth that just when it looks like winter, it is spring.

These chapters form the biography of an idea that exists without a current definition. When we don't have a word for an inherently fleeting idea, we speak about it differently, if at all. There are all sorts of generative circumstances—flops, folds, wipeouts, and hiccups—yet the dynamism it inspires is internal, personal, and often invisible. As legendary playwright Christopher Fry reminds us:

> *Who apart*
> *From ourselves, can see any difference between*
> *Our victories and our defeats?*[12]

It is a cliché to say simply that we learn the most from failure. It is also not exactly true. Transformation comes from how we choose to speak about it in the context of story, whether self-stated or aloud.

———————

On that cold day in May, I watched the Columbia archers and saw why errorless learning does not lead to certain wins. Some archers spend months practicing rhythmic breathing to release the arrow at the rest between their heartbeats, miming the motions, training their bodies to have impeccable bone alignment and scapula motion. They start by using just their hand and an elastic band at very close range on a target with an extremely large face. Their aim has to be nearly flawless before they can move the target farther and farther back. Yet triumph means dealing with the archer's paradox, handling what lies out of our control: wind, weather, and the inevitably unpredictable movements in life. Hitting gold means learning to account for the curve embedded in our aim.

This book is not an Ariadne's thread, not a string that prescribes how to wind our way through difficult circumstance. It is an *exploration*, an atlas of stories about our human capacity, a narrative-driven investigation of facts we sensed long before science confirmed them. The many who appear on these pages gave me their trust to present their journeys and offered me a critical reminder, one that created the unintended thesis of this book. It is the creative process—what drives invention, discovery, and culture—that reminds us of how to nimbly convert so-called failure into an irreplaceable advantage. It is an idea once known, lived out, taken for granted, and now, I hope, no longer forgotten.

THE UNFINISHED MASTERPIECE

Lord, grant that I may always desire more than I can accomplish.

—MICHELANGELO

Last year, I drove out to a place where our sight extends far enough to glimpse the curvature of the Earth. There the familiar relationship between earth and sky fractures. No orienting horizon, foreground, mid-ground, or background is there to guide our path. The phenomenon occurs on a short list of locales: where I went, the salt

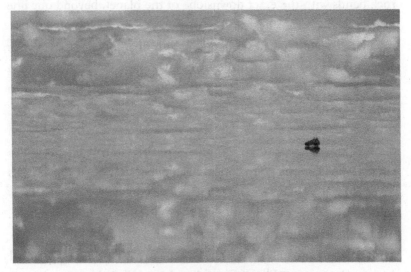

Anna Batchelor, *Driving Bolivia's Salt Flats*, 2012.

flats, the bone white, briny swath of a prehistoric lake bed in Bonneville, Utah, just shy of its border with Nevada; Lake Eyre in Australia; the Salar de Atacama in Chile; and the larger Salar de Uyuni on the Bolivian Altiplano, where those near-mythical pink flamingos come to nest. In these regions, sea evaporation has outpaced precipitation year after year, and arid winds have buffered down the miles of remaining salt to a plane so level that it is isotropic—it appears with the same flatness, the same dimension in all directions.[1] Last I was there, I met a man at the edge of the salt flats who told me, perplexed, that he had driven across the entire state of Illinois on less gas than it took him to drive across the Bonneville Salt Flats. To walk it, to drive on it, feels like standing on a ball—each step forward on the blindingly white ground feels unexpectedly new. It creates an endurance walk, one that seems to extend how much we think we can traverse.

Mountains are what create the illusion on the Bonneville Salt Flats—the massifs can appear as if sky-suspended mounds of earth. The eye catches what we think must be their bottom, but that pile of rock bends with the exact downslope of the planet, beyond our line of sight.

The distortion creates mountains with floating edges, sharp like an arrow's tip. The flint blade-like ends hover, as if pinched by a giant. Set down before us as if a materialized taunt, they seem to show a future within our sights, but just out of our grasp.

Few get out on the salt flats. It is the kind of site you visit when there is nowhere left to go—you have to drive through it to get to your destination, or you venture out deliberately, as if the Earth's other natural wonders can no longer move you and what's left is this alien locale. When it's dry, the land is a place of seeming freedom. After all, there's little there. Some head there to set land racing records of up to 450 miles per hour. Others go for the annual National Archery Association Flight Championships. When I went, it was so

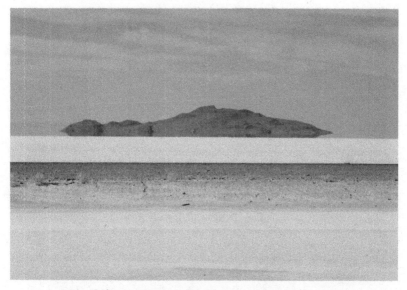

Mike Osborne, *Floating Island*, 2012 (Bonneville, Utah).

quiet that for vast stretches I heard only the sound of my shoes on the crinkled land. Except for the occasional sound of a thunderclap shearing the air, a race car breaking the sound barrier, this is a silent ground.

It mirrors the process in ourselves, when the road before us is flat, when we've accomplished much of what we've set out to do. When any direction seems possible, we walk forward with the clarity that comes from contrast. Save one large obstacle in our sights, we could be disoriented, aimless, adrift.[2]

They say we never walk in truly straight lines, but on the salt flats, a ruler-lined walk is impossible. A seemingly direct forward march turns out in hindsight to be a series of curves. Without realizing it, we constantly autocorrect, covering more ground than we knew we could.

A friend, an artist who has gone to the Bonneville Salt Flats more times than I have, tells me that even with the assistance of a naviga-

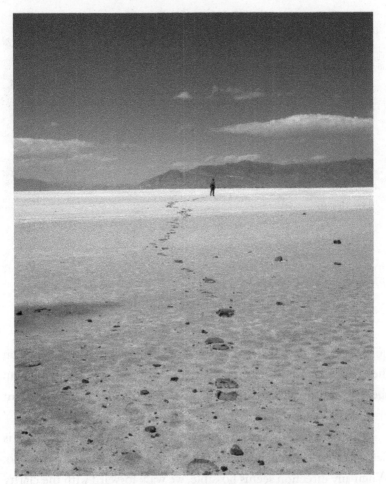

Chris Taylor, *Impossibility of straight lines*,
2003, Bonneville Salt Flats, Utah. Photo: Bill Gilbert.

tor, she has never made it fully across, never walked an arched path
all the way to the edge to meet the foot of the massifs that ring the
salt flats like a bowl. Last we spoke, she had attempted it three times.
We agree that it is an uncanny walk, "like trying to climb up a mountain and not being sure if you're at the top or not, so you keep trying
to rise higher, and by the time you get to what you think is the high-

est point, you're at the edge, can't really see, and realize that you've managed to go beyond the peak."[3]

To walk on the salt flats is to live out archer's paradox, an off-center logic that the best archers use to thrive.

How often have we designated a work of art or invention a masterpiece or a classic, an inexhaustible gift, while its creator considers it incomplete, permanently unfinished, riddled with difficulties and flaws?[4] More times than we could possibly know. I considered a partial list: William Faulkner wrote sections of *The Sound and the Fury* five different times after it was already published, adding new writing as an appendix to the novel's later editions.[5] Paul Cézanne worried that he would "die without ever having attained this supreme goal": to create a work of art that came directly from nature, as he put it. He found his painting oeuvre wanting.[6] Cézanne identified with Frenhofer, the protagonist of Honoré de Balzac's 1831 short story *Le Chef-d'oeuvre inconnu* ("The Unknown Masterpiece"): a Pygmalion figure whose aesthetic ambition to re-create reality by painting the female form ends in inevitable failure.[7] Frenhofer probed the meaning of color, of line, "but by dint of so much research, he has come to doubt the very subject of his investigations"—a dynamic that Maurice Merleau-Ponty would later call "Cézanne's Doubt."[8] Frenhofer was a favorite literary character of Cézanne's. Émile Bernard recounted that during a visit to Cézanne in Aix in 1914, the conversation turned to Frenhofer and "The Unknown Masterpiece" and the painter "got up from the table, stood before me, and striking his chest with his index finger, he admitted wordlessly by this repeated gesture that he was the very character in the novel. He was so moved by this feeling that tears filled his eyes."[9] When he sketched self-portraits, he labeled some FRENHOFER. Cézanne rarely thought that his works were finished, but put them aside "almost always with the intention of taking it up again," which meant leaving most of his works unsigned.[10] Less than ten percent of paintings in his catalogue raisonné bear his signature.[11]

Nobel Prize–winning poet Czeslaw Milosz was one of many who repeated this coda as if on a constantly extending crystalline ground. After every book of his poetry came out, he said, "There is always the feeling that you didn't unveil yourself enough. A book is finished and appears and I feel, Well, next time I will unveil myself. And when the next book appears, I have the same feeling."[12]

We thrive when we stay on our own leading edge. It is a wisdom understood by Duke Ellington, whose favorite song out of his repertoire was always the next one, always the one that he had yet to compose. Like trying to find the end of a sound wave, the endeavor is never complete.

———

The pursuit of mastery is an ever onward almost. "Lord, grant that I may always desire more than I can accomplish," Michelangelo implored, like a perpetual Adam with his finger outstretched but not quite touching the Old Testament God's hand in the Sistine Chapel.[13] When Michelangelo was commissioned to paint the vaulted fresco ceiling sixty-five feet above the ground, he complained of his brain nearly hitting his "back," and that he nearly had "goiter" from "the torture" of having his "stomach squashed" beneath his chin and his face doubled as "a fine floor" for the "droppings" of paint from his brush above him, as each gesture had become "blind and aimless." "My painting is dead. Defend it for me. I am not in the right place—I am not a painter," he implored his friend Giovanni in a letter written as a sonnet.[14] Next to it he drew what looks like a self-portrait: a figure stands, cranes his head, and paints a devil-like face on the ceiling. While laboring over his second cycle on the vault of the Sistine Chapel ceiling, *The Flood*, his plaster mixture sprouted mildew and

Michelangelo Buonarroti, *Sonnet V (to Giovanni da Pistoia)*
with a caricature of the artist standing, painting a figure on
the ceiling over his head, c. 1510. Pen and ink, 11 x 7"
"To Giovanni da Pistoia When the Author Was Painting
the Vault of the Sistine Chapel," 1509. Casa Buonarroti,
Florence, Italy. Photo: Studio Fotografico Quattrone, Florence.

a lime mold plagued the work, as if some crude joke. Michelangelo wrote to his patron, Pope Julius II, "I told Your Holiness that this [painting] is not my art; what I have done is spoiled," and asked to be replaced.[15]

He had left commissions unfinished before. He would leave works deliberately unfinished so often that it became a style—the *non finito*, as scholars call his sculptures of figures emerging from rough-hewn stone.[16] His public came to know his habit. In the midst of creating a costly bronze statue of the pope in Bologna for the Basilica of San Petronio, he admitted to his brother, "The whole of Bologna was of the opinion that I should never finish."[17] Yet his aesthetic of the intentionally incomplete became a metaphor for humility and thriving.

There are enough forms of the unfinished to create a taxonomy. Some works seem complete to the outside world, but remain truncated in the eyes of their makers, stopped short perhaps by an imposed deadline. Others are abandoned out of pure defeat. More still are curative works, ones that remain incomplete, but have helped an artist improve. Some are cut off by death and then completed posthumously by others.

We often linger over this final form of unfinished works, wondering how far what we are viewing, hearing, or reading is from that vision that just shimmered out. When an artist dies before finishing what we expect might have been a classic, we often continue the enterprise, frustrated by a sense of foreclosed possibility. We may ask if it is right to expose a work that the artist did not have time to complete for public scrutiny. Yet often, we finish the work anyway, as we did with Ralph Ellison's *Juneteenth* and *Three Days Before the Shooting*, culled from the two-thousand pages of notes that the writer left when he died, or David Foster Wallace's multi-stranded, titled but unfinished novel, *The Pale King*, as if we must know what would have come from the artist's continued efforts.[18]

Franz Kafka, who saw incompletion where others would see only work to praise, purportedly had one "last request" upon his death. He wrote it in a letter left on his desk in Prague just before he passed: "Everything I leave behind me . . . in the way of diaries, manuscripts, letters (my own and others'), sketches and so on, to be burned unread."[19] He addressed it to his friend of over two decades, Max Brod. Three years before, he had told Brod that the request was coming.[20] Brod refused to honor it and published all the novels we now have by Kafka: *Amerika*, *The Trial*, and *The Castle*, which even stops midsentence. During Kafka's lifetime, he had only published 450 pages of text yet "according to a recent estimate" the *New York Times* reported "a new book on his work has been published every 10 days for the past 14 years."[21]

To fill in based on the fragment is part of the mechanism of vision itself. This skill can be attributed to the brain's ability to reconstruct a complete image out of a once-spotted sliver of information—the back of a person's head, for example, though we haven't seen them in years. As neuroscientist Semir Zeki bravely describes it, the unfinished "stirs the imagination of the viewer, who can finish it off mentally."[22] Artist Romare Bearden considered this fragmentary viewing central to his definition of being an artist: "An artist is an art lover who finds that in all the art he sees, something is missing; to put there what he feels is missing becomes the center of his life's work."[23]

We thrive, in part, when we have purpose, when we still have more to do. The delibrate incomplete has long been a central part of creation myths themselves. In Navajo culture, some craftsmen and women sought imperfection, giving their textiles and ceramics an intended flaw called a "spirit line" so that there is a forward thrust, a reason to continue making work. Nearly a quarter of twentieth century Navajo rugs have these contrasting-color threads that run out from the inner pattern to just beyond the border that contains it; Navajo baskets and often pottery have an equivalent line called a "heart line" or a "spirit break." The undone pattern is meant to give the weaver's spirit a way out, to prevent it from getting trapped and reaching what we sense is an unnatural end.

There is an inevitable incompletion that comes with mastery. It occurs because the greater our proficiency, the more smooth our current path, the more clearly we may spot the mountain that hovers in our gaze. "What would you say increases with knowledge?" Jordan Elgrably once asked James Baldwin. "You learn how little you know," Baldwin said.[24]

The technical term for this, if you like, is the Dunning–Kruger effect—the greater our proficiency, the more clearly we recognize the possibilities of our limitations. The converse is also true—ignorance protects us from the knowledge required to perceive just how unskilled we may actually be. Albert Einstein, who left his desk with a splay of papers at his Princeton, New Jersey, office at the time of his death, still at work on the Theory of Everything, summarized the effect in a quip to a young girl, Barbara, who wrote to him upset that she was a little below average in math.[25] "Do not worry about your difficulties in mathematics," Einstein told her. "I can assure you that mine are still greater."[26]

The Near Win

At the point of mastery, when there seems nothing left to move beyond, we find a way to move beyond ourselves. Success motivates. Yet the near win—the constant auto-correct of a curved-line path—can propel us in an ongoing quest. We see it whenever we aim, climb, or create with mastery as our aim, when the outcome is determined by what happens at the margins.

The Olympic Games, one of the few sporting events where such a pursuit is on full display, once included alpinists and artists alongside athletic categories during the first half of the twentieth century. Between 1912 and 1952, entrants in the categories of architecture, literature, music, painting, and sculpture were listed among the world-class athletes at the Olympics in Stockholm, Antwerp, Paris, Amsterdam, Los Angeles, Berlin, and London. There were a few well-known judges and participants, such as Igor Stravinsky and Josef Suk.[27] Yet it was hard to consider artists selling their work as amateurs and not professionals, an early stipulation for Olympic competition, and the art competitions went the way of the alpinists, the shorter-lived competition of the two on that world stage. Odd as it may seem to consider artists and athletes side by side, there is a high level state to both endeavors where outcome is determined by our inner resources—our spirit, will, belief, and focus. All those who do more than compete, who strive for mastery, play on a field that exists largely within.

We glimpse the phenomenon with silver medalists, according to Thomas Gilovich, a psychology professor at Cornell University, who was fascinated by the particular responses of silver and bronze medalists during the 1992 Summer Olympics. His research team assessed all that he could from visual and verbal responses, differences in their answers in post-competition interviews, to their postures on the medal stands, and found that silver medalists seemed far more frustrated and were more focused on follow-up competitions than those who earned bronze—those farther away from *fama*, the glory of victory. Silver medalists can be plagued by "if only" thoughts about their near win.[28] Bronze medalists, often projecting satisfaction on the medal stand despite being in the lowest rank order on the podium, Gilovich found, are often just thankful that they medaled and were spared fourth place.[29]

The illogical swap occurs because of counterfactual thinking, ideas we have about "what might have been." Daniel Kahneman and the late Amos Tversky first discovered this through a thought experiment that asked people to imagine their level of frustration after missing a scheduled flight by five minutes or thirty minutes. It is easier for the slightly late traveler to conceive of how she could have made it—if only she had driven to the airport faster or found her keys more easily when trying to leave. Arriving at an airport thirty minutes earlier than planned is harder to imagine. The more frustrating scenario is more likely to result in a change in future behavior.[30]

The jolt of a near win is so enduring that slot machines and instant lotteries are often programed to display a higher than expected amount of one-number-off misses, to encourage follow-up play. Near win scratch-off tickets, called "heart stoppers," so consistently manipulate the duration of sustained play that in the 1970s, Britain's Royal Commission on Gambling put them in the category of industry "abuses."[31] Slot machines and games hold the probability of winning at a constant on each throw of the dice or pull of the lever, yet near-win tickets give players the feeling that a win may be close at hand.

On the field, in a game of preparation, not chance, bronze medalists often think like Jackie Joyner-Kersee. In the 1984 Olympics, she came in one-third of a second behind the frontrunner in the 800 meters and missed taking the gold in the heptathlon. Her coach and husband Bob Kersee predicted that it would give her the tenacity she needed in her next Olympic competition in 1988. There, she set the heptathlon world record of 7,291 points. No athlete has come close to her score since. When she lost again in the 1991 qualifiers in Tokyo due to injury, Kersee knew that it would propel his wife to win the gold again in the heptathlon. "I think she can," he said, not because of new training methods, but simply because "the ghost of Tokyo has been bothering her." She took the bronze in the long jump in 1992. True to counterfactual form, the woman then known as the world's greatest all-around athlete expressed no frustration. She had competed through injury. The bronze became her "medal of courage."[32]

The near win is all around us, fabricated or anticipated, even when it's not. As I was leaving the Columbia team archery practice, I called Andrea Kremer, a veteran reporter respected for her probing, tough questions covering teams and players for HBO's *Real Sports* and NBC for the past thirty years, who told me stories about how winning athletes find ways to eat "humble pie," "to manufacture failure, manufacture weakness just so it can be further motivation."[33]

The pressure that comes before winning is one thing that fascinates her. Without it, we often lack some of the drive that we need. This might be part of the reason, she believes, why no NFL team has ever "three-peated," taken the championship three years in a row. Just as a seasoned professor might rattle off facts from decades of study, she listed the few other teams that could seem to invalidate her theory with ease. "[In basketball] the Bulls have done it twice, the Lakers have done it once, yet no team in the NFL has ever three-peated. There have been a couple of repeats—the Steelers, the Patriots, the Broncos—but it's very difficult because you get yourself so up and to maintain that level of euphoria is difficult." The mental discipline and flexibility required to sustain excellence is different, and often harder, than the exertion it took to get there in the first place.[34]

When the ground is too level, high-level performers can manufacture mountains, creating the experience of a not quite, the thrust forward of the incomplete. James Dawson, the affable and ebullient headmaster of the Professional Children's School (PCS) near Lincoln Center in New York City, has a unique lens on it. For nearly twenty years, he has run this school for ballet dancers, Olympic-caliber athletes, and gifted actors, which offers the same classes as public and private schools, but scheduled at times to accommodate the lives of its students—elite working professionals who are still children. Over 40 percent of the dancers of the New York City Ballet are PCS alumni. Some of the school's 200 students are actors on

Broadway or Off-Broadway. Yo-Yo Ma, Sarah Jessica Parker, Uma Thurman, and Berenika Zakrzewski are part of their long list of graduates, out of whom 95 percent apply to college and 85 percent attend.

Over breakfast in a restaurant near Columbus Circle, Dawson ordered pancakes and ate every last one while telling me about how exacting his students are in self-reviews. With their permission, he described one Russian pianist who asked if Dawson had noticed that he missed the third bar on the fourth movement in one of his concerts. "Of course, I hadn't," Dawson said, his face deadpan, then he smiled and shook his head.[35] He told me about a violinist who was in a major competition, came in second place, and told Dawson afterward that his minor mistakes made him feel as if he had failed Mozart himself. The student wallowed. He stopped practicing for some time, then told Dawson in a "whispered aside" one day in the halls that he had picked up the violin again. "Half of my job is being able to let students come in and close the door," Dawson said about the safe space that he offers to these often public young performers, for whom the inner landscape of striving can make coming close feel like the most common place of all.

With trash talk, however playful, we often see propulsion on this fabricated near win terrain. The inimitable German filmmaker Werner Herzog famously dared his friend and colleague, filmmaker Errol Morris: "If you finish the film, *Gates of Heaven*, I will eat my shoes." He didn't think Morris could bring his projects to completion. Morris finished the film. Herzog boiled and ate one shoe. Restauranteur and chef Alice Waters helped him prepare his footwear at the Chez Panisse restaurant in Berkeley, California, with a little spice, garlic, stock, and herbs, stewed for five hours.[36] At the premiere of Morris's *Gates of Heaven* at a Berkeley campus theater, Herzog ate it in public, cutting the shoe with sharp scissors and a knife on a white plate rimmed with black, tossing aside the only bit of the shoe he didn't eat—the sole—like discarding chicken bones, talking about the importance of film between his chews.

———

A near win can feel eternal. One boxer, Byun Jong-Il, was so devastated by his loss at the 1988 Seoul Olympics that he sat in the ring on the mat with his head in his hands for over an hour after the match; officials didn't ask him to leave.[37]

Former Vice President Al Gore spoke to me candidly about one of the most excruciating kinds of near win—to win the U.S. presidency and then, after a drawn-out battle in public adjudicated by the Supreme Court, to be told that victory was not his. I asked him about whether it forced him to reinvent himself, to intensify his core principles, and I mentioned a comment, often attributed to Winston Churchill: "Success is going from failure to failure with no loss of enthusiasm." He laughed. He knew that quote, he said, nodding, then paused and said Churchill later admitted that while the idea was true, success had a damn good disguise.[38]

The sort of random testing a sociologist might loathe gave me countless other glimpses of everyday ring sitting. I was riding home on the train one night, drafting this chapter, papers surrounding me, when a man across the aisle asked me what I was writing. He had boarded with little more than a folder. He looked to be in his midthirties, a banker, I guessed. He was. He worked for UBS. I told him about the phenomenon of the near win. Off he went, telling me about how horrible he still feels about losing a badminton game at age thirteen. "I was just inconsolable," he said, turning to stare off at the gritty window. "And I was winning!" he said loudly, beyond the code of commuter decorum, then regained composure and said more softly, but still resolute, echoing silver medalists I had heard, "I mean, I should have won."

It can be such a strong force that a preeminent healthcare organization, the Mayo Clinic, and Mayo Medical Ventures created a "queasy eagle" award after their Innovation Work Group realized that a low tolerance for failure might preclude medical breakthroughs. The Mayo Clinic had generated only thirty-six new ideas for patents in one particular field in the eighteen years prior to this initiative. Just over a year after the initiative, meant to honor near win, yet abandoned, efforts, there were 245 new ideas, many of which merited new patents.[39]

A near win shifts our view of the landscape. It can turn future goals, which we tend to envision at a distance, into more proximate events. We consider temporal distance as we do spatial distance. (Visualize a great day tomorrow and we see it with granular, practical clarity. But picture what a great day in the future might be like, not tomorrow but fifty years from now, and the image will be hazier.)[40] The near win changes our focus to consider how we plan to attain what lies in our sights, but out of reach.

While the thrust of coming close does not always translate into triumph, it can help us outdo ourselves. The story of such a feat by twenty-three-year-old Julie Moss has contributed to the popularity of Ironman competitions. In 1982, she was a college senior at California Polytechnic State University in San Luis Obispo, majoring in Physical Education, and entered the competition in Kona, Hawaii, to collect data on herself for her college major's requisite senior project. She procrastinated, left the training to the last minute, and prepared during a two-month period before the triathlon and after finals. Her guidance was "limited to one article in *Sports Illustrated*." So dissimilar was it from anything she had done before, it seemed like fiction. "Fiction gives you the freedom to imagine the impossible and make it up as you go," she said.[41]

After the first leg, a 2.4-mile rough-water swim, a 112-mile bike race and the final leg, the 26.2 mile run, she found herself winning at the twenty-fifth mile. She had a six-minute lead. Her closest competitor was a mile behind her. With a half-mile left to win the Ironman, her victory clearly unfurled on the ground before her, Moss began cramping, shifting her gait to a bizarre irregular motion. Within feet of the finish line, her legs gave out. She fell with such unnatural movements on the side of the final stretch that it appeared nearly fatal.

In the footage captured by helicopters and a ground camera from ABC's *Wide World of Sports*, she seemed oblivious to the penetrating gazes on her or the attention that such a dramatic scene was causing for the crowd of spectators. She tried to rise and walk, lost control of her body and starfished—her limbs spiraled down on the ground.

At one point when Moss struggled not to lay supine, the footage shows her competitor Kathleen McCartney's pair of tennis shoes going past. It put Moss in second place. "I thought, 'That's her. She's gone by me.' I just thought, 'I quit,'" Moss said, narrating what was going on in her mind as she did with Jad Abumrad and Robert Krulwich of WNYC's program *Radiolab*, and as she had for others before. "And all of a sudden, there's this voice that just said," with force this time: "Get up."[42]

"I thought, 'I can't get up again. I've sort of worn out that tactic. But I can *crawl*.' I don't know if it was a surge of new-found competitiveness or if I'd just become territorial about my position in the lead, but I didn't want to come this far and have it taken away from me," she explained.[43] She lay on the ground, leaning on her arms and legs like a tripod to stagger to a walk and start again.

Moss crawled the last ten yards of the race. She pushed herself to the point of losing control of bodily functions. "I pooped my pants on national TV," she revealed to Krulwich and Abumrad. This is what was happening as she forced herself to cross the finish line, crawling low to the ground of those Hawaiian lava fields with its banyan trees. "In my mind's eye, I was making good time. The replay on tape reveals a slower, more truthful version," she said on another occasion.[44] She shooed off those trying to help her up, not wanting to be disqualified for outside assistance, and even, by accident, her mother Eloise offering her a lei, as she tried to stand to cross the line still running, but she kept falling. A pained creep was the only option she had.

NBC's Jim McKay spoke for the many who have seen it when he called Moss's finish "the most inspiring sports moment he had ever seen." The Ironman entrant pool doubled over the following three years.[45]

During that ordeal, she says, "My life was going to be different. I felt my life changing. I made a deal with myself. A deal was struck. And I don't care if it hurts, I don't care if it's messy, I don't care how it looks, but I would finish. I would *finish*."

She completed those last ten yards, twenty-nine seconds after McCartney, the competitor who had passed her. It remains the smallest margin of victory for any Ironman competition.[46] Moss still thinks about what it would have been like to win, but credits her near win for leaving her irrevocably changed.

"It was a pivotal moment in my life, that voice that I hadn't ever called upon that just said, 'Keep moving forward . . .'"

"That's the thing that gets me," Krulwich said. "It didn't say to you, 'YOU CAN'T.' It actually said exactly the opposite,'" reflecting on the fact that Moss was recharged when the mountain was in her sights.

"Isn't that cool?" Moss said.

Abumrad said, "I would have thought it would have said, 'Stop. Come on, Stop. Lie down.'"

Constant walking is not just a mode of movement; it describes how we live. "When we imagine ourselves, we imagine ourselves walking," author Rebecca Solnit reminds us. "'When she walked the earth' is one way to describe someone's existence, her profession is her 'walk of life,' an expert is a 'walking encyclopedia' and 'he walked with God' is the Old Testament's way of describing a state of grace."[47] Indefatigable painter Mark Bradford, talking about the process he goes through to find the foundational material of his monumental works, says, "Well, what I need is not here, so I just have to make myself available to the universe, so I start walking around, looking for paper, for the right paper."[48] What we want but do not have creates our onward march.

Moving forward on those arid playas is to live out a *saudade*, the Portuguese term for persistent longing for what we sense may never come. It is to live with the sense that Wynton Marsalis, despite his virtuosity and that of the greats who have inspired him, believes: "All you can do is get in the ocean, try to swim, look at some of the fish, catch somethin' you want to eat. . . . You can't make it across. . . . Its course was set in motion long before you were born. You can't do nothin' but participate in it and love it, because if you hate it, you still got to be out in the ocean."[49]

Masters are not experts because they take a subject to its conceptual end. They are masters because they realize that there isn't one. On utterly smooth ground, the path from aim to attainment is in the permanent future.

———

Michelangelo never gave up his walks to search the stark white marble quarries in the mountains for just the right *pietra viva*, "living rock." There was still moisture in this marble attached to the mountain vein, or quarried so recently that it still had its sap, and could create sculptures to best "emulate the ancients."[50] He was the only artist in fifteenth-century Italy of such renown to personally search for his own materials in this way. He would hire another, but would also spend the better part of a year in this quest himself—eight months in one stretch.[51]

At Carrara in the Apuan Alps, he looked out to the ocean and envisioned carving one of the mountains into a gigantic colossus, a sculpture so large as to be seen by all mariners who approached. He was a man enthralled by the marble that came from mountains and how he could release the images that he saw within stone. This dreamlike vision produced a kind of productive delirium. He held onto it for five decades. When it was time for Condivi to write the biography of the artist's meticulously documented career, Michelangelo wanted this vivid example of his unfinished path to be a part of his life's record.[52] It is one of the only times in the biography where Condivi quotes from his conversations with the artist directly for emphasis. Michelangelo called the lingering thought "a madness that came over me, so to speak. But if I could be sure of living four times as long as I have, it's there I would attempt this."[53]

For Michelangelo, art was "an unending succession of contests."

"David with his slingshot, I with my bow." This was Michelangelo's view of his famous work, his journey, and his tools.[54] His achievements came from focusing on what more there was left to do, by keeping a gaze on the mountain constantly set in his path.

Now, it made sense that the archery coach told me toward the end of practice, standing out of earshot from his team, that many of his colleagues feel that they can never do enough for their archers. Some just quit, he said, sensing that their entire trove of techniques is insufficient. There are never enough visualizations and posture drills to help his archers address whatever blocks them. It didn't sound like a complaint exactly, but a tender admission, a way to let me know that he was giving himself over to a voracious path that always required more.

We build out of the unfinished idea, even if that idea was our former self. "Utopia is on the horizon," author Eduardo Galeano said. "When I walk two steps, it takes two steps back . . . I walk ten steps, and it is ten steps further away. What is utopia for? It is for this, for walking."[55] It gives propulsion to what we might never have created without it. If we created utopias, we would still have the incomplete. Completion is a goal, but, we hope, never the end.

BLANKNESS

Creativity is allowing yourself to make mistakes. Art is knowing which ones to keep.

—SCOTT ADAMS

The Gift

As the lights dimmed in Lincoln Center at the start of the evening program, I curled my Playbill and wondered irreverently: Did the woman seated to my left and the young girl to my right have any idea about what happened one of the first times that choreographer Paul Taylor's company danced, long before they arrived at this famed performance hall, and before the hall was even built? It must have been Taylor's good nature that saved him from calling that 1957 performance an out-and-out disaster, or the wisdom to know that it would one day become an unheralded advantage. He had debuted his program, *7 New Dances*, at the 92nd Street Y's Kaufmann Concert Hall. One of the few people I talked to who did know about it was choreographer Bill T. Jones. The response to it was a scandal, he told me. Few others outside of the field of dance remembered it. But, then again, why would they? The eighty-three-year-old Taylor has held the rotating position of head of the vast dance-making knighthood as "the world's greatest living choreographer." With a repertory of over 135 pieces, he is central to American modern dance. His influence is vast. Pina Bausch, Twyla Tharp, and David Parsons, among other giants, all first earned spots in the Paul Taylor Dance

Company and then went on to establish dance companies in their own right. Robert Battle, the artistic director of Alvin Ailey Dance Company, was admitted, but he didn't drop out of his junior year at Juilliard to take his spot. Ailey himself admired Taylor, paying homage to him in a section of *Streams*.[1] Taylor once earned the moniker Martha Graham gave him: the "naughty boy" of dance, but as Taylor recounts in his autobiography, *Private Domain*, his nicknames became "Sir Paul" after being knighted by the French government, "Master Taylor" after countless honorary degrees, and "Mr. Smarts" after a MacArthur "Genius Grant."[2]

"All hot water is is cold water heated," Taylor once said in an award speech—a comment that his friend painter Robert Rauschenberg told him as they came to understand how close together the extremes of life could be.[3] The two men, flat broke and living on optimism before they would go on to be legends, had met by chance in the basement of the Stable Gallery near Columbus Circle. They struck up a conversation right after one of Rauschenberg's "dirt paintings," homages to the everyday, fell right off the wall. It could have been a sign about what would happen that night in October 1957. Taylor had saved enough money over the course of years for the chance. He scrapped what he called "dancy dancing" for his own homage to daily life. It was by no means perfect, but he felt sure it would at least be a first.[4]

Taylor wanted to make gestural dances out of everyday movements and ordinary posture—what most then felt dance certainly was not. He beaverishly catalogued people on the street "doing what they usually did": waiting, running after a bus then slowing to a walking gait, sitting in a car, or just milling around.[5] The "moves" and "stillnesses" of ordinary folks were his "found objects."[6] He broke down these movements into five categories, divided them by their dominant working body part, then began choreographing a new piece.[7]

A few days before the debut of 7 *New Dances*, he started to question whether the program's austere minimalism would sustain the crowd's interest. The movements for 7 *New Dances* required such little exertion that muscle memory had barely taken over after eight months of rehearsals. The counts of the accompaniment were also so arrhythmic that learning it was "like memorizing a page of numbers in a phone book."[8] It might have bothered others more fixated on how people would respond, but he was just performing dances he knew he would enjoy ("otherwise, what's the point?").[9]

There were some clues about what might happen that night back in 1957. Questions kept running through Taylor's mind as he reflected on the dances he created prior to 7 *New Dances* such as: "There must have been some kind of structure somewhere, but where? What was the point of view, if any? And what was dance in the first place?"[10] With this new work, he would posit an answer.

The first piece, "Epic," was just twenty minutes of Taylor dressed in an everyday business suit (Rauschenberg's costume direction) standing still then assuming a new posture every ten seconds. At that point, a recording of a woman's nasal voice would say "at the tone the time will be," then stated the correct time.

Taylor remembered seeing people in the audience walk out "at a polite but firm pace," as he was on the stage after just five minutes. At first, he thought that the timestamp repetition just reminded them about some forgotten obligations. That was until he saw the majority of the audience bolt, "accumulate into a solid mass and practically canter up the aisles." It was a flood. Over half the audience was gone. Inside, he felt like he was sinking. His neck was ticking out of "nervousness."[11]

The second piece, curiously titled "Events I," went off with no more incidents in the front of the house. In the third work, "Resemblance"—the act that Taylor performed with Duchess, a rented dog from Animal Talent Scouts, still foggy from the tranquilizer she got at the dress rehearsal—she was scared by pianist David Tudor performing part of John Cage's composition, banging down the piano lid and striking it occasionally. During practice, Duchess ("the only one of us who is being paid") had darted to the theater's basement as fast as the audience cantered up the aisles. Now, at the live performance, she sat sedated, half-risen on her mat, spying the piano warily. Midway through, her eyes started to glaze over, her ears laid back, and she began creeping off stage. The animal trainer, standing behind a curtain drape, pointed menacingly to force her back onto the mat. Duchess returned at first, then backpedaled, tail between her legs, and tried to sneak off again. Rauschenberg had suggested the animals. A llama would have been his preference, but it was too expensive. What remained of the audience now seemed to stare at the dog. Taylor swore off any more of Rauschenberg's suggestions for "anything live, even his stuffed angora goat with a tire around it."[12]

"Panorama" was next. Its audience-facing mirror-filled set optically doubled the number of empty seats. Taylor had envisioned that the reflection would act as a reminder that the dancer's pedestrian movements were mimicking the audience's own. Yet with so few people left, the mirrors doubled an image of the mainly vacant house.

"Duet" followed. The curtain rose. One dancer sat in an evening dress, propped up on one hand. Taylor, dressed in a suit, stood next to her feet. Stage directions called for looking "calm in an exciting way," then staying motionless for four minutes. They did. The pianist played a counterpart to Cage's now famous *4'33"* composition of silence; he just sat at the piano. The curtain fell. "This time everything has come off perfectly," Taylor said, relieved.[13]

By the finale, "Opportunity," the stalwarts in the house were mainly a few of the dancer's friends. The manager of the concert hall had also stayed. He waited backstage to tell Taylor never to rent out the theater again.[14]

Dance critic Louis Horst never did find the words to describe 7 *New Dances*. He just listed its title and the performance location. Then he signed it at the bottom with his initials—L. H. There was no type whatsoever. Horst, the founder, editor, and chief critic of *Dance Observer*, printed four nearly square inches of blank newsprint. If Taylor would not "dance," Horst would not write:

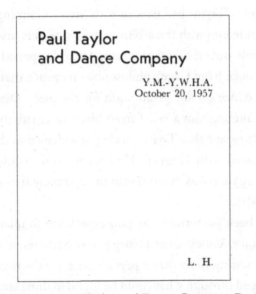

Louis Horst, "Paul Taylor and Dance Company Review," *Dance Observer* 24.9 (November 1957), 139.

This rebuke was as creative and singular as the minimalist performance itself. His indifference and dismissal was prominent all the more because of how scant dance coverage was in print. Horst was one of the field's elders. His magazine was "a voice through which modern dance spoke."[15] He had composed for Martha Graham in the 1930s and established the *Dance Observer* in 1934 as a forum dedicated to the field's emerging aesthetics. The prominent magazine was one of a tiny handful dedicated entirely to dance at that time.

Horst was not alone. *New York Herald Tribune* dance critic Walter Terry, whom Taylor characterized as "a nice guy who can be counted on to like almost everything," only managed to stay for five of the seven pieces of flamboyant minimalism.[16] For his efforts, Terry's review stated: Taylor was "determined to drive his viewers right out of their minds."[17]

Terry expected more of this new sprout on the landscape with talent for miles. Taylor had danced with Merce Cunningham's company, but got fed up with the arbitrary, everyone-gets-an-object-that-someone-pulls-out-of-a-basket routine that happened onstage. It was an influence from Cage's philosophy on chance that determined who would dance on any given night for the piece *Dime a Dance*.[18] It offered Cunningham a relief from bouts of creativity-stifling indecision.[19] It meant that Taylor rarely got a chance to dance. Taylor had also danced with Graham. He later formed his own company, founded in 1954. It has evolved into the company that still exists in his name today.

He had been performing to gain experience in quarterly events through Dance Associates at Henry Street Settlement House. This was back when modern dance performance production costs were often managed through what could be found in dime stores and with donations, rehearsal space was whatever they could sneak into, and the concerts that came with no notice in any newspaper were "performed practically in secret."[20] The Kaufmann Concert Hall production was a major outing.

When Taylor saw Horst's review, he confessed, "My first reaction is outrage."[21] "Louis's review wasn't even a very *big* blank," he said.[22] "Folks have indeed misinterpreted my beautiful ABCs of posture as being a nightmare alphabet."[23] What he considered a near win looked to others like failure.

He wasn't the only one with that frustration. "I loved it of course. I wasn't bored," dancer Aileen Passloff told me about watching 7

New Dances. "I didn't get restless. It was alive. Oh, it was beautiful. He changed how we thought about time, about stillness. It *imprinted* on me." She clutched her heart with her left hand, leaning forward with her right on her leg, and nearly fell out of her chair with enthusiasm. "You know," she said, pausing to reflect on it more, "people just got uptight back then if it wasn't wanton frolicking."[24]

Word of Taylor's blank review traveled. A year later, he was in the landlocked Umbrian town of Spoleto for his engagement at its month-long dance festival. Everyone was running late on the night of the dress rehearsal in the small theater of Caio Melisso. Pina Bausch couldn't fit into the mysteriously stitched-up armholes of her costume. The musicians had left for a favorite café. Taylor was adding new dances at the eleventh hour. The festival's founder, Gian Carlo Menotti, warned that the critics were getting impatient. What critics? Taylor didn't know the custom in Italy of reviewing rehearsals. He tried to accommodate them on the fly, located the musicians, and prepared the company to start. When the curtain rose, Taylor stepped out onto the stage, was confused that no sounds were coming from the pit, spied that the musicians still weren't there, and signaled for the curtain to come down. The critics broke for the exits. They thought they had seen another of Taylor's minimalist pieces. To ensure that the critics didn't miss Taylor's actual dance, the ushers had to secure the doors until the company regrouped.[25]

Like flypaper, the blank review stuck. Nearly fifty years later, the octogenarian dancer said, "I've never lived it down."[26]

There are reviews and there are reviews. All artists are bound to feel the sting of a blistering critical attack from some quarter. In 1966, the London-based *Evening Standard* review of a work read: "Three girls, one named Twyla Tharp, appeared at the Albert Hall last evening and threatened to do the same tonight."[27] Some of the best performers have started off with audiences as small as the one that Taylor was left with after they flooded out.

If all art is an exchange, an inner idea made manifest and delivered to the outside world, the blank review says that the offer wasn't just condemned. It was refused. Yet the blank review also offers a gift along with its barb.

———

The problem couldn't have been Taylor's dedication. To rent the Kaufmann Concert Hall, he had saved money while living on a meager budget, camping out illegally in an apartment with no bathroom, no water, no heat, and large holes in the roof from a fire. He covered them in plastic, trying to imagine that he had skylights. He didn't use the fridge in winter—the whole place gave off the same icy chill.[28] He also wrote in pencil—ink would only freeze and crack the bottles—and he rarely used the cast-iron gas stove; he feared that the fumes from the neighbor's piles of garbage and cat urine would set off an explosion.[29] His furniture? Things he picked up off the street—"objects trouvés," as he liked to kid.[30] Money ran low and he took to pilfering what he thought would go unmissed from supermarkets: cans of dog food—immoral, but a necessity, he said—and caviar "for dignity."[31] At least he could laugh at himself looking at a mouse on his table one night, stingily refusing to give it a crumb, as he had in earlier days—he had nothing to give.[32]

In that icy studio, he and his three dancers, Donya Feuer, Toby Armour, and Cynthia Stone, had rehearsed for eight months through the winter in hats and coats.[33] They found time late in the day, after he worked at odd jobs that paid little and for too short a time to collect unemployment when each stopped.[34] Taylor worked so many jobs that he considered it a feat to just remember his schedule and make it to rehearsals on time after school—Juilliard, after first studying at Syracuse on a swimming scholarship—before he dropped out to dance with Cunningham and Graham. Still, he was content. He had enough room to rehearse his own routines.

The issue couldn't have been Taylor's talent as a dancer. Back at Graham's dance company the year following 7 *New Dances*, Taylor was singled out for acclaim despite his small role in Graham's masterpiece *Clytemnestra*. He triumphed in the premiere. Lincoln Kirstein, the cofounder and director of the New York City Ballet, asked Taylor to dance with George Balanchine's company in Spoleto in a new ballet, despite being a staunch opponent of modern dance, especially what Kirstein described as Taylor's "maverick talent for oddball dancing." Kirstein didn't extend the offer that way. "Geek, you big piece of irrational pulp, you're getting another chance" is how he invited Taylor.[35]

If there was an issue back in 1957, it was a common artistic state that can look like failure to others. Taylor was dealing with the stretch to clear the gap that Leonardo da Vinci described, and many other artists know: the crevasse "when your views are in advance of your work."[36]

The Gap

Coming to the edge of this gap between work and intentions can be an engine-house of all kinds of artistic practice. It's the edge that made artist Mel Chin confess to me that, years ago, he stole away into his tony Midtown gallery just off Fifth Avenue during the night of his opening, while his guests were at his celebratory dinner, just to take back a painting to keep working on it. It is the place where August Wilson found himself when his poems didn't have the form he needed to express his ideas and turned to plays instead.[37] It's the period where Ezra Pound tossed failed novels into the fire as he realized that he was trying "to get the novel cut down to the size of verse" and turned to poetry.[38]

It is the state of development that Pound described unmercifully to poet Hart Crane after his submission to *The Little Review*. Pound served as the foreign editor. This is "all very egg," Pound said, "there is perhaps better egg. But you haven't the ghost of a setting hen or an incubator about you." Crane, just around eighteen years old, was in the middle of a gap. All that he had was still raw; it hadn't yet congealed. The first book of Crane's poetry contains a picture of Pound, an advertisement for *Personae*, and the coincidence revealed what Crane's letters showed. Crane had kept Pound's rejection letter throughout his short life, "like a kind of diploma that in some way he was a member of modern poetry" as Crane scholar Langdon Hammer put it, since Pound had taken the time to write while Crane was in the crevasse.[39]

Trying to bridge the gap between work and vision can be like hearing the notes to a song without being able to finish hearing the complete tune. As with earworms, snippets of songs that we hear and then repeat in our minds, the unfinished scenario often crops up in our thoughts over and over again until we discern how to complete it. It is a bit like unconsciously living out the Zeigarnik Effect, the experience of replaying notes in an attempt to try to piece together an entire melody. This phenomenon, researched by Bluma Zeigarnik and Kurt Lewin, isn't the result of the mind "nagging" us to follow through on things until we complete them, as people once thought.[40] Ruminating on the incomplete snatch of a song or an overdue task is the unconscious posing a repeated question to the conscious mind: Can you please "make a plan" to resolve this incomplete endeavor? "The unconscious mind apparently can't do this on its own, so it nags the conscious mind to make a plan with specifics like time, place, and opportunity. Once the plan is formed, the unconscious can stop nagging the conscious mind with reminders."[41]

We can sense the Zeigarnik Effect, though we would rarely refer to it that way. Expanding, stretching to cross the chasm between ambition and proficiency, is an internal, invisible process. It is like the Catalan saying that Joan Miró once mentioned about artistic endeavors—it's a parade, but it marches inside you.

At the gap, artists are in competition with themselves, like brilliant painter Jennifer Packer. Once in the MFA program at Yale University, Packer, who used to compete against Goya, now tries to best her own works with each successive painting, hanging the current victor up on her studio wall.

Closing the gap means coping with the blank review. It diagrams the riddle that can come after an artist takes a risk. Artists have to learn to shield themselves from criticism. They also have to know when to engage with criticism to see their work anew.

Private Domains: Studios and Inner Worlds

Taylor knew how and when to ignore critique. Up until this point, as he tells it, his attitude after rejection had been that obstacles could be solved by disregarding them. If he didn't push through obstacles, he had let them drift off into the air. He did this through a ritual with Rauschenberg after their first collaboration, Taylor's premiere public performance—*Jack and the Beanstalk* in 1954. The audience "just sat there. No boos, no clapping, nothing," Taylor said.[42] The two men went to the alley behind the theater. As they let loose the balloons tethered on a string—Rauschenberg's beanstalk stage set—the two talked about how wonderful it was that dances were so fleeting. Rauschenberg agreed. The painter had, after all, embraced impermanence in his own way, famously erasing a celebrated Willem de Kooning drawing that he had received the year before. Taylor thought that "the main idea was to flush a painting or a dance out of your system and then go on to the next one."[43]

An artist's act of refusal, deciding to ignore criticism, isn't always the same as obstinacy. Often, it is an act of integrity. To some, insisting on an inner vision amidst a chorus of complaint can seem like madness, especially when declining opportunities that might lead to greater popularity. Despite the criticism of 7 *New Dances*, Taylor was offered countless chances to engage full time with other dance forms such as ballet, after an invitation from Balanchine to join his company. The "flabbergasting" honor would have meant broader popularity, he said, but "I have to keep heading in my own direction."[44] "Modern dance is what I set out to do . . . come whatever."[45]

Like leading an orchestra, you have to know how to turn your back to the crowd, as the saying goes.[46]

Taylor's dances still have those pedestrian movements at their core, no matter how kinetic the piece. They occur in his best works. "There's no question these dancers are virtuosos," *New York Times* dance critic Alastair Macaulay said, but "it's remarkable how frequently basic features recur in many of his finest works: walking, running, falling, tilting, kneeling . . ."[47] In the 1982 piece *Lost, Found and Lost*, Taylor returned to the terrain he laid for himself in "Epic" and "Events I" from 7 *New Dances*: Dancers lined up single file, popping their hips, slouching and shifting their weight before stepping offstage, nailing the feeling of fidgeting and frustration on an interminable queue all set to Mantovani Muzak. It mimed everyday movements in just the way that Taylor hoped to show back in 1957.

Ignoring criticism as Taylor often did requires keeping others out. Part of the creative process requires "undisturbed development" in what poet Rainer Maria Rilke described as some "dark" and "unsayable" place. While speaking to young poet Franz Kappus about the importance of learning how to immunize creative work from criticism, he emphasized that "each embryo of a feeling" should have the benefit of this cocooned space.[48]

I saw it as a new Critic on the faculty at Yale School of Art in the artists' studios I would visit. Completed paintings, or at least ones in a confident state of incompletion, were out for discussion. Others would be back-turned, hidden in plain sight. As I would restrain myself from asking to see tucked away works in studios, I often imagined the story about an event that occurred in Rodin's studio in 1904. Rodin gave Virginia Woolf and her friends permission to look at any work, but not what was under the sheets. Woolf cheekily tried to lift the linen on a sculpture. Rodin slapped her hand.[49]

Back-turned paintings and sheeted sculptures are often how artists give their process amnesty from premature critique. They create safe havens for good reason, sometimes to preserve innovation. Innovative ideas, after all, are often so counterintuitive that they can, at first, look like failure.

We make discoveries, breakthroughs, and inventions in part because we are free enough to take risks, and fail if necessary. Private spaces are often where we extract the gains from attempts and misses.

Private domains—created by time away or time within—can last years. Celebrated soprano Renée Fleming recalls that it took a decade before she could sing anything in front of anyone, then another five years before she could sing consistently. "It wasn't until my late thirties that I could get on stage and reproduce what I was doing in the practice room," she said.[50]

Philosopher and novelist Umberto Eco creates havens anywhere by learning to inhabit the "empty spaces in our lives." He can detach from his surroundings at will and focus, even if just for a few minutes, on a problem he's working through, even while standing on line at the grocery store. Here is Eco: "Say you are coming over to my place. You are in an elevator and while you are coming up, I am waiting for you. This is an interstice, an empty space. I work in empty spaces. While waiting for your elevator to come up from the first to the third floor, I have already written an article!" These empty spaces in life are massive, just as they are in the universe. "What will happen if you eliminate the empty spaces from the universe, eliminate the empty spaces in all the atoms? The universe will become as big as my fist."[51]

No haven, room, or back-turned painting is required to shield work from premature critique in the improv of jazz. There, it happens naturally. In this state of play, the brain generates a barricade from self-judgment. This is what Allen Braun and Charles Limb, a neck surgeon who is also a saxophonist with a recording booth in his office at Johns Hopkins Medical Center, have found in studying jazz musicians' minds as they improvise. Together they devised a study to replicate it as closely as possible. They invited musicians to the National Institutes of Health, asked them to memorize a piece of music, and then to improvise to the same exact chord changes while hooked up to an fMRI imaging scanner. During improvisation, areas of the musician's brain involved in self-expression lit up and parts that control self-judgment were suppressed, freeing up all generative impulses. Neuroscientists describe this permissive state where the mind allows for failure without self-condemnation as disassociation in the frontal lobe.[52] The rest of us call it a basic tenet of improvisation in jazz—not to negate, but to accept all that comes and add to it, the foibles, the mistakes, the exquisite beauty and joy. Playing jazz is "like a conversation," Wynton Marsalis said. "You can't evaluate yourself while you're having it. You're playing in time."[53]

The closest the mind comes to this state is during reverie-filled REM sleep; to ignore judgment amounts to living in "a waking dream."[54] Suppressing judgment of yourself and others has translated into the legend of the jazz musician's self-assurance. We've seen it so often that it has resulted in the age-old saying that jazz musicians are cool. I remember seeing it in my grandfather, painter and jazz and blues bass player Shadrach Emmanuel Lee. Little could ruffle him, down to his last days in his eighties. Ill and in a place of pain, he never let on. There are echoes of what I saw in my grandfather in the testimony of sons and daughters of bluesmen around the world. "The scuffling jazzmen around my father were so self-assured," Marsalis remarked, "they didn't mind you knowing who they were."[55] Quelling self-judgment, "jazz leads you to the core of yourself and says 'Express that,'" Marsalis continued. This means that every player has the ability to convey their own unique sound, to use that personal language to communicate how the world feels to them. They learn to accept all that comes, keep their equilibrium in the midst of it all, and do it in the time signature of swing.

Safe havens sometimes mean shielding the work even from our own overgrown self-censors. In a *Paris Review* interview, August Wilson recalled the moment when a waitress at a restaurant noticed he often came in and wrote on a paper napkin. She asked, "Do you write on napkins because it doesn't count?" "It had never occurred to me that writing on a napkin frees me up," the playwright said. "If I pull out a tablet, I'm saying, 'Now I'm writing,' and I become more conscious of being a writer. The waitress saw it; I didn't recognize it, she did. That's why I like to write on napkins. Then I go home to another kind of work—taking what I've written on napkins in bars and restaurants and typing it up, rewriting."[56] His napkin became an incubator, a safe haven, a way of silencing the brash inner critic before it was time for it to have its say.

Some force themselves into a physical isolation of extreme kinds to silence unwanted commentary. Other artists incorporate mistakes to silence their own inner critics. Brooklyn-based artist Shane Aslan Selzer makes what she calls "single-session sculptures" where she doesn't go back and let herself edit, persevering with the same commitment to continual process as Ellsworth Kelly's single-line drawings, where we see no unbroken mark, no inner critic that forced the hand to a halt.[57]

Knowing when to ignore criticism is a riddle.

In a world where we are increasingly blasted by the stories of others, retreating to recover our own is more vital than ever before. The critic, whether internal or external, who speaks up when the work isn't coming together is a healthy part of the psyche and our environment. The inner critic, Jungian analyst Clarissa Pinkola Estés says, has a role to play when it is not overgrown, and "can be useful when it poses such questions as: How will this work best? Or how does this fit with that? Or I think you made a false start here, begin over again."[58] It is perhaps what a lab study cannot fully account for, but our life stories can—how the act of playing in time allows for jazz musicians to be permissive enough not to condemn themselves for a mistake, but reflective enough to know when they've made one.

Art has long been created in private domains, but creation requires feedback of some kind. Seclude yourself away from most criticism for too long, and you can distort your perceptions entirely. One artist serves, for me, as a cautionary tale—Jacopo da Pontormo, whom Duke Cosimo I de' Medici secured to paint the frescoes in the chapels and choir of Florence's Basilica of San Lorenzo in 1545. Pontormo labored over his commission, a biblical postdiluvian flood scene, and forbade anyone to view it. Like Balzac's protagonist Frenhofer in "The Unknown Masterpiece," who painted a portrait for a decade in isolation to deleterious effect, Pontormo worked on his piece for eleven years behind various enclosures and coverings. When Pontormo died, he had not completed the commission. None of it survives today. The Italian painter, writer, and Renaissance-artist biographer Giorgio Vasari described Pontormo's painting as a distortion of forms, positioned in ways that were so entangled, so jumbled, that if he had to live with the work for eleven years, Vasari said, "I believe that I would drive myself mad with it . . ."[59] Pontormo had imprisoned himself with his work through extended isolation and, like a bird caged too long, plucked his feathers out.

Letting Them In: On Critique and Pressure

A few days before I went to see Taylor's company at Lincoln Center, all of the tickets were priced at $3.50 for one day only. In 1962, this was the top price of admission to see *Aureole*. Forty years later, that won't even buy a round-trip subway ride to Lincoln Center to see the ever-present pieces that took Taylor's company around the world. *Aureole* made dance history, signaled Taylor's seminal place in the field, and was the final piece that he performed before retiring from dancing altogether in 1974. In *Aureole*, he learned what to listen to and what to ignore. It was a conduit he used to express his artistic vision that remained after 7 *New Dances*. "In every work of genius we recognize our own rejected thoughts: they come back to us with a certain alienated majesty," Ralph Waldo Emerson wrote.[60] Many audiences have seen Taylor's thoughts, rejected by others (but always accepted by him), take their place in his work.

This dance had none of the sharp breaks and stillness for which he was skewered in 1957. Yet the pedestrian vocabulary he put out on the Kaufmann stage—the kneeling, walking, running, the extended hold on a position, the exaggerated swinging of arms and rushing forward—was intact. He found a more fluid approach. He set it to selected movements from Handel's *Concerti Grossi*, as much of a contrarian compliment to modern dance as were his selections for the 1957 piece, the sounds of everyday life: heartbeats, wind, rain, and often silence. *Aureole* is the essence of Taylor's basic lyric vocabulary.

With the exception of compliments from Merce Cunningham and José Limón, who came to the *Aureole* premiere, the roar from the crowds that came after its debut was lost on him. "I wasn't doing it for them."[61] When people were applauding the celebrated 1962 piece, Taylor felt that they were also, without knowing it, acknowledging the painstaking work to create the less-acclaimed, even panned dances that had come before. "I couldn't forget how relatively easy the dance had been to make and how previous dances, both larger and smaller scaled, had stretched my goals much further. *Aureole* had been child's play compared with others that I had to dig for, grapple with, and slave over, ones that had a more developed craft to them but weren't as popular."[62]

What Taylor needed were "seed steps," as Horst called them—signature moves repeated with variation in sequence, speed, and direction. Horst had taught Taylor composition at the summer American Dance Festival at Connecticut College just before Taylor went to Juilliard. Taylor appreciated how open-minded Horst had been about his work despite their stylistic differences—he had reviewed Taylor's earlier pieces in *Dance Observer* before 7 *New Dances*—no mean compliment given the draconian style of Horst's exceptional drills.[63] (At the American Dance Festival, Horst's students dubbed him "the resident ogre."[64] He was known for pushing his students just enough. Dance critic John Martin argues that through Horst's rigor, Martha Graham clarified her technique: "Without Louis standing there beside [Graham], day in, day out, adamantly refusing to let her improvise . . . she would have changed the choreography . . . until it finally became diluted."[65]) Taylor saw that the seed steps would give him a more "kinetic" movement to communicate his idea.[66]

Taylor, unsurprisingly, twisted Horstian rules. In his hands, they were "unreasonably transmuted beyond recognition."[67] His deliberate misinterpretation of Horst was the kind, as Harold Bloom explained, many artists engage in to "clear imaginative space for themselves."[68] In his classic text *The Anxiety of Influence*, Bloom develops his idea of this strong misreading, where an often younger figure sees the work of a previous master and bends that work into a new form that fits the immediacy of his or her moment. An intentional misinterpretation can also lead to a unique approach perhaps not otherwise pursued. Sticking to our own views might be best achieved by finding lessons from the people who oppose us.

Incorporating criticism can benefit from pressure. Enclosure builds an intensity that can become an aid. Taylor began *Aureole* in Paris at the Théâtre des Arts, a nineteen-show engagement that gave him free time and full access to a stage during the day. He could work for the first time and get perspective from the audience's vantage point, where he started to notice the effects of distance and stage lighting on movements and even facial features in a way he hadn't before. Yet he scrapped it upon seeing it in New York light.[69]

Aureole, a piece that would have five parts, lacked a finale days before the rehearsal for its debut at the American Dance Festival. He tried to eliminate it. He had envisioned it as a solo that would feature him, a piece done largely on the left leg and that would be full of adagios, one of the ways that he wanted to change what was considered contemporary dance. But a rehearsal visit from friend and champion, poet and influential dance critic Edwin Denby, who suggested that the piece needed an ending, changed Taylor's mind. With little time, he refused to use the same "old used-up steps." He crafted his finale's steps out of "the first that come to mind. A bunch of dizzy tilts, turns, breakneck cavorting."[70]

Head to a retreat, give yourself a deadline, make it nearly impossible to get something done, and a new reservoir can often open up. As composer Leonard Bernstein said, "To achieve great things, two things are needed: a plan, and not quite enough time."

There is a reason why so many residencies are successful, ritualistic places for artists to work: time is in short supply. In artist residencies—such as MacDowell, Skowhegan, and Yaddo in the United States—each has a condensed time frame that allows for an ameliorating shift, "a move from the creative process to art-making" as choreographer Liz Lerman calls it.[71] In the beginning, all ideas are let in, more or less. "We talk, we listen, we generate, we gather, we teach, we make stuff, and it is all okay." Then there comes a point when you start to shut down the gates of what ideas get to be realized. She calls this the phase when you "flip the funnel" and whittle down your work to a more polished piece, a refining point where art making can become "excruciating."[72] The structure that a residency gives turns the process of making—a step into an inevitable unknown—into a kind of frame.

Author and neurologist Oliver Sacks, in a fit of desperation, once made a lethal dare with himself: He would write his book in ten days or else commit suicide. The hypothetically mortal threat terrorized him, he said. He had gone for months without writing anything. After the dare, he began to stitch together ideas in unexpected ways, and to take a sort of inner dictation as if he was just the "bridge," just "the transmitter," finishing the book a day early.[73] Handling such limitations can result in breakthroughs, as it can create a sense of uncertainty that often leads to more creative solutions.[74] Under pressure, we can see creativity when we expect to see regression.[75] Steve Jobs put this productive constraint on himself his whole life. He told his colleague John Sculley, "None of us has any idea how long we're going to be here, nor do I, but my feeling is I've got to accomplish a lot of these things while I'm young."[76]

––––––––––

At the end of Taylor's show that night at Lincoln Center, I walked up the diagonal Broadway blocks and passed another Kaufman Center on an unusually tiny block, 67th Street, where Broadway dives toward Amsterdam. I stopped in front of that Kaufman Center's glass-walled entrance. It gives a view of audience members milling around, coming in or out of the sunken entryway. To jot down some notes about Taylor's show, I reached into my bag and pulled out my blank-paged, curved-cornered, leather Moleskine notebook. I started buying them about eight years ago. They had me when I heard that the notebooks' design is based on ones that Vincent van Gogh, Pablo Picasso, Ernest Hemingway, and Bruce Chatwin used. I've since found out that this advertising pitch was a slight exaggeration.[77] Not that I believed it anyway. But I liked the reminder that everyone needs to sort out how to handle starting anew, that we all confront a blank page. I still use them. Now they remind me of Taylor.

Whenever we deal with blankness, we are in lineage.

"If I did a perfect dance, I think I'd quit, you know?" Taylor said.[78] Even the title of his dance *Lost, Found and Lost* hints at this cycle.[79]

Managing the gap between vision and work, which often looks to others like being swallowed by failure, is a lifelong process. It is perhaps the one thing that any artist or innovator can control. As the sage dancer reminded us on the eve of his fiftieth anniversary celebration of *Aureole*, "You never know how a dance is going to go with an audience. I never know. I never care as long as I think it's what I wanted to make. It's nice if they do like them, but that's not why I do it. I just like to make things."[80]

THE CRUCIBLE

ARCTIC SUMMER:
SURRENDER

If you surrender to the wind, you can ride it.
—TONI MORRISON

Within days of the news, more people walked into to St. Paul's Cathedral in London than had after the sinking of the *Titanic*.[1] In January 1911, Captain Robert Falcon Scott had set out to trek through Antarctica, covered in reindeer fur, on a journey to reach the South Pole, the "Holy Grail" of exploration. Nations had raced to see who could be the first to plant a flag on the Earth's southern end; "the Pole, and nothing but the Pole, was the talk of the day."[2] For Scott and his crew, the "journey to the Quiet Land" became a "living hell."[3] Rest eluded them at night and found them during the day. Some men fell asleep while trudging on the icy turf amidst "roaring" wind speeds that meant that they could "only talk in shouts" and move forward at a rate of about six inches per step as they dragged 200-pound loads on sledges in -30 degrees Celsius weather at best.[4] Sweat from these man-hauling exertions froze into ice on their clothes, thawed at night, then refroze and turned their sleeping bags from "wet blankets" into solid "sheets of armour-plate."[5] One man shattered his entire set of teeth from uncontrollable chattering in the frigid cold. The men felt "bruised all over, nearly dead."[6] No one has since bested the record that Scott and his crew set: all the men perished during the trip. The remaining five died within twelve miles of a camp where they had stocked food to refuel. It is often considered the great, un-

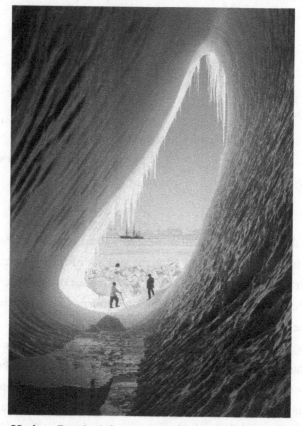

Herbert Ponting, *Grotto in an iceberg, Antarctica*, 1911.
Licensed with permission of the Scott Polar Research Institute,
University of Cambridge.

finished journey of the Edwardian golden age of exploration and "the world's most tragically famous failure."[7]

"The twenty-something biographies of Scott seem to be fairly evenly split between 'he was a courageous, quintessential British hero who was desperately unlucky,' or 'he was a lunatic who was driven by his ego which led to his death,'" Devon-born Ben Saunders told me in one of our first conversations, his electric-blue eyes flashing.[8] He is one of the world's greatest polar explorers. I wanted to understand why he was about to set out to complete Scott's journey a century later. At 1,800 miles, the length of sixty-nine marathons back to back, it would be the longest unsupported polar expedition in history.

I knew that Saunders had already set a record—he became the third person in the world to reach the North Pole solo and on foot.[9] No one has achieved this feat since. To depart from Cape Arktich-eskiy, he shared a flight with three other unaffiliated explorers in February 2004, splitting the cost to reach the seam where that north-ernmost Siberian land meets the Arctic Ocean, the start of their jour-ney. Two men had to be rescued. A French marine fell through the ice and developed frostbite and an American was airlifted out because of an ankle injury. The third, a Finnish woman, was never found. Saun-ders alone made it.

That day came on May 11 when he stood on the sea ice under the Arctic sun at the geographic North Pole, warmed his satellite phone battery, sticking it under his arm, and called his mother. She was on the cashier line at the grocery store.[10] She started to cry, became overwhelmed, and asked him to call her back. He rang his girlfriend. The call went to voice mail. After seventy-two days of trudging alone on the pack and pressure ice, at times swimming through the "inky black water" of the Arctic Ocean over three miles deep, he had no cheering squad, no flag to plant.[11] Besides, he said, any flag he could have planted would inevitably drift off, "usually towards Canada."[12] Framed on his desk at home is a report card from when he was thir-teen years old that begins, he recalled: "Ben lacks sufficient impetus to achieve anything worthwhile."[13]

Everyone has their own Pole, Saunders believes, an outsized dream that can involve a paradox: "We often need a few failures to get to the goal we're trying to reach." His occurred before and during the Arctic journey, an ingrown loss that had propelled, not paralyzed. I wanted to understand how he had surrendered to what he thought were his absolute limits and realized that there was still another frontier.

Being an explorer today is an unusual choice for a profession. Flag planting on the North and South Poles was once done in the name of science—specimen gathering, geographical discoveries, and magnetic research.[14] When Scott set out for Antarctica, Saunders reminds me, "We knew more about the surface of the moon" than we did about frigid planetary climates.[15] Yet by the end of the nineteenth century, with so much territory around the planet mapped, "explorers had nearly worked themselves out of a job."[16] Neither the term explorer, which calls to mind "a colonial chest-thumping image," he said, or adventurer, which can be a job description that "unfortunately, can suggest that you have nothing better to do," captures his central mission—to unearth a capacity stored within himself to shatter his own geography of human limits. As abstract painter Ed Moses likens his work to discovery, Saunders finally inverted the logic and told me that he has settled on the term *craftsman* or *artist* to describe his life of exploration.[17]

People driven by a pursuit that puts them on the edges are often not on the periphery, but on the frontier, testing the limits of what it is possible to withstand and discover.

With the exception of those whom Saunders considers his peers (a few "very obscure Norwegians"), it is hard for most to understand how ice-encrusted wilderness still pushes women and men to the edges of human endurance, and what it takes to endure.[18]

Yet now, since it is possible to fly to the Poles, or fly and ski the last sixty miles, some may see Saunders's work as little more than a "contrived stunt." Saunders tells me how amused he was that a "Random Person from the Internet" back in 2004 told him "in no uncertain terms" that any of his failures to reach the North Pole would be the result of "attempting the impossible," and that he should just "get a job." Saunders feigned an apology. "I'm normally all for changing my entire life on the half-baked advice of a ranting blog commenter. Instead, I've stuck to my guns, returned my nose to the spinning grindstone of the useless but meaningful, and pumped every penny, every fizzing joule of energy and every ticking second I have into the expedition I'm about to start."[19]

"How do we talk about the Arctic? How do we think about the Arctic? How do we relate to the Arctic?" Subhankar Banerjee wrote to open his volume on the region, anticipating the relational concern.[20] The imagination alone cannot conjure the realities of frozen realms.

"It's so far outside of most people's scope of experience that I might as well talk about going to outer space," Saunders told me, his voice lowered as if resigned.

Surrendering to negative drift, the fact that the ocean floes will move ice sheets backward as you're trying to advance forward—this is one reason that the Arctic is an alien experience. The ice landscape lies over much of the 5.4 million square miles of Arctic Ocean (about one-and-a-half times the size of the United States), which acts as a cistern for 10 percent of all the rivers around the globe—the Lena, the Yenisei, and the Ob in Siberia—and those ice layers are increasingly thin. "It's not, like, one big ice cap. It's lots and lots of sheets of ice, some of them miles across, some of them just a few feet across. It's always moving, always drifting," Saunders said breaking into a wry smile, "and chances are, if you're having a bad day, the ice starts drifting backward." One day when Saunders still had over a thousand miles to go, he skied north for over eight or nine hours as the ice drifted south over two miles. At night, alone and farther north of the Arctic tree line than any native Inuit for miles and miles, he would write in his diary about how far he'd gone after checking his GPS; it was a ritual he looked forward to most. In the morning he would check again, and often found that he had floated away from his goal as he slept. As if by a cruel trick, the rest he needed to continue could erase the gains from the previous day.[21]

Yet reaching a goal by walking on ever-mobile ground possessed a kind of magic. He enjoys "that it's never a well-traveled path. And particularly being alone out there, there's always this knowledge that this scenery and the icescapes were unique to me; that someone could come back to the same point, at the same time, a day later, and it would look completely different."

Eventually, he started to tune into the wind, the temperatures, and the climate's cues. "Clearly you can't change anything that's going on in this harsh place, but you start to understand its rhythms and seasons. You come to a place of surrender to the physical environment." Still, when the glassy, snow-packed ground was drifting backward and he had another thousand miles to go, it was "absurdly tough," he admitted, and took a long pause as if the feeling had rushed in again:

> There were days where it seemed completely impossible, and I couldn't even contemplate the ultimate goal. There were days when I'd just look at a bit of ice in front of me on the right bearing north, and just think, 'All I'm going to think about is getting to that bit of ice there, that's thirty feet away, and when I get there, if I get there, that will be a success. It'll be in the right direction, and then I can think about the rest of it.' So there were days like that where I just had to break it down into the smallest possible steps.

To avoid mental tailspins, he tried to keep the pain at bay by refusing to linger over any downbeats. His determined tone often

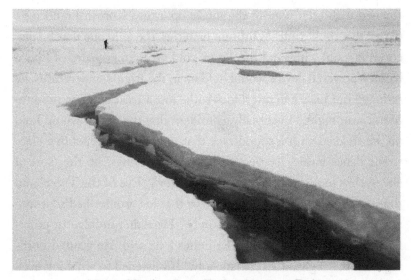

Martin Hartley, *Route Finder, Adventure Ecology
Trans-Arctic Expedition*, 2004.

Martin Hartley, *Navigator, Adventure Ecology
Trans-Arctic Expedition*, 2004.

rhymed with each note in the music on a tiny, Korean-brand mp3 player that took triple-A, lithium batteries, the only one that he discovered could withstand the Arctic cold. At first, not sure of how a battery-powered device would hold up in the frigid temperatures, he rationed out his sonic interludes with "just a treat of a few minutes of music at night." Eventually, confident that the device would hold up, he trekked with a soundtrack that ranged from repetitive electronic dance music, "some weird, wonderful songs," to the "sort of cheesy, but motivational" music—Survivor's "Eye of the Tiger" and the soundtracks of *Rocky* and *Top Gun* that his brother had sent him and labeled "for emergency use only." He didn't indulge in popular music from the time, like Radiohead, he said. He wanted nothing even the slightest bit melancholy. "If I listened to anything even mildly somber," in that depopulated landscape, "I would just be spiraling. It had to be upbeat."

Those before him have sustained themselves on the ice by reading poetry like Lord Alfred Tennyson's *In Memoriam* and "Ulysses," which famously closes with the final lines: "To strive, to seek, to find, and not to yield."[22] Saunders chose two books instead: *The Life of Pi* and *Courage from Piglet (The Wisdom of Pooh)*. *Courage from Piglet* made sense. Breakdancing to the sound of creaks in the ice, bum-rushing down snow-packed mountains, and pretending to spy out of the window on emptiness—a barren landscape of snow—these are the playful, likely sanity-saving stunts you can catch him doing in a video chronicling daily preparation activities for an upcoming expedition and his breaks from strenuous training.[23] So taking along Pooh and Piglet seemed appropriate.

Yann Martel's *The Life of Pi*, however, is about as unlikely a story as you might expect Saunders to be burying his head in alone on the high Arctic Ocean. Yet it, too, resonates with Saunders's life. Martel's novel is about a young boy, Pi Patel, who lives in a zoo in India; is told he is moving with his family to a place (Canada) he feels to be as "permanently far away" as Timbuktu; endures the loss of his father, his mother, and his brother en route; and survives as a castaway alone in a boat with a 450-pound Bengal tiger. Saunders has dodged polar bears, journeyed to an alien locale with the most ferociously inhospitable conditions imaginable, and sets off on the kind of trips that can be described akin to how Martel writes about Pi's survival as a castaway: "You reach a point where you're at the bottom of hell, yet you have your arms crossed and a smile on your face, and you feel you're the luckiest person on earth."[24] The power of the polar environment, the extreme nature of the task forces Saunders to discover a rarely used resource within himself.

When he told me about those brutal days, he often unconsciously slipped into talking about it in the first person plural, as if distancing himself from it was the only way to describe it. He referred to himself as "we" despite being alone on the ice, not out of arrogance, but perhaps, I wonder, as an unconscious sign of how much he needed to feel connected, to see it as a supported enterprise, even as he recalls the experience from the comfort of his apartment on vacation with his girlfriend on a warm day in July.

He'll admit that he embarked on his trip with a sense of trepidation. He boarded a Russian airline ("pronounced 'crash air,' spelled K-r-a-s,") to reach a place called Khatanga in the far north—a flat, desolate spot in the middle of miles of pack ice with a population of roughly 3,500. "It isn't the end of the world, but you can see it from there."[25] Saunders then flew by helicopter to a snow-covered spot where the land meets the Arctic Ocean with his preparation crew and his girlfriend. The group stayed on the ice for about forty-five minutes, documented it with video and photographs, and then got back into the helicopter, leaving Saunders. They had arrived on the day of a full moon, not a good time to start an Arctic expedition on the pack ice; the coastline can get pretty "smashed up" then as this lunar phase brings the highest and lowest tides. NASA described the ice conditions in the Arctic in 2004 as "the worst since records began," Saunders recalled. "All I could think about was running back up to bang on the door, and saying, 'Look guys, I haven't quite thought this through.'"[26]

On stage, when asked to deliver his life as a story, he is all confidence, wit, and self-deprecation—often he'll mention that he trekked for an entire day only to find that he had drifted backward a precise measurement of miles. Yet offstage, over the phone, I ask him about the most he ever drifted backward and he shows a bit more of his inner life. "I think my worst was . . ." he said, then paused and stayed silent for what felt like an uncomfortable length of time in our fast-paced conversation, as if glimpsing pain still lurking around him. He never completed his sentence. "Well," he said, "I can't remember."

Out in the Arctic, he said, "I was aware that I was responsible for my own survival," but eventually settled into a "wonderful feeling of 'Well, I can't think of a better word than surrender,'" as he described the process of nonresistance to wind, temperatures, and the pain that had brought him there.

It is a bit like living out Hooke's law—the force of an extended spring is equivalent to how far it is stretched. To convert our own energy and operate at full force, often we must first surrender.

I wondered for two years after first speaking to Saunders about this idea of surrender. How do you lean into pain when you're trying to forge ahead in one of the most inhospitable places on our planet? Why is that helpful? Talking about the martial art of aikido and how we can use it to manage pain is one of the things that helped me to grasp what Saunders was describing. *Surrender*, we both admitted, might be an imperfect word to describe it. The term is often synonymous with the white-flag retreat of loss in the context of battle. Yet when feelings of failure come with their own form of pain, empowerment through accepting it—surrender—and pivoting out of it can be more powerful than fighting. The kind of surrender that Saunders means is more akin to Nietzsche's idea of *amor fati*, to love your fate. "The demon that you can swallow gives you its power, and the greater life's pain, the greater life's reply."[27]

The power in the martial art of aikido comes from strategic non-resistance. If you have ever watched martial arts footage and seen a person abscond, retreat, and reemerge—calm and smiling and in a stronger position before the attacker or group of attackers even realizes they're gone—you have been viewing the Japanese martial art of aikido, perhaps even the film of O Sensei himself, the founder of aikido, Morihei Ueshiba (1883–1969). Aikido is the art of being thrown, falling, and standing up in a different, more stable place. It is the martial art with no kicks, the one that deals with perfecting both dimensions of life, how to go down and rise stronger.

Some who have studied its physics consider it the hardest of all the martial arts to learn, in part because it gets the body to do what thousands of years of conditioning has trained us not to do—relax when we feel threatened, so as to maintain access to our internal resources.[28] Our primitive survival reflex is to tighten up in the face of stress. "It's a part of us that kicks in faster than the cognitive part that thinks, oh, I can relax and open," said six-degree aikido black belt Wendy Palmer, one of the most prominent American aikidoists. She teaches how embodying mindfulness and the martial art's principles can enrich one's life, not just one's practice on the mat. She often hears that she looks huge when she's on it, much larger than her 5'5" frame, so surprising are her feats of neutralizing attacks from those twice her size. The contrarian nature of it all, she tells me, "is why we practice over and over in the intense simulator that aikido provides until that alternative neural pathway is deep enough that surrender becomes an actual choice that we can make."[29]

Aikido embodies the idea that when we stop resisting something, we stop giving it power. In aikido, an *uke*, the person who receives an attack from the thrower, or *nage*, absorbs and transforms the incoming energy through harmony and blending.[30] There is no word for competitor, only for the one who is giving or receiving the energy. If boxing is about meeting force with force, Peter Gombeski, who practices aikido, emphasized that with this martial art, the idea is about "either getting out of the way or accepting it, and diverting the energy right back to the ground."[31] The goal is to blunt the force of an aggressive incoming attack not by kicks, blows, or otherwise overpowering the attacker, but by "blending" as if in "liquid flow," absorbing instead of fighting against, "like entering a pool of warm light." It is a focused, fluid way of being that is akin to "being out in the world and being in the zone of the 'flow' state."[32]

Surrender heightens perceptions. Palmer offered me a tactile analogy of how we can hold two objects of the same size and density, say two glasses, one empty and one full of water, and feel their different weights, but if we tighten and squeeze our arm and hand muscles more, we won't perceive the difference in the two weights nearly as much. "When we are stressed, we lose access to information," she explained, "and when people are out there on the edge, they need to have access to all the information they can." That edge can be conflict. Yet the founder of aikido saw that edge as the energy of the world itself, as Saunders seems to, whether it is the winds of the Arctic or the ground shifting beneath our feet.

To surrender and draw on other resources to redirect our animating energy (*ki* in the Japanese and *chi* in the Chinese martial arts) turns aikido into a "reliable magic," said Sensei George Leonard, who owned a dojo with Palmer for thirty years.[33] Bodies are porous, "more space than particles," Palmer said, and she helped me to understand it: "In aikido, that space is as important as the object. It's the collective of the energies working together that control the technique." She offered the analogy that when you put two musical notes together, they become dissonant, but if you put space in between them, they can become melodic. What creates the magic is that you become so "congruent" with the energy coming at you that it takes very little to shift it in the advanced states of the martial art. Just as "a note can be implied but not played, in advanced states of jazz . . . it only looks like the person is not doing much in aikido; like they're just standing there and the other person falls down," but it's all being done by surrender.

When you surrender enough, you feel the heft of a situation or an environment and can better judge how to move with it.

If we haven't anesthetized ourselves to it, people can often experience relief from chronic pain in this counterintuitive way. Some pain-management specialists remind patients of advice that Aikidoists themselves might give: "tensing against chronic pain, or hating it, only increases the discomfort," yet instead, if the person surrenders, "allowing the pain and relaxing at the same time let the body self-organize so that more circulation can occur."[34] It is akin to heeding the warning that James Baldwin offered: not to be "panic-stricken at the very first hint of pain" and instead to understand "a very physiological fact: that the pain which signals a toothache is a pain which saves your life."[35] To transform from failure, you first have to let yourself feel really badly about it.[36]

This is still understood in Iceland—a place where people are happier than seems reasonable for a country in near-perpetual darkness for many months at a time. This country, with a national drink nicknamed "black death," *svarti daoui*, knows that the key to coping with pitch darkness and the many shades of night in Iceland, as author Eric Weiner discovered on his trip around the world to find the "geography of bliss," is to "embrace it" and not fight it, not wish it away.[37] It is easier said than done, but there are some forms of pain for which struggling and resisting is worse than acknowledging it and letting it be.

Shakespeare put this insight into Edgar's lines in *King Lear*: ". . . the worst is not / So long as we can say, 'This is the worst.'"[38] I came to understand this after losing seven friends in a little over a year. They died in a quick succession of independent accidents right after I graduated from college. All but one was younger than twenty-four years old. I was born on the same day a year later as one, one of my closest friends. Updrafts of laughter, deep, crevice-making smiles streamed throughout our conversations either in our dorm rooms or at L.A. Burdick Chocolate, her favorite—an all-dessert restaurant a block down from the American Repertory Theater in Cambridge. They were probing, intense conversations. She thought about others more than herself. She sensed that her life was not just her own. So when I got a call that Anna had drowned in an attempt to save her young cousin one day when she was watching him alone, died jumping in to save him although she herself could not swim, died and, in so doing, saved her young cousin's life, I remained shattered for the better part of a year. But somehow, I was not surprised at how she met her end.

When we surrender to the fact of death, not the idea of it, we gain license to live more fully, to see life differently, as I have to imagine Anna must have done to have surrendered herself. She decided in a split second that life must go on, even if it meant losing hers; that a young one, a sapling idea, that promise, must be given a chance.

For me, a gift of a steady, guiding thought transcended my compound grief—if life was indeed so fragile, if so many friends were departed, and I was still left, doing what was proscribed or expected simply because I could was no longer an option. If my life was to have a soul-stated meaning, I needed to be unafraid to walk down paths of my own choosing, which to some might seem like failure, to pursue all that mattered most to me. My gift from grief was the knowledge that I may never become my fullest self if I do not come to live from that place.

Surrendering, as I see it, is a bit like this. It is about giving yourself over to another mode of being. I often think of a story I heard Harry Belafonte tell about his friend, the late Martin Luther King Jr. King developed an emotional response to all that he faced that manifested itself in the form of a tic—a speech hiccup. "He constantly was . . . tic," Belafonte said, imitating this prodigious leader and orator's "flawed characteristic," as he called it. The tic didn't occur all the time, but it did happen during a few speeches, he said. King had confronted difficulties with speaking earlier in his life. He earned the passing grade of C in his oratory class in Seminary not once but twice, and yet went on to lead a nation through the power of spoken truth. Eventually Belafonte noticed that the speech hiccup had gone away. He asked King how he overcame it. King replied, "Once I'd made my peace with death, I could make my peace with all else," and the tic just disappeared.[39]

How leaders handle pain is something rarely discussed. Kathleen Kennedy Townsend was struck that her father, U.S. Attorney General Robert F. Kennedy, mourning the loss of his brother, President John F. Kennedy, in 1963, would retreat into his bedroom and read the work of his favorite poet, the Greek tragedian Aeschylus, on the wisdom that comes from letting in discomfort, "to really feel the pain," and grief to move through it. "He said, 'I'm going to dwell in the pain. I'm going to understand that something terrible has happened,' and I think it made him a really stunning, extraordinary leader because a lot of the time, people in the public life don't go deep into pain, and he was willing to do that," his daughter recalled.[40]

Having disempowered what threatens to do us the most harm, we are shored up with the knowledge that nothing else truly can. "It is not often that poets, psychoanalysts, sociologists and economists give the same advice: we fail because we have not learned to die," Scott Sandage writes in *Born Losers*, a history of failure in nineteenth- and twentieth-century America.[41] John Kenneth Galbraith echoed this refrain when he observed in *The Age of Uncertainty* that death is one of the greatest sources of anxiety for humankind.[42]

This is part of the paradox within the Axial Age spiritual traditions—the period between 800 and 200 BCE, from Socrates, Plato, and Aristotle and the emergence of Greek rationalism; to Buddhism and Hinduism in India; along with Confucianism and Taoism in China—that Karen Armstrong reminds us each has at its core. Their philosophies made paramount the inextricable relationship of suffering to life.[43] This is what natural childbirth reminds us, that life only comes when you acknowledge the pain that might come with it, not by fending it off. It is why, I imagine, the Sumerian goddess Ereshkigal is the Queen of Hell and also the Mistress of Life, constantly portrayed in a position of giving birth. It is what we see in the Indian Vedic myths or in the intertwining of life and death in the myth of Persephone and Demeter, where gods of death are also gods of harvest.

It is found even in physics, in the fiction of absolute zero. In theory, there can be a point when atoms have no life and no more energy.[44] Yet in a natural state, there is no such thing. When William Thomson, known as Lord Kelvin, taught this idea to the world, it revolutionized physics, creating a new field—thermodynamics. No object is immune from deriving some energy from its surroundings. No material can be cooled to the point of having no energy.[45] Perhaps surrender is equivalent to this idea.

Zero is the oddest number. Its value is foundational and yet unstable; it has what seems to be inexplicable properties. It can threaten some—multiply or divide a number by zero and you wipe it out. Or it can act neutrally—add or subtract zero from any number and it remains. For centuries, it has been a limit that most civilizations have preferred not to consider, with the exception of Hindu societies, which embraced it.[46] It is on the threshold, separating positive from negative, all that we want from all that we don't. Surrender, like zero, doesn't translate into an appreciable form. It is like the *duende* of the artist, living on the line in between worlds where intellect, intuition, and force meet, and unendurable beauty is born of enduring travails.[47]

For all of our attempts to describe surrender, discerning its place in our lives feels like trying to engage with that elusive number without which nothing makes sense, and through which all that we thought we knew falls down slack like a rag doll in our lap. And this is the trouble with the rebounding effect of zero: we have to first let ourselves get extremely low to go there.

———

Saunders has some help with the counterintuitive act of being vulnerable in the presence of pain; a ferryman often acts as a guide. This is a man with whom the artist-explorer talks regularly, Jerry Colonna. The former venture capitalist, an Italian American from Brooklyn who once worked in private equity at J. P. Morgan, has become a sought after counselor to entrepreneurs seeking more balance in their life. "Listening to and bearing witness to the suffering is part of what I was put here to do," Colonna told me, ensconced in his office on Broadway in the Flatiron District of downtown Manhattan. He is unassuming in his demeanor, but to be on the other end of his lupine gaze is to sense a probing heart and mind at work. Saunders counts on Colonna to help prepare him emotionally and mentally for his journey.

The men were, to me, an unexpected match. Saunders first went to Colonna for practical reasons. "Ben can be one of the representatives of Land Rover, but will not have enough money to put gas in the tank himself," Colonna told me. Saunders isn't doing this work for fame or financial gain. But in Colonna, Saunders has also found a well-suited coach. "Jung talked about the fact that we all have unlived lives within us. And as I've grown into my own adulthood, and become more comfortable with the second half of my life, I allow more of those unlived parts of myself to come forth. There's a photographer in me, a teacher, a writer, and a crazy wanderer in me."[48]

Hearing him describe Saunders's resilience and ability to accept the pain of his arduous feats from the comfort of his office, it sounded as if helping this world-class explorer accept the lows was easy. "I essentially mirror back to him and say, 'Okay, so this thing that you're trying to do that no human being has done before is hard. And you're shocked? If it wasn't tough, there would be queues or hoards of people out here!' which first gives Ben a sense of perspective again, a way to be more gentle with himself." But then he goes deeper.

Learning to accept pain and then move through it "is not just a simple mental cognitive trick," Colonna emphasized as if sensing my initial skepticism. "One of my Buddhist teachers, Sakyong Mipham Rinpoche, whose father brought the Shambhala warrior teachings to the United States, says that 'pain is not a punishment. And pleasure is not a reward.' You could argue that failure is not punishment and . . . success is not reward. They're just failure and success. You *can* choose how you respond."

As I questioned whether he was positing that a response to failure is mere choice, he said, "We have to be careful, because we can't just say, 'I'm going to reframe this experience.' It actually requires a kind of connectedness, what I often refer to as radical self-inquiry. It is a courageous looking in the mirror that says, the ugly stuff that I don't like to look at and acknowledge as well as the aspirational stuff that I do like to look at is okay for me to see and it's all there. Building that as a foundation for a kind of centeredness allows a kind of equanimity to emerge. Saunders is an extreme example of this."

When he finished that thought, my mind flashed back to Saunders's comment that Pema Chödrön's book *When Things Fall Apart* was one of Colonna's recommendations. Her message about accepting "the off-center, unresolved state" resonated with him.[49] When he is over the Arctic Ocean, he's aware of his full responsibility for his own survival. Yet the floating ice is a reminder that many things are out of his control.

"I've had to learn to become more relaxed about what I can change and disregard the rest," Saunders said. "If I can't change it, it's not worth worrying about"—even something as extreme as the ground constantly moving beneath his feet.

During his 2004 expedition, his example had inspired. He told me about a policeman in Chicago, Paul Christian, who had been shot and paralyzed from the waist down, and would leave comments on his website each day about his progress in regaining control of his body, spurred on by Saunders's trek. Saunders had no Internet connection from his tent, but his team in the UK received these messages and they would read them back to him when he needed encouragement during the limited contact time he had on his phone. His site chronicling his journey had 7.2 million hits. The fact that he wasn't just "doing a long walk on my own, and growing a beard, going slightly mad, but that it had a wider impact and what it was doing was actually providing the inspiration for other people was something that definitely, definitely, kept me going," he said.

––––––––––

"When Ben is out on the ice by himself looking for his father," Colonna told me, "I basically encourage him to not push it away, but to acknowledge it."

Colonna presumed I knew what he was talking about. I had no

real idea, not fully, and also felt that it wasn't my place to know more. I let the statement dangle in midair. What Colonna described came out in later conversations with Saunders. Early on, he had told me that his father had disappeared when he was five or six years old. Later, he told me that his father left their family's home one day, then just started showing up on weekends once a month for a few years. When Saunders was eleven or twelve, he stopped turning up altogether. He severed all contact without explanation. Saunders has no idea if his father, an orphan with no surviving relatives, is dead or alive. He hasn't been able to reach him in over twenty years.

The most paternal endeavor he could find to replace his father was exploration, Saunders said, that and mentorship from invented father figures whom he has found along the way. When he was young, he remembers being impressed by tough-looking British soldiers getting off ships, coming back from the Falkland Islands. John Ridgway and cyclist Jan Ullrich are among his heroes. Saunders identifies with Ullrich—his father also left the family early on, then came up to him at the starting line of a cycling race, and passed him his phone number on a sheet of paper that stayed in Ullrich's jersey during his many hours of racing and sweating in the rain. At the end, the cyclist had nothing left but blank, illegible, wet paper.[50]

Colonna may not be a father figure, Saunders told me, but still, "he says things I wish I had heard from him."

"A man travels the world over in search of what he needs and returns home to find it," novelist George Moore once wrote.[51] If he can't, he may continue the pursuit.

In an age where we can skip from idea to idea, with countless distractions to divert us, absconding from painful places is easy. How do we stand in a place where we would rather not and expand in ways we never knew we could? How do we practice the aikido move of surrender? The perception of failure, the acceptance of the low, is often the adhesive.

Saunders's admission to the prestigious Royal Military Academy Sandhurst had been taken by his family as a sign that "Ben has made something of himself." He dropped out after only eleven months. "My dad was a penniless, orphaned bricklayer, so there certainly wasn't an expectation I'd be a high achiever (or had an inheritance to cushion the journey)." His friends and family thought he had lost the plot of his life.

He was an accidental journeyman. After leaving Sandhurst, he ran a marathon, realized that he loved extremes, and sought out one of his heroes—Ridgway, a former army officer who rowed across the Atlantic in a wooden boat back in 1966. Ridgway runs the School of Adventure, a place that offers leadership development courses for corporate clients similar to Outward Bound, but in the Scottish Highlands. Saunders worked at the camp during his gap year between high school and university, mentored by this paternal figure. "[Ridgway] was very, very good at using his own experiences to get other people thinking differently about their own potential. So when he said 'Why not?' rather than, 'Of course it's not going to work, don't be ridiculous,'" Saunders hatched a serious plan to go on an Arctic expedition.

It began with what he considers "baby steps." The first was a try at a North Pole hike with an experienced explorer, Pen Hadow, in 2001. At twenty-one years old, Saunders was the youngest person ever to attempt this journey. It was a rough near win. He had "this strange idea of coming home to this hero's welcome," he told me through laughter, describing his staged reverie at London's Heathrow Airport with Union Jack flags waving to greet him. Yet the reality was more like a scene from Randall Jarrell's poem "90 North," where the childhood dream that gave meaning to reaching the North Pole faded in reality. Saunders realized midway to the Pole that he hadn't trained hard enough, hadn't prepared properly—"a catalogue of errors." They were attacked by a polar bear on their second day. Saunders developed frostbite in one toe and lost thirty pounds in eight weeks. They couldn't afford a satellite phone that year, so they used ski poles for their high-frequency radio antennae, which meant having only two hours of communication in a period of two months, and they started too late to make it to the Pole before the temperatures melted the ice. They had completed two-thirds of the trip—four hundred miles with nearly two hundred more to go—when Russian pilots told them that they had to turn around; they wouldn't survive the trek.

Saunders landed at his mother's house malnourished, suffering from frostbite on his left big toe that he worried might leave permanent damage. While he resumed working the job at the sports equipment store that he held as a high school student to pay back his sponsors, many of his friends had positions as commissioned officers. Sitting on a sunken couch in his childhood living room watching daytime television—anathema for strivers—he remembers getting a text message from his brother quoting *The Simpsons*: "You've tried your best and you failed miserably. The lesson is: never try."[52]

The circular arc of his life had contorted and careened. It left him "broken." "There was no shortage of others who would bluntly bluster, 'What the hell were you thinking?'" "Depression" set in, which "as an Englishman," he admitted, "I feel sort of ashamed to say. I could only see it as a failure." After a seemingly endless set of weeks of being laid flat, "I could only feel that I'd been sort of . . . beaten . . . by this challenge."

"It's not like I came back in 2001 thinking, 'When's the next trip?'" But something in him started to sway. He still can't pinpoint the moment, but after a while he started to realize, "This hasn't been a giant failure. In many senses, I've got an enormous amount of experience under my belt, a very hard-won first experience and, actually, I've come closer to achieving the skill than anyone in my position on the planet. I just haven't quite finished it, so I need to get back out there and finish the job."

Two years later he tried again, before a third, successful attempt. His journey is not "a grand achievement," but a universal one born of "trying and failing and stumbling."

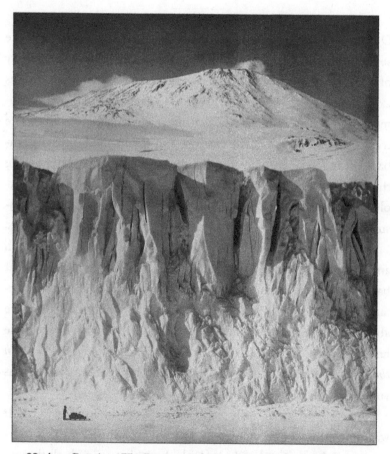

Herbert Ponting, *The Ramparts of Mount Erebus, Antarctica,* 1911.
Licensed with permission of the Scott Polar Research Institute,
University of Cambridge.

Saunders finally reached the North Pole as a midway point on his intended trek. His aim was to go to Canada straight across the Arctic Ocean from the Arctic coast of Russia, a solo journey that no one has ever completed. He traveled onward for another week before he made the decision to stop.

To reach an audacious goal, we sometimes benefit from having it lie just beyond our grasp.

———

During one of my last conversations with Saunders, it was as if the season of his life had shifted. London was celebrating the centenary of Scott's last expedition. The city's Natural History Museum was exhibiting a re-creation of the Edwardian explorer's lodgings, equipment, and tools. Saunders was getting ready to leave for a practice trek to extend Scott's failed mission, and then would officially embark during springtime in the Southern Hemisphere. After seeing this exhibition and reading the reams of paper dedicated to the explorer in biographies and articles, he had started to feel some pressure, especially as one of Scott's grandsons is now among his patrons.

Saunders is part of a long "lineage," one that he considers both an "honor and a burden," words that Colonna once said to him that have stuck. "I never anticipated the feeling of pressure and expectation and the weight of the story," but after understanding more about Scott, he started to identify with him. He learned how fallible he was, how he felt out of place in society. He had read the book *In the Footsteps of Scott* by Roger Mear and Robert Swan when he was young, but then it was more abstract.

"At first, I didn't really care about Scott as an individual. It was more the fact, initially, that this physical challenge, this journey, hasn't been completed yet. And why is that so, with all that we know?" Scott and his men traveled 1,570 miles, what could be considered the apex of a human psychological and physiological endeavor in Antarctica. "Despite having climbed the highest peaks, visited the moon, rowed and sailed the oceans, paddled lunatic rivers, mapped underwater caves, and crossed deserts, ice caps, and continents on foot and bicycle," Saunders said, no human has ever covered this distance. Antarctica has "people's desires and aspirations," both past and present, etched into the tundra.[53] It remains an unfinished path.[54]

Golden age explorers long ago reminded the world of the force of the incomplete: "It is true that we failed to bring home the North Pole as a national present to the world, but those that regret that circumstance may be consoled with the knowledge that failure implants more deeply in all breasts the desire to excel," Navy explorer George Nares said.[55] The near win is a likely outcome for even the most prepared explorers. Discovery can be a gold medal quest that never ends.

———————

One of Saunders's biggest fears is not a catastrophe, "it's someone not wanting to continue." Not that he expects it. His partner on this journey is his friend Tarka L'Herpiniere, who has been on at least twenty-two polar expeditions, but has come out of early retirement for another trek. Their chances are good. Many believe that Saunders and his new partner are the best prepared for this expedition in recent times. Saunders still worries. It's a "high-pressure relationship, being in this enormous expanse of nothingness, and yet spending all this time together cooped up in one tent." He also worries that his partner, a man who now works as a computer programmer but doesn't own a cell phone, might not tell him when he's struggling. "The legend about Tarka is that he's a machine," quiet, meditative, strong, and without much ego. Scott's team was used to the dance of collaborative work. Being in the Navy gave them practice with "living together on leaky wooden ships." Saunders has now prioritized strengthening team dynamics that could otherwise unravel them on the ice.

Perhaps we have grown impatient with the incomplete. We are part of a generation that, as the African proverb goes, wants to eat dinner in the morning, that longs for the immediate, fully prepared for consumption.[56] Yet the strength to linger over the long-left unfinished reminds us that something inexhaustible in us is empowered by striving, that we sense unnaturalness in blunt ends of journeys, of lineage. And that power comes from where we least expect to find it.

Saunders's journey south will not be the end. He had hoped that the trip "might scratch the itch for good. I hope I won't be bashing away out there in my sixties," he told me through a smile.[57] Yet he knows that there's something addictive about living at one's own edge. For now, he feels unfit to do anything else. We talked about what other job he could have, and if he could even bring himself to fill out an application. "If I tried to write one now I'd probably come across as an egomaniac, a lunatic, or both."[58]

There will be some changes to this polar trek. The trip to the South Pole ends with a climb—the plateau is at 10,000 feet, which comes with much higher winds than in the Arctic and with poorer visibility. Saunders told me that he was thinking of taking some poetry or verse along and learning to recite it by heart.

Arctic Summer, the title of E. M. Forster's unfinished novel which he started writing in 1911—an image meant to conjure "a period when all is light"—requires accepting the season that we're in.[59] To surrender means not giving up, but giving over. "For after all," Henry Wadsworth Longfellow wrote, "the best thing one can do / When it is raining, is to let it rain."[60]

When it gets cold in parts of the American Southwest, the Chinook winds are so fierce and warm that you can stand out in them, lean down at a near 90-degree angle and be supported. There is, too, a force that comes from surrender—a supportive, benevolent current. We come to our own edge, the precipice where we threaten to fall over into what feels like an abyss. Yet we often find a way to trust the wind.

There is no way to measure surrender's impact. We know its efficacy when we see it: After the deep pain of coming close, of failures of all kinds, we break open enough to contain, invite, and triumph over more.[61]

BEAUTY, ERROR,
AND JUSTICE

Over the long run of human history, the constant presence of beauty helps call us to the work of repairing in-
juries in the realm of injustice.

—ELAINE SCARRY[1]

It fixed me like a statue a quarter of an hour, or half an
hour, I do not know which, for I lost all ideas of time,
'even the consciousness of my existence.'

—THOMAS JEFFERSON[2]

In the face of war, he would ensure that they remembered the power
of aesthetic force. Few else would have dared. After all, the crowd
was living out the consequences of America's greatest failure with
their lives. Nearly one in four men would die for it during the na-
tion-fracturing Civil War.[3] They had come to Boston's Tremont
Temple to hear what the path toward a true union might mean. No
one was expecting to hear what the speaker thought it would take
to mend the nation's foundations, though they would listen. For it
came from this man, the "volcanic," near-peerless orator, one of the
nation's greatest statesmen in importance if not in title, who had
earned an oracular reputation as that of a "prophet," advocating for
acts that, soon after, came to pass—the freedom of enslaved men
and women who crossed over into Union territory, arming African-

Americans in the military, and a president-issued Emancipation Proclamation.[4] At the age of twenty-three, at a time when orators "were analogous to star athletes" and "the stage" could resemble a "boxing ring," his will, skill, style, and intellectual prowess proved to nearly all that "this is an extraordinary man" as one journalist put it, "cut out for a hero . . . As a speaker he has few equals."[5] He may have sensed that what he was to advocate was unexpected. He was, after all, a man of action. President Abraham Lincoln, then considered by many of his close advisors to be a failure before his reelection, sought his counsel on the subject of emancipation. In a two-hour, one-on-one meeting, Lincoln requested, should the war end without abolishing slavery, that he spearhead a federally sponsored underground railroad, helping the enslaved to go North.[6] Now in Tremont Temple, what the orator was about to tell the audience seemed like a mere trifle in contrast, but Frederick Douglass was sure, even in the face of war, that the transportive, emancipatory force of "pictures," and the expanded, imaginative visions they inspire, was the way to move toward what seemed impossible.[7]

An encounter with pictures that moves us, those in the world and the ones it creates in the mind, has a double-barreled power to convey humanity as it is, and, through the power of the imagination, to ignite an inner vision of life as it could be. The inward "picture making faculty," Douglass argued, the human capacity for artful, imaginative thought, is what permits us to see the chasm accurately, our failures—the "picture of life contrasted with the fact of life." "All that is really peculiar to humanity . . . proceeds from this one faculty or power."[8] This distinction of "the ideal contrasted with the real" is what made "criticism possible," that is, it enabled the criticism of slavery, inequity, and injustice of any kind.[9]

It helps us deal with the opposite of failure, which may not be success—that momentary label affixed to us by others—but reconciliation, aligning our past with an expanded vision that has just come into view.

––––––––

It may have seemed unusual, even unthinkable, as if Douglass was asking the gathered crowd to look at a single flower while flying down a perilous path on the back of a galloping horse. They had likely come expecting to hear a lecture about the Civil War and its Union-slashing effects rather than an ode to the power of visual imagination. Yet there Douglass stood in Boston's famed Tremont Temple—the integrated church one block from Boston Commons where he had delivered a commemorative address on the anniversary of John Brown's execution a year earlier, and where he would go on January 1, 1863, to hear the news of Lincoln signing the Emancipation Proclamation "on the wires" via a Samuel F. B. Morse–devised telegraph.[10] Lincoln, too, had spoken at the church, as had abolitionists of the day, from Brown to William Lloyd Garrison. Now, early in 1861, with the war just begun, the crowd was beginning to pay for combat's consequences with their lives. We will never know how he said it, in a stentorian or a subdued tone, but we do know that the audience was largely silent— his speeches "completely carried away" his audience, Elizabeth Cady Stanton recalled—as he focused on the critical role of what some might consider irrelevant in the face of a nation-severing conflict.[11]

Douglass made the case for art before science would show it: The "key to the great mystery of life and progress" was the ability of men and women to fashion a mental or material picture and let his or her entire world, sentiments, and vision of every other living thing be affected by it.[12] Even the most humble image held in the hand or in the mind was never silent. Like the tones of music, it could speak to the heart in a way that words could not. All of the "Daguerreotypes, Ambrotypes, Photographs and Electrotypes, good and bad, [that] now adorn or disfigure all our dwellings," Douglass said, could allow for progress through the mental pictures that they conjured. He went on to describe "the whole soul of man," when "rightly viewed," as "a sort of picture gallery[,] a grand panorama," contrasting the sweep of life with the potential for progress in every moment.[13] From the famed orator and abolitionist came one of the earliest articulations of how the private function of aesthetic force operates in public life. He was interested in the emancipatory quality of an aesthetic experience and the way it permeates the everyday.

Perhaps most surprising may not be that he said it, but when he did—at a time of unthinkable retrenchment and national fracture, when there was blood on the fields. In his first meeting with Lincoln, Douglass had turned up at the White House in August of 1863, traveling down by train without an appointment and sitting down with those who looked as if they had been waiting a week (and some had). Douglass sent the card announcing his arrival up the stairs. Within minutes, Lincoln received him. The Civil War president considered Douglass to be "one of the most meritorious men, if not the most meritorious man in the United States."[14]

The crowd would recall, too, what Douglass had once uttered—violence and force may be the only way out. He would not have been surprised if "Old Testament retribution" broke out through a Southern slave insurrection. It would have been as natural as the eruption of "slumbering volcanoes."[15] It was a time when most saw incendiary force as indispensable; "I have need to be all on fire, for I have mountains of ice about me to melt," abolitionist William Lloyd Garrison had said.[16] Douglass took it further, saying that "it is not light that is needed, but fire; it is not the gentle shower, but thunder. We need the storm, the whirlwind, and the earthquake . . . the propriety of the nation must be startled; the hypocrisy of the nation must be exposed."[17] Yet he had hinted at times that talk and action were not all that it would take to mend the nation's fracture as he addressed the more serious mood of the country. Those expecting to hear a two-hour speech the week that Emancipation would take place only heard a "ten-minute homily" that day at A. M. E. Zion Church in Rochester. "This is scarcely a day for prose," but instead, "a day for poetry and song, a new song."[18]

On the eve of Emancipation, eliminating the line between liberty and slavery by law, the nation was focused on another kind of justice that no law could correct—the ability to reconcile your dream with your reality.[19] The older notion of a "self-made man" was tested after the abolition of slavery upheld the two main tenets of American life—equality and what Lincoln called the "new birth of freedom."[20] Erasing the dichotomy of liberty and slavery would put even greater pressure on what "success and failure"—increasingly unmoored from financial position, but determined by character, agency and vision—would come to mean in public life.[21] Douglass was not only speaking about national justice, but what reconciliation would mean for each individual.

The course of our lives, Douglass argued, resembles "a thousand arrows shot from the same point and aimed at the same object." After leaving their starting position, the arrows are "divided in the air" with only a few flying true, as he put it, "matched when dormant" but "unmatched in action." Bridging the gap between sight and vision, which often comes through aesthetic force, is part of what made the difference.[22]

The words to describe aesthetic force suggest that it leaves us changed—stunned, dazzled, knocked out. It can quicken the pulse, make us gape, even gasp with astonishment. Its importance is its animating trait—not what it is, but what it does to those who behold it in all its forms. Its seeming lightness can make us forget that it has weight, force enough to bring about a self-correction, the acknowl-edgment of failure at the heart of justice—the moment when we rec-oncile our past with our intended future selves. Few experiences get us to this place more powerfully, with a tender push past the praeto-rian-guarded doors of reason and logic, than the emotive power of aesthetic force.

What forces us to see our errors, collective failures, ones too large to ignore and personal, perceptual ones of our own? Argument alone is not enough to make men good, Aristotle said.[23] Reason does not govern completely, as the example of Odysseus lured by the Sirens' song shows us. A cogent lecture on the topic by Yale philosophy pro-fessor Tamar Gendler outlined the way in which the non-rational takes over in everyday life, using an example of what would happen if we were to stand on a piece of glass at a peak point at the Grand Canyon over the coursing Colorado River. The rational part of us would know that we're safe on the glass, but being "affected by this visual stimulus" is enough to cause physiological sensations, which we may sense as trembling.[24]

"We all have a blind spot around our privileges shaped exactly like us," Junot Díaz has said, and it can create blindness to failures all around.[25] It results in the Einstellung effect: the cost of success is that it can block our ability to see when what has worked well in the past might not any longer. In the face of entrenched failure, there are limits to reason's ability to offer us a way out. Play helps us to see things anew, as do safe havens. Yet the imagination inspired by an aesthetic encounter can get us to the point of surrender, making way for a new version of ourselves.

Our reaction to aesthetic force, more easily than logic, is often how we accept with grace that the ground has shifted beneath our feet.[26] "Art is a journey into the most unknown thing of all—oneself," architect Louis Kahn stated. "Nobody knows his own frontiers."

Aesthetic force can alter vision. When an experience astonishes us, we can conjure up an image that we mistakenly recall as fact. Academy Award–winning visual effects supervisor Robert Legato discovered this phenomenon when working on feature films from Martin Scorsese's *Hugo* and *The Departed* to James Cameron's *Titanic*. Legato's powerful cinematic moments re-create historic events, but he doesn't reproduce them with fidelity. He makes up a compilation of images culled from what viewers state that they recall seeing, feeling, and in turn believing was in front of their eyes. He grew curious about how the audience viewed his scenes—the ones he wanted to astonish, to evoke poignant, powerful emotion—and had a conversation that became an experiment. When he was creating footage for the Ron Howard–directed feature film *Apollo 13*, an astronaut who had been on this seventh Apollo mission came to the film set as a consultant to check on the veracity of the events shown. The astronaut viewed footage of the actual shuttle blasting off with the red gantry arms rotating out of the way alongside the fabricated footage from the film. *Both* looked "wrong" to him. "When we're infused with either enthusiasm or awe or fondness . . . it changes what we see," Legato said. "It changes what we remember."[27]

Daniel Schacter, the Harvard psychologist whose research on memory may one day change how we consider its function in our lives, posits that instead of simply recording the past, "memory is set up to use the past to imagine the future" and "its flexibility creates a vulnerability—a risk of confusing imagination with reality."[28] This can result in "false memories," the ones that so stunned Legato. Factor in our "positivity bias," our tendency to recall the impactful and positive over the mundane, and it becomes clear that astonishment can change our view of the world.

Recently psychologists such as Jonathan Haidt and Sara Algoe have begun to measure how awe or elevation systematically results in generosity and altruism. A sense of "vastness" seems to inspire that in us.[29] Yet philosophy considered it before psychology ever would. Beginning with Plato, philosophers have had a common concern about how our responses to aesthetics can sideline cognitive defenses. Two thousand years ago, in the first century CE, Longinus understood that something akin to "transport" happens when we feel moved by "elevated language," that does not occur with rational "persuasion."[30] It was a truth that Leo Tolstoy declaimed a century or so ago: our response to art has the agency to do what "external measures—by our law-courts, police, charitable institutions, factory inspections" cannot.[31] Centuries later, we sense it still, as did Tolstoy, John Keats, and art critic Michael Brenson made the rare argument that "the aesthetic response is miraculous. Such an astonishing amount of psychological, social, and historical information can be interwoven into a single connective charge that a lifetime of thinking cannot disentangle the threads."[32]

We permit a new future to enter the room with these startling encounters. A young boy from Austin, Texas, Charles Black Jr., stood and knew it when he was just sixteen years old, thinking he was going to a coed social at the Driskill Hotel in his hometown in 1931. It was a dance, the first in a session of four, yet he remained transfixed by an image that he had never seen before. The trumpet player, a jazz musician whom he had not heard of, performed largely with his eyes closed, sounding out notes, ideas, laments, sonnets, "that had never before existed," he said. His music sounded like an "utter transcendence of all else created." He was with a friend, a "'good old boy' from Austin High," who sensed it too, and was troubled. It rumbled the ground underneath them. His friend stood a while longer, "shook his head as if clearing it," as if prying himself out of the trance. But Charles Black Jr. was sure even then. The trumpeter,

"Louis Armstrong, King of the Trumpet" as it turned out, "was the first genius I had ever seen," Black said, and that genius was housed in the body of a man whom Black's childhood world had denigrated. The moment was "solemn." Black had been staring at "genius," yes, "fine control over total power, all height and depth, forever and ever," and also staring at the gulf created by "the failure to recognize kinship." He felt that Armstrong, who played as if "guided by a Daemon," all "power" and lyricism, "opened my eyes wide, and put to me a choice"—to keep to a small view of humanity or to embrace a more expanded vision—and once Black made that choice, he never turned back. This is what aesthetic force can do—create a clear line forward, and an alternate route to choose.

Later Black would say that, in many ways, this was the day he began "walking toward the *Brown* case, where I belonged." Black would go on to join the legal team for the 1954 *Brown v. Board of Education* case that persuaded the U.S. Supreme Court to unanimously

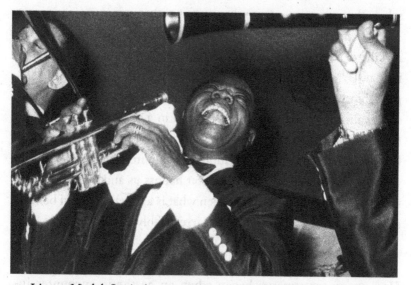

Lisette Model, *Louis Armstrong*, c. 1956. National Portrait Gallery, Smithsonian Museum. © Lisette Model Foundation Inc. (1983).

declare segregation unlawful, and become one of the preeminent constitutional lawyers in the country.[33]

Like an unwelcome guest at a tightly guarded affair, the power of aesthetic force can be "haughtily dismiss[ed]," though it can get us to a point of self-correction.[34] It has a hidden life in the personal form of justice. Black never forgot it. He held an annual Armstrong listening night at Columbia and Yale, where he would go on to teach constitutional law, to honor the power of art in the field of justice and the man who caused him to have an inner, life-changing shift.

Out of the "great artists in my time . . . it just happened that the one who said the most to me . . . was and is Louis," Black said. Whatever is melodic, lyric, or poetic that gets us to this place can be catalytic in a way that few other things can. Yet it was fitting that for Black it was jazz, built as it is on the art of sounding out longing, as we hear in much of American roots music, specifically the blues. The melody of a song about heartbreak suggests that we believe life will improve, yet in its bittersweet tones we remind ourselves that sometimes the only way out is through.[35]

"Pictures have a power akin to song," Douglass said. "Give me the making of a nations [sic] ballads, and I care not who has the making of its Laws."[36] The foundations of progress rest on twice-stamped improbability, once from the fractured foundations we need to mend, and again from stomping on its ground in a protracted tangle with failure, attesting to the desire for more. Social justice, no matter its kind, comes from more than critique and counterstatement, but from wrestling with seeming failure—what haunts us and what we would rather not inhabit, the gulf between what is and what should be. The tool we marshal to cross our gulf is irrevocably altered vision.

How many movements began when an aesthetic encounter indelibly changed our past perceptions of the world? It was an abolitionist's print, not logical argument, which dealt the final blow to the slave trade—the broadside of *Description of a Slave Ship* (1789). The London print of the British slave ship *Brookes* showed the dehumanizing statistical visualization with graphic precision—how the legally permitted 454 men, women, and children

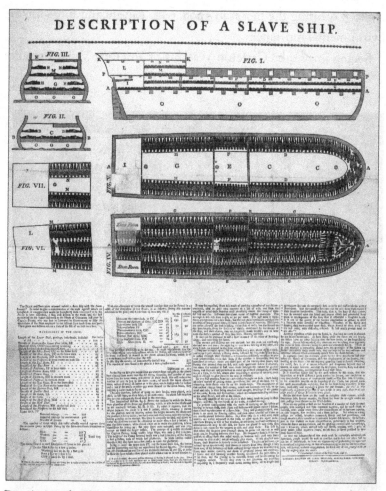

Description of a Slave Ship. (London: James Phillips, 1787). © The British Library Board. All Rights Reserved. 1881.d.8 (46).

might be accommodated (though the ship *Brookes* carried many more, up to 740).[37]

The contrast between reality and the image it conjured in the mind was intolerable enough to abolish the institution and was the evidentiary proof of slavery's inhumanity used in Parliament hearings.

Many credit the awe over *Earthrise*, the photograph taken from Apollo 8 orbiting the moon in 1968, with galvanizing force for the environmental movement.

Seeing images by Carleton Watkins of Yosemite Valley's granite

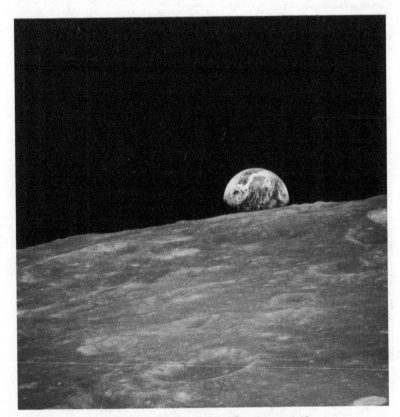

NASA / William Anders, *Earthrise*, 1968.

cliffs convinced Lincoln to sign legislation in 1864 that would lead to the establishment of the National Park Service.[38] It is embedded so deeply in the private lives of our more public shifts that we can forget it is there until a poet is jailed in a repressive regime, when his books are banned—there is a force to the images that they inspire that has a straight line to justice, and its mechanism can spark an inner alteration.[39]

It is similar to the phenomenon of the unfinished. When we're overcome by aesthetic force, a propulsion comes from the sense that, until that moment, we have been somehow incomplete. It can make us realize that our views and judgments need correction. It can give these moments "elasticity" and "plasticity"; as Elaine Scarry writes about the force of being moved by beauty—"momentarily stunned by beauty, the mind before long begins to create or to recall and, in doing so, soon discovers the limits of its own starting place, if there are limits to be found . . ."[40]

Douglass knew this from his own life. Born into bondage, he decided to seek his freedom after he saw a simple, seemingly innocuous image of sailboats on the Chesapeake Bay, gliding with a rightful ease that he had never felt. He stood and "traced" their path moving off to the ocean, powered by the currents, and then thought that he, too, would "take to the water" and go one hundred miles north.[41] He would set down these moments in words—probing and exact— with a pen that he would often lay in the bored-out "gashes" in his feet. They had been cracked open by frost from times when he had endured winters enslaved in Maryland.[42] He told his story through autobiographies that garnered him wide acclaim (and a warrant for his life—as we know, he fled to Britain to escape capture and a return to slavery). *My Bondage and My Freedom* (1855) sold 5,000 copies in the first two days.[43] John Whittier was not alone in considering it the headwaters of a "new, truly national literature."[44] Yet Douglass knew that the key to change lies in the literature of thought pictures we carry born out of contrast. "Poets, prophets and reformers are all picture makers—and this ability is the secret of their power and of their achievements," he said. "They see what ought to be by the reflection of what is, and endeavor to remove the contradiction."[45] This penetrating vision went far beyond a theory of our response to pictures. It described the chrysalis nature of becoming.

———————

Today, saturated with images, we live in a world where aesthetic force is alternatively so self-evident, so easily dismissed, that we move forward through its veracious power without realizing it. Douglass was speaking at a time when aesthetic force could not be forgotten. Then the new inventions of photography, microscopes, and telescopes had begun to give validity to what people could before only imagine. Many had started trying to take pictures of the granular surface of the moon as soon as Daguerre's photographic method was announced—constructing images of what we could envision, but not yet fully see.[46] Rampant visual deception, from frauds to humbugs to optical illusions, also had the power to confound and challenge the authority granted to sight alone. Each prompted the question, "How do I know what I am seeing is real?" Being skeptical of what the eye could see was a sign of wisdom; seeing reality justly meant accepting the limits of sight.[47]

The authority then lost by the eye was the gain of the imagination. Not seeing what was in front of everyone's view was disconcerting. Perhaps our most well-known example came from the time in 1872 when California tycoon Leland Stanford was curious about whether all four legs of a running horse ever leave the ground at the same time while galloping. At that point, before the invention of stop-motion photography, it wasn't clear. He decided to hire Eadweard Muybridge to photograph his horses mid-run.[48] It was a similar impulse to the one that occurred just after the invention of the daguerreotype, when all around the world people tried to take images of what the eye could not fully see such as the lunar terrain. Muybridge inaugurated a technique to freeze physical motion, a device comprised of twelve cameras, twenty-four inches apart set on Stanford's 8,000-acre estate in Palo Alto. The cameras went off at 1/1,000 of a second, triggered by the horse galloping on the track. On the third day, he got the adjustment right, proving that "unsupported transit" did in fact take place. It took him until 1878 to create a more refined system and revisit the Palo Alto track.[49] We focus on what would come out of this: Muybridge published his project *Animal Locomotion* (1872–85) to show the other physical movements that human vision cannot capture, which led to the birth of motion pictures. Yet we may forget what it conveyed—wonder through the mysterious act of sight was all around.[50]

Astonishment was bi-directional. People could lose themselves in both "minuteness" and "vastness."[51] The act of looking through a microscope could "lay bare a land of enchantments" and offer "revelations" that were "astounding."[52] The turn-of-the-century invention of the X-ray (a discovery, too, based on an accident taken as a route to a new possibility) was seen as a "new light, before which flesh, wood, aluminum, paper, and leather became as glass" which then many thought seemed "like some aged Arabian fiction."[53] Not only did scientific discoveries challenge the presumed accuracy of vision, but so did visual entertainments, from trompe l'oeil paintings to P. T. Barnum's humbugs. This "diminished credibility of the seen world" around the turn of the twentieth century placed greater value on what cannot be glimpsed.[54]

The mechanics of how we see and remember when we are moved is one way that we move forward out of near ruin. Douglass was describing, as he saw it, our pictorial process of creating reality.

It is as true of vision as it is of justice—distorted, flat, horizontal worlds become more full when we accept that the limit of vision is the way we see unfolding, infinite depth. Painted and printed images used to be just flat bands of color until the invention of perspectival construction and with it, the vanishing point—the void, nothing, the start of infinite possibility.[55] Moving toward a reality that is just, collectively and for each of us individually, comes from a similar engagement with an inbuilt failure. A fuller vision comes from our ability to recognize the fallibility in our current and past forms of sight.

——————

When I visited Douglass's estate high on a hill in Anacostia, overlooking the Capitol building, I saw that his irregularly shaped study, where he wrote speeches and correspondence, was angled to face three things at once—glass-paneled bookshelves, a wall of pictures and photographs, and a window with a view of pure expanse. There are homes, and there are *homes*. Douglass's residence in Anacostia was a political act, not a retreat.[56] His study has a curious tripartite vantage. It was off the parlor next to the main entrance without a division: there was no door. The arrangement of his study displayed his life lived with those powers—of oratory, of pictures, and through the window, a new imagined world. Behind his home, in view from his study, was a cabin—a windowless, one-room brick house, only ten by twelve feet—that he had built to replicate the slave cabin where he was born. Out on the house's hilltop front lawn, he could face the arc of his own unprecedented rise—to the right, a green expanse of Maryland where he was born enslaved, and to the left, Washington DC, where he became a man so prominent that a bill was introduced in the Senate for his body to lie in state in the Capitol upon his death.[57]

He had no doubt, he said, that his topic would need further exploration. "The influence of pictures" upon our thoughts "may some day, furnish a theme for those better able than I, to do it justice," he said.[58] It has since become a timeless idea, articulated by national leaders and sages in our age.

What we lose if we underestimate the power of an aesthetic act is not solely talent and freedom of expression, but the avenue to see up and out of failures that we didn't even know we had. Aesthetic force is not merely a reflection of a feeling, luxury, or respite from life. The vision we conjure from the experience can serve as an indispensable way out from intractable paths.

What is the future of how we think about so-called failure, these dubious starts and unlikely transformations? This was the apt question that came from a friend, a photographer, as I was writing this book. We can answer it by finding ways to honor them, by not letting the path out of them stay hidden, by letting them be generative, even indispensable. Seeing the uncommon foundations of a rise is not merely a contrarian way of looking at the world. It has, in many cases, been the only way that we have created the one in which we are honored to live.

THE BLIND SPOT

If a pot of wisdom is broken, it could mean wisdom will
spill out of the world or, on the contrary, it could mean
it will permeate every nook and corner and be accessible
to everyone.

—EL ANATSUI[1]

Once we reached a certain height we could see it. Until then the
path—high, strong, hidden, and burnished with the patina of use—
was nearly lost. Honoring or preserving it at first seemed unthinkable,
and then inevitable. The mile-and-a-half-long track had long cut a
swath largely above Tenth Avenue, the gills of Manhattan Island's
Lower West Side, and looked as if it would never be much more than
what it was—an engineering feat built nearly a century ago to haul
meats, dairy, and produce. The city demolished parts of the viaduct in
the 1960s, and shut it down completely in 1980, but it remained alive
as a fantasy repurposing project for architects for decades, a kind of
Holy Grail, while a succession of mayoral administrations had tried
to scrap it.[2] Pedestrians in New York's Chelsea neighborhood would
often scurry under the aging tracks with accumulated debris and
grime to avoid being bombed with droppings, while at night on the
tracks above there were rumored to be raves.[3] How to scale and enter
the risen path was largely unknown. It all might begin in darkness, but
it cast a shadow that, when viewed from the ground, was too bleak.
Demolition was once a question not of "whether, but when," until one
photographer spent a year on the trail documenting what was there.[4]

The scenes were "hallucinatory"—wildflowers, Queen Anne's

lace, irises, and grasses wafted next to hardwood ailanthus trees that bolted up from the soil on railroad tracks, on which rust had accumulated over the decades.[5] Steel played willing host to an exuberant, spontaneous garden that showed fealty to its unusual roots. Tulips shared the soilbed with a single pine tree outfitted with lights for the winter holidays, planted outside of a building window that opened onto the iron-bottomed greenway with views of the Hudson River and the Statue of Liberty to the left and traffic, buildings, and Tenth Avenue to the right.[6] Wading through waist-high Queen Anne's lace was like seeing "another world right in the middle of Manhattan."[7] The scene was a kind of wildering, the German idea of *ortsbewüstung*, an ongoing sense of nature reclaiming its ground.[8]

"You think of hidden things as small. That is how they stay hidden. But this hidden thing was huge. A huge space in New York City that had somehow escaped everybody's notice," said Joshua David, who cofounded a nonprofit organization with Robert Hammonds to save the railroad.[9]

They called it the High Line.

"It was beautiful refuse, which is kind of a scary thing because you find yourself looking forward and looking backwards at the same time," architect Liz Diller told me in our conversation about the conversion of the tracks into a public space, done in a partnership with her architectural firm, Diller Scofidio + Renfro, and James Corner, Principal of Field Operations, and Dutch planting designer Piet Oudolf. Other architectural plans proposed turning the High Line into a "Street in the Air" with biking, art galleries, and restaurants, but their team "saw that the ruinous state was really alive."

Joel Sternfeld, the "poet-keeper" of the walkway, put the High Line's resonance best: "It's more of a path than a park. And more of a Path than a path."[10]

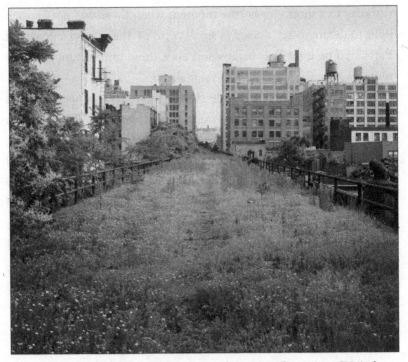

Joel Sternfeld, *Looking South on an Afternoon in June*, 2000. Digital C-print; 39 1/2 x 50 in. (100.33 x 127 cm). Courtesy of the artist and Luhring Augustine, New York.

From a certain elevation, with the benefit of a view of the ground and into the distance, we see how a rise often starts on a outworn, maligned foundation; the threshing floor of our endeavors becomes a kind of consecrated ground.[11] It has the authenticity of a careworn luster that comes with use. We hear more about dignity and "pensive luster" from cultures where the patina of age is highly valued, from the *shutaku* (soil from handling) in Chinese culture or the Japanese concept of *nare* that garners a reverence over "shallow brilliance," objects with too much finish.[12] In France, low radiance, the mere shine off a coin, was once enough to mark the start and end of the workday in winter, it was "the moment when there was not enough light to distinguish a denier [a small coin] of Tours from a denier of Paris."[13] The light that begins and ends these uncommon journeys requires a similar sensitivity to their sheen.

It often takes a blaze to see things anew. So age upon age has had its icons who went unsung during their lifetime. When Herman Melville died as a customs agent at the Port of New York in 1891, his widow complained that the copyright of *White Jacket* (1850) and *Moby-Dick* (1851) had no worth; they "give no income and have no market value."[14] It took nearly seventy years for *Moby-Dick* to receive its critical acclaim. In the final months of writing the book, Melville suspected as much, and acrimoniously foretold his fate: "though I wrote the Gospels in this century, I should die in the gutter."[15] Our lodestars often shine a few foot-candles below the level we are prepared to see.

A rise often falls into the blind spot of vision, and so we tell the stories that I have in this book because we are hardwired not to be able to glimpse them. Like a type II error in statistics, a "false negative," when we have the evidence but can't see that an alternative hypothesis is correct, these rises are a perceptual miss. We tell the story of Muhammad Ali's eighth-round win against George Foreman that night in Kinshasa, Zaire, even though we know how it ends, for while it happened, no one could see it. Ali upset most of the 60,000-person crowd who favored him as he spent the first seven rounds, 180 seconds long each, learning against the ropes while enduring brutal frontal attacks from Foreman, known to have bored a hole in his practice punching bag. No amount of screaming from his trainers could get Ali off the ropes, never mind the shouting of those sitting near the ring, from George Plimpton to Norman Mailer—counting how many right-hand leads Ali took, and remembering how Ali, being pummeled, still managed to whisper to Foreman in the seventh round, "Is that all you got, George?"[16] Yet no one but the fighters in the ring could sense it—there is a difference between being beaten and being strengthened, for as it happens, it is hard to perceive.

We extend the reach of these stories through repetition, as if to create the feeling of a Danish *hygge*, a word with no cognate in English that describes the feeling of sitting around a campfire in the cold with friends.

Entrepreneur Sara Blakely has often described the influence of her father's unique way of asking about her activities when she was a young child; the lessons gleaned from his perspective became part of the foundation that helped her become one of the youngest self-made billionaires at age forty-one. Sitting at her family's dining-room table at night meant hearing him constantly say, "What did you fail at today?" She and her brother disclosed their failed attempts at school activities like sports tryouts. After each one, he raved the way other parents might over a stellar report card.

"Blakely, you know you're gonna change the world," her closest friend, school teacher Laura Pooley, would often say, flopping onto a bed in their shared apartment. Blakely wanted to go to law school, but had twice done so poorly on the LSATs that she felt as if she had failed.[17]

"But I sell fax machines," Blakely replied. Going door-to-door with office equipment was Blakely's work for seven years.

"I know, but it's your destiny," Pooley said.

Blakely is the founder of the girdle-redefining line Spanx, valued at one billion dollars in 2011. She founded the company before the age of twenty-nine, and currently owns it outright. She is one of a handful of female billionaires who created wealth without a husband's income or an inheritance.

She attributes the conversion, in large part, to her father's childhood reconditioning about failure and its definition. Failure became not the outcome, but the refused attempt.

The equivalent of Blakely's childhood dinner table conversations now exists as a conference called FailCon, a summit in Silicon Valley, which also takes place around the world from France to Australia, helping people "be wrong as fast as they can," and speak publicly about how they did it.[18] The rule there is that people can't speak about their successes, only their failures.

"This is the only time that I've ever called someone to ask if I could speak at their conference in the last ten years," said Vinod Khosla, founder and CEO of Sun Microsystems and Khosla Ventures, speaking to the audience gathered in the ballroom of the Hotel Kabuki in San Francisco in 2011. PayPal cofounder Max Levchin, Mark Pincus, founder of the social gaming company Zynga, Travis Kalanick, cofounder of Uber, and Kholsa are just a few of the speakers at this conference in the past few years, attended by tech entrepreneurs, investors, and founders.

I found a seat at the back of the hotel ballroom next to a slight man with blond hair and sun-weathered, tan skin who told me in a heavy Australian accent that he is a surfer, a harpsichord player, and also an entrepreneur. (He later told me that he had sold his company, astrology.com, with five million unique visitors to iVillage in 1994 for approximately $28 million.) He came to FailCon looking for a to-don't list and to hear Khosla, who is fluent in failure. Khosla has thought about the many permutations of failure in entrepreneurship so much that his insights are either condensed quickly into pithy, insightful comments or are so deeply nuanced that they beg for clarification—and Kalanick, who stated that he was putting in his bid for "the unluckiest entrepreneur of the year" with his speech. After Kalanick's synopsis about his ten-year-long slog, his astounding serial setbacks so heinous that if even one of the things he talked about had happened, it would be a failure, the post-lunch crowd, sluggish when he first stood on stage, was left rapt, pin-drop still, and few heads moved except to offer a sympathetic laugh.

"The problem is that when you do the fake-it-until-you-make-it strategy when you're failing, it will crush you," he said, then stopped, looked down, and said under his breath, partially caught by the microphone: "I said that so casually, so lightly, '*it will crush you.*' Maybe I should sit down." He sat down and the table crashed.

"Oh, okay, that just happened," he said as if suddenly remembering that he is, in fact, in front of five-hundred people, sitting next to a falling table, and not alone, reflecting on a painful period in his life. "This is what I love about FailCon," he said. "Whatever I do up here, it's totally okay."

Kalanick left time for questions but not for nearly as many as the almost fifty hands I counted that bolted up and stayed raised as he scanned the crowd. The first question was about his mental health and whom he was relying on for advice and mentorship.

"When you go this long, all the people who were giving you advice in the beginning start to think you are crazy," Travis said. "So ultimately, by the time you get this far in, you don't have anyone to talk to.

"Are there any other questions?"

The woman next to me leaned over. Despite writing about failure for years now, I had still needed the reminder of the dingy gleam of these rises, and I must have had a stunned look on my face. She touched my arm and whispered, "What's the point of FailCon if we can't talk about those things?"

Development aid organizations are also beginning to create spaces to process unintended outcomes with more transparency.

"If we all knew exactly what we were doing, we wouldn't still be at it fifty years after we said we were going to solve the world's problems," Tim Brodhead told me from his office in Montreal when he was president and CEO of the J. W. McConnell Family Foundation in Canada, which since 1995 has specialized in funding difficult projects in the development sector.[19] Success means something is wrong, Brodhead said. "It means that we're either choosing very simple issues, or we're deluding ourselves about our results."

Brodhead was one of the earliest investors in Engineers Without Borders, Canada (EWB), an NGO based in Toronto, which recently dared to speak publicly about the organization's setbacks in their development initiatives across sub-Saharan Africa. Years ago, EWB began to publish Failure Reports in addition to an Annual Report, pushing their level of acceptable disclosure beyond what many organizations would dare for fear of losing funding.

"The big organizations are driven by a need to raise donations. The dominant view is, well, the public won't understand because we've made our pitch on the fact that if you give us a donation, then we'll produce miracles. Well, everybody knows that's not true. Everyone in the field of international development knows that's not true." The result, he says, is that development organization fund-raising appeals often simplify the message down to: "Give us the money, we'll solve the problem. So if you say, 'You gave us money but we haven't been able to solve the problem,' that's a pretty dangerous thing to venture into."

EWB Canada's cofounders, George Roter and Parker Mitchell, along with Ashley Good, who runs an interactive web portal, Admitting Failure—a ground-clearing operation for other NGOs to disclose failures—were undaunted. As engineers, they had trained to understand systems analysis, the practice of predicting potential failure.[20] They hold to a premise that we make breakthroughs in part because we are free enough to acknowledge when we have fallen short of our stated goals. The organization's courageous self-criticality has been groundbreaking, one of the great catalytic moments in the field.

"After sixteen years of doing work in the NGO sector, I don't know of anything that broaches this subject in the way that they have done it," Samantha Nutt of War Child Canada told me about EWB's initiative. "A lot of the time NGO groups will come together in cluster groups, and there you'll have that dialogue, but never in this kind of big, cohesive, multifaceted way."

Conversions are aided by a collective re-envisioning of what can come from alternate terrain. It was a West Side community board meeting that brought High Line cofounders Hammond and David together. Both were concerned about preventing the railroad's demolition. They were the only ones. Everyone else at the meeting was "verging on apoplectic about the need to tear the whole thing down."[21] The tenor only became more aggrieved when they tried to preserve the "blight" that some thought would collapse any day.[22]

For a while, any materials about converting it into a route for all to enjoy went into a folder in the office of early supporter Christine Quinn called "Good Ideas That Will Never Happen," who was then Speaker of the New York City Council. Yet Sternfeld's images of the rusted, out-of-use tracks sparkling like the inside of a geode turned the landscape into a metaphor, an accurate view of how we live, one that had political force enough to transform public sentiment about the aerial path. Soon after, the paperwork started to outgrow the file.[23]

There is no word to describe exactly what the High Line is to the non-architects among us, nor the collective reframing process required to see beyond its dingy path.[24] The promenade's landscaping and minimal architectural interference is meant to find a balance between "melancholia and exuberance," Diller told me. "Whatever that intermediate thing is, it's ineffable and is kind of what makes the High Line so popular."

"Part of what is so successful about the High Line is that it looks like it's about nothing," Diller said. Everything is prohibited on the promenade but the act of moving forward or stopping to look at the vistas from that vantage point. A dedicated place for strolling, where there are no dogs, no bicycles, or wheeled objects of any kind, it is "radically old fashioned," designed to let us do what we ordinarily don't, like taking time to linger and gaze at passing traffic. There is even a "sunken overlook" viewing station with movie-theater-style rows of descending seats and a window instead of a screen to see Tenth Avenue's traffic instead of a featured film. Looking at the path beneath our feet and the view before us are the High Line's activities.

The High Line's path will extend up the island in nearly interminable stages, "perpetually unfinished."[25]

As if to underscore it, on the west-facing side of the High Line, with views of the skyline and the Hudson River, sculptor Anatsui erected a monumental mural, *Broken Bridge II*, a three-dimensional painting the size of a city block made of flattened, dull-finish tin and mirrors with expert placement and hours of scaling. The vista in its upper reaches blends sky and land "in such a way that you do not know where mirrors end and sky begins."[26] Anatsui, known for his radiant, monumental murals with a unique luster, fashioned as they are out of recycled metal bottle caps from his studio in Nigeria, starts his work from an approximate center with exquisite discards. He then builds outward, unscrolling the once-scattered shards so that they shine in their new form, as if they could unfurl to the full extent of vision.

For me, walking the High Line has always felt like a land-bound *immram*, a passage tale where physical roads weave with new, imagined geographies without differentiating one from the other.[27] It is an alternate bridge, offering entry, surrounded by the company of others, who walk, cavort, sit, or stroll around me, all enjoying previously inaccessible terrain.

THE GIFT

THE ICONOCLAST

How, as a human being, does one face infinity? How
does one attempt to grasp the incomprehensible?
Through lists . . . the origin of culture.

—UMBERTO ECO[1]

Lists only seem flat. We live in them and look through them.
Through repetition, they give coherence to what eludes form. We
cling to lists even when their contents burst at the seams. From
Homer to Joyce, Dante to Whitman, we have long comprehended
the universe through this vertiginous linear form.[2] Rudimentary as
they can seem, they permeate our interpretation of culture, down to
how we catalogue our DNA. "Wherever you look in cultural history,
you will find lists," Umberto Eco said. They order our mental walk
through innumerable paths. Their presence reminds us that there is
ever more to evaluate on the horizon, more that otherwise might escape our view.

———————

"There is this list, I gather, that travels around through all of the
offices in Hollywood and everybody knows about it," Meryl Streep
told Charlie Rose at the start of an interview, recounting the unlikely
journey that a screenplay had taken to get to her. "It's the Black List.
It's the greatest scripts that are not produced," Streep said, then
paused giving a wry smile, "and maybe not producible."[3] Streep
knew of it because one of her recent film roles came to her that way.[4]

The screenplay had been around Hollywood for a while, gaining no traction. Being voted on to the Black List garnered the script attention and then an all-star cast.[5]

The Black List is a way of getting at the truth that few expected—many iconoclastic scripts were the ones that executives thought had true merit, but studios were often too risk-averse to approve. After landing on the list, much can change. The list revealed the unproduced screenplays secretly beloved by major film industry dealmakers. By granting importance to iconoclastic talent, the Black List has altered how the film industry does some of its most lucrative business and has expanded the idea of what constitutes excellence in a screenwriter's craft.

Seven of the last twelve Oscars for Best Screenplay went to scripts that were on the Black List. Three of the last five Best Picture Oscars were movies based on Black List scripts. The Black List has become a king- and queenmaker, a Hollywood institution, a triumph for screenwriters, particularly for those making scripts too "quirky," as Jodie Foster said, to ever get made.[6]

If the Writers Guild of America logs approximately 50,000 new screenplays every year and major studios release only 150 films annually, the tight bottleneck means, as Scott Meslow of *The Atlantic* reminds us, that "all things being equal, an unproduced screenplay has a .3 percent chance of being made into a feature film by a studio."[7] Out of the 168 screenplays on the debut of the Black List, sixty-eight have been made into feature films. This produces a miracle of a statistic—40 percent and higher of the films that land on the Black List get produced and distributed.

I was in Los Angeles to figure out why its originator didn't want anyone to know who he was, and how a simple list could shift an industry's perspective.

"I was just an aggregator of information," the Black List founder tells me, looking down at the table in the booth where we sat in Soho House's glass-walled room, revealing a splayed aerial view of Los Angeles above the Sunset Strip, moving his copper dreadlocks off his shoulder.[8] Though lightning-quick and handsome, he says that he's grateful to have a job that is nowhere near the camera. Most of his conversations are on the phone, or sometimes over drinks. His restrained ambition has remained what it was when we attended Harvard College together (separated by a year): to be the person behind the person in charge. He created the list as a way to be better at his job as a development executive at Leonardo DiCaprio's production company, Appian Way. He kept his Black List-related anonymity for two years. But public curiosity became too great and, in 2007, a reporter identified the originator as Franklin Leonard, who had then become vice president of creative affairs at Will Smith's production company, Overbrook Entertainment.

It started as an anonymous e-mail. In 2005, Franklin wrote to seventy-five colleagues in Hollywood asking them to send him a list of up to ten of their favorite screenplays. There were three conditions. First, they had to love it. Second, it could not be in theaters that year. Third, the script must have become known in the previous twelve months. Nearly all did as the anonymous e-mail asked. Three declined. A handful of others joined, which brought the final voting count to ninety. Franklin then tabulated a ranked list based on the number of votes each screenplay received, aggregating the information with just a few "simple moves on Excel," he said. He slapped on a "vaguely subversive name," and e-mailed it out anonymously to the people who had voted.[9]

The list's name is only partially a reference to the historical Hollywood industry anticommunist blacklist—the group of studio executives, directors, producers, and writers questioned in Washington by the House Un-American Activities Committee (HUAC) and prevented from working in Los Angeles by the Motion Picture Association of America. Franklin wanted to refute the idea that black stands for something undesirable.[10] As a student back in a middle school in Georgia, he remembers having a teacher tell the class when talking about symbolism in literature that white is often considered good and black is bad.

"There was no racial animus there," he clarified. "It was more, if you see a cowboy with a white hat, that's probably your good guy, and if you see one with a black hat, that's probably your bad guy. Yet even as a young boy," he tells me, "I remember thinking, I don't like the implications of this." Neither did writer James Baldwin, film scholar Manthia Diawara, or any of the other artists, poets, and scholars who have detonated bombs of scholarship on the color-sign logic in literature and film noir, rooted in biblical texts, equating blackness with darkness and evil, and whiteness with purity and light.[11]

Like architect David Adjaye, who aimed to deftly invert color symbolism with his famed black buildings, such as the one designed for artists Lorna Simpson and James Casebere, Franklin turned the list's black association into a statement. The tag line on the frontispiece of the list the first year was "THE BLACK LIST is well aware of the irony of its name. The second year, it was "BLACK is the new white." In 2010 it was a reference to Jay-Z's lyric, "all black everything." "In a very subtle way, I'm trying to be black positive," and he said, "in some way, Hollywood has embraced that element too." People have pulled him aside and complimented him on the subtle inversion of racialized symbolism, particularly noticeable in an industry where power often comes in one color. Lisa Cortes, an executive producer of the Oscar-winning film *Precious*, said that she "loves that a seemingly subversive term could be something that is so empowering." She went on to say, "As we all know, what is on the edge today becomes the mainstream tomorrow."[12] Though it was never the list's explicit intention, highlighting improbable scripts from its inception gave it a deft political point of view. Works once on the brink of failure from lack of public acclaim can be more powerful than we often realize.

After he sent out the list, Franklin went on vacation as the Black List began circulating through Hollywood. "Everyone is in each other's offices, calling each other, and debating the order of the list," said William Morris Endeavor agent Cliff Roberts, who had a client on the 2005 Black List. "Traffic in the development community stops," as agents read this free, unadorned tabulation of the secretly loved screenplays.[13] Hundreds had e-mailed Franklin about it, unaware that he was the one who created it. Some agents would even call Franklin and pitch a client who they said they had on good authority would be on next year's Black List, an impossible claim given the voting process required. Directors and screenwriters fixated on it as well. *Precious* director Lee Daniels told Franklin (without knowing he was the originator of the list) that he gets on the phone with Julian Schnabel and Wong Kar-wai once a year to talk about the scripts on it. With the creation of an anonymous e-mail, screenplays that failed to find any notice or acclaim were now ranked and recast as the ones to watch. An institution was born.

Franklin had a sense of what was happening mid-vacation when he checked his e-mail: he saw that his anonymous list had been forwarded back to him many times. Everyone was like, 'Oh my God, what is this document?'"

"What did you think about the Black List becoming so public?" I asked.

"'I'm going to get fired.'"

The list had exposed a fissure in the film industry that would be present in any field with pressure to conform to a particular formula of past success.

Here is the Black List from 2005, the first year it was released, truncated at the screenplays with more than six votes:

THE BLACK LIST			2005
twenty-five mentions			
THINGS WE LOST IN THE FIRE	Allan Loeb	CAA	Carin Sage
twenty-four mentions			
JUNO	Diablo Cody	Gersh	Sarah Self
fifteen mentions			
LARS AND THE REAL GIRL	Nancy Oliver	UTA	Tobin Babst
fourteen mentions			
ONLY LIVING BOY IN NEW YORK	Allan Loeb	CAA	Carin Sage
thirteen mentions			
CHARLIE WILSON'S WAR	Aaron Sorkin	Endeavor	Jason Spitz
ten mentions			
KITERUNNER, THE	David Benioff	CAA	Todd Feldman
nine mentions			
FANBOYS	Adam Goldberg	WMA	Ken Freimann
POWER OF DUFF, THE	Stephen Belber	BWCS	Todd Hoffman
eight mentions			
AGAINST ALL ENEMIES	Jamie Vanderbilt	Endeavor	Adriana Alberghetti
seven mentions			
A KILLING ON CARNIVAL ROW	Travis Beacham	WMA	Cliff Roberts
PEACOCK	Michael Lander & Ryan O. Roy	Endeavor	Elia Infascelli-Smith

Franklin Leonard, *The Black List* (detail), 2005.

Of the top five screenplays on the Black List in 2005, two would be nominated for Oscars: Diablo Cody's *Juno* and Nancy Oliver's *Lars and the Real Girl.* [14] Before landing on the list, these scripts by often then-unknown, obscure, or first-time writers were passed over by film industry producers and studios. Some of the featured screenwriters now command the highest figures in the business. [15]

When Franklin came up with the idea for the Black List, he was ending a three-month stretch of reading bad scripts that made him wonder if he was "either not very good at my job or this *was* the job in which case I needed to get the hell out of there." Trying to find good screenplays had felt like trying to reap a mountain's harvest with hand tools. If someone only read scripts all day each day, perhaps they could read 1,000 in a year. But in his best year, Franklin says he probably knocks out 500. For him, the quest to find those elusive 150 out of 50,000 seems like "walking into some kind of members-only bookstore that has all of the best and exclusive titles in the world. But it's all organized alphabetically, and all of the covers are exactly the same. And your job is basically to not come home until you find the best book there."[16]

"How bad are we talking?"

"The best way I can explain it is to tell you about a script that I was pitched from a manager who called saying that he had Leo's next movie. It was a call I'd get every Tuesday and Thursday."[17] He describes it, a screenplay called *Superstorm*. It's about an oil company lobbyist, DiCaprio if he played the part, whose girlfriend, a meteorologist in DC, wants to end their relationship because there's a massive hurricane off the coast of Africa that is going to destroy the East Coast from Maine to South Carolina. DiCaprio, distraught, does more research into the hurricane and discovers that its path over the Atlantic Ocean will cross over an active volcano, making it spew toxic sludge into the air, turning it into a biological weapon, destroying all civilization in the eastern part of the United States.

"At that point, I stopped the guy and said, 'So basically, you're pitching me, Leo versus the Toxic Sludge that will Destroy Humanity.' And I wish I was making this up, but he said, 'Well, when you say it like that, it sounds ridiculous.' But here's the sad part. Because of the way this town works, I still had the guy send me the script and read the first thirty pages of it before I felt confident enough to say, 'Yeah, this is terrible.'"

Franklin was facing what he felt was the one thing worse than reading a morass of terrible scripts: another family getaway where he would face questions about his meandering path. It started when he survived a car crash that altered the course of his life. He had one thought on his mind now: You get one go around. A rigid model of success that stipulated being either a doctor or a lawyer had been ingrained in him since childhood. His mantra became, "Life is short. If I don't enjoy it, I just have to find something else."

The number of screenplays Franklin has read comes through in his three-minute synopsis of his search—from campaign organizing to journalism, to management consulting at McKinsey & Company in New York City in 2001, where he felt "instantly miserable," though he was earning enough to pay off debt and found some enjoyment in his work on deals for nonprofit cultural organizations. He decided to quit a day before his entire analyst class was laid off, but luckily waited one more day. He ended up receiving five months' severance pay and health insurance.

After that, he said, "I just threw myself into the wind." This meant wandering around Manhattan and Brooklyn with his three roommates, an actor, a playwright, and a graphic designer, all without day jobs. "No matter what ridiculous plan we had," Franklin said, he ended up watching three movies a day rented from Kim's Video & Music on St. Marks Place, or going to the Union Square Barnes & Noble and reading about films so often that when he'd walk into the bookstore the employees would let him know if "his chair" upstairs was free. During the night of a snowstorm, he set up an all-night triple feature for himself: *Amadeus*, *Dr. Strangelove*, and *Being There*. At six A.M., he walked into his bedroom and booked a flight to Los Angeles. He found a job as an agent's assistant within a week and has been there ever since.

The story of the Black List is not only about how many blockbuster and Oscar-winning and nominated screenplays it helped get made, but also about how many of these nearly never did. Landing on the list is often "the difference between a script that keeps getting passed from hand to hand without really being read and a script that gets an actual look from a studio and starts to get some money behind it."[18]

Most scripts on the list are long-odds contenders from the stand-point of how studios make decisions. They were scripts written on spec where often the premise is very strange, very niche, but because the writer set a relatively high bar and then cleared it, they transcend the expectation that the premise is too weird to be good.

One of the most implausible films that came from the Black List is a movie about a mentally-ill man so lonely that he buys an inflatable sex doll for companionship and a town so humane that they go along with the mentally-ill man's scenario. *Lars and the Real Girl* screenwriter Nancy Oliver felt that the list "gave permission for other people to like it."[19] Before the Black List, "*Lars* had been making the rounds for a few years, but it was still an invisible property," she said. Imagine asking another executive to spend precious time reading a script about a young man who treats a sex doll like his girlfriend. "I'm very confident in my taste," Franklin says, "and even now, I would still doubt myself before going to James Lassiter (co-founder of Overbrook Entertainment) and saying, 'You have to read that script.'" The list gave *Lars*, once lost in a holding pattern, so much cachet and exposure that actor Ryan Gosling, cast as the lead, admitted that since it had become "such a respected script . . . there was a certain level of fear on my part because whenever I'd mention it to people, there was always a 'Don't ruin it' involved."[20]

The efficacy of the Black List propagated a UK version in 2007: the Brit List.[21] It has been particularly effective since in Britain there is no studio system as there is in Hollywood, no systematic way to get attention for this smaller set of more tightly guarded scripts. "It's very much about bumping into, knowing, or meeting the right person," the Brit List's current organizer, Alexandra Arlango, tells me. While she admits that she likes the democracy of this process, where "anyone can pitch up and write a script," represented or not, she is not alone in finding the process so loose—when even established producers struggle to find financing—that "it's kind of scary."[22]

The King's Speech's inclusion on the Brit List in 2008 garnered it attention in Hollywood, amplified when it landed on the Black List the following year. When David Seidler wrote the screenplay, his career, he felt, was "truly in the toilet" along with nearly everything else.[23] He had just sold his family's home, his second marriage was crumbling, and he was depressed after being diagnosed with bladder cancer. Even after the surgery to remove it, the doctors told him that there was an 80 percent chance that the cancer would be back in a progressed state in six weeks. He wrote *The King's Speech* as his "last will and testament." It was one more attempt for Seidler, who had come to Hollywood at age forty ("the age when most people are thinking about leaving"), and endured a series of near wins with no breakthroughs. He had first written a script for Francis Ford Coppola, *Tucker: The Man and His Dream*. Over the next twenty-five years, he had a run of constant work—at times, this meant television movies for markets in Germany and New Zealand when he couldn't get work in the United States. But it wasn't the work he wanted. One of his scripts had Michael and Kirk Douglas attached to it for a spell, but it fell apart. None of his feature-film scripts made it to the screen. "I'm not proud of myself for thinking this, but I began to think that I was jinxed," he told me.

So when it came to *The King's Speech*, he said, "It had to be made. If it didn't, basically my life was over." He wrote a draft, scrapped it, and finished a second version from his Pacific Palisades rental in those post-surgery six weeks. The drama chronicles Prince Albert's unexpected ascension to the throne as George VI (played by Colin Firth) and his struggle to overcome his stutter with the help of unlicensed therapist Lionel Logue (played by Geoffrey Rush). Seidler also stuttered. He was born into an upper-middle-class family in England, raised in his early years by a caretaker who vanished after the Blitz, which took the roof off of his London home during World War II. German U-boats bombed the boat he was on en route to America to relocate from Britain. His stutter emerged. Seidler's parents urged him to listen to George VI's radio broadcasts for encouragement ("The King was far worse than you," they'd say).[24]

Seidler hadn't even pitched *The King's Speech* to Hollywood studios. He didn't think it had a chance. "If I had pitched a film about a dead British king who stutters, I would have been asked what I was smoking, where they could buy some, and then asked to leave. I didn't even try," he told me. His longtime manager said he loved the script, but he didn't think a major studio would invest. Even Seidler's son Marc questioned his judgment in choosing the script's subject: "No one is going to spend an hour and a half watching someone trying to go through their lines."[25] Seidler had it sent to Geoffrey Rush's agent, but it was initially rejected.[26] So he created a semaphore game, giving it to his Cornell college roommate's nephew, Tom Minter, an actor in London. Minter gave it to Joan Lane, a producer earning her living producing events for the royal family, such as the Queen Mother's birthday. Some time later, she showed it to Simon Egan, who runs Bedlam Productions, and they optioned it. The aspirations for *The King's Speech* were modest. "We were hoping to get maybe a one million or two million pound BBC Four camera production, that's it. It was going to be a humble, tiny TV movie." That was, until Harvey Weinstein saw the script when it appeared on the Brit List.

Made for just $15 million, *The King's Speech* grossed nearly $500 million in box-office sales. It went on to earn twelve Academy Award nominations, winning Best Director, Best Actor, Best Picture, and Best Original Screenplay. In that year, at age seventy-three, Seidler was the oldest person ever to win an award in that last category. Woody Allen bested his record the following year, setting up a joking rivalry between the two men. ("I told Woody, last one to win an Oscar over one hundred is a rotten egg.")

———

The impact of landing on the Black List has become so seismic for some people's careers that it's often no longer seen as a tabulation of underappreciated scripts. Marquee name writers so often populate it now that some wonder whether the list is being manipulated by screenwriters' agents wrangling as many favors as possible to get their clients enough votes to get on.

"It's no longer a 'best liked' list at all, but more of a 'browbeaten executives' begrudging choices' list," one commenter ranted in 2009 on *Deadline Hollywood*. Others call it a popularity contest for films and agencies.[27] Another screenwriter typified the complaint using the example of *The Social Network*, number two on the Black List in 2009 even though the film was already in production. "I don't know what the spirit of the Black List was when they founded it, but I can't imagine it was a way to recognize scripts Aaron Sorkin and Sony Pictures already decided they were producing," a blogger said.

Franklin counters the stream of similar comments this way: "There's something special about a place where Aaron Sorkin's script for *Social Network* is number two behind a script by a total unknown who wrote a spec script about Jim Henson's life by doing research from his home in Australia. It legitimizes Christopher Weekes's work in a way that being at the top of the heap of previously undiscovered writers will never do."[28] Franklin also reminds me that the earliest Black List log lists (the few lines of text saying who is representing or producing the script) didn't state whether a script was in production already. The later lists do publicize this, a difference that has skewed people's perceptions, he believes. While before the screenplays were often unproduced and had no one attached, they often now have both going for them.

It was inevitable that the Black List would change. If it suffers from anything, it is the hipster complaint of "now that everyone loves them, they can't be cool," Franklin says, like listening to Radiohead before they were popular, but feeling like "now that everyone loves them I can't listen to them driving down Sunset Boulevard and Silver Lake."

The Black List shines a spotlight so large that for some writers the platform can help transform their world. Diablo Cody's semiautobiographical script *Juno*, her first attempt at writing a feature-film screenplay, one that she says "nobody thought was going to be this blockbuster," became a phenomenon aided, in part, by her exposure through the Black List. The movie grossed over $140 million, and Cody admitted to Scott Myers that she didn't know how to handle massive success after obscurity. Cody felt that the time period where that level of recognition was permissive, when she knew that she "could do anything I want," wasn't at all helpful or healthy. One day she's a writer who, she admits, made so many "mistakes" that certain lines in *Juno* still make her cringe. "When I wrote *Juno*—and I think this is part of its charm and appeal—I didn't know how to write a movie. And I also had no idea it was going to get made! It was really just a hypothetical in every way." Soon after, nearly anything she wrote could get a green light. There can be a cost to the permissive state that comes with constant achievement.

Too much success can make you overconfident, she said, describing how people often make "rash decisions when the wind is at their back. When it's just 'Yes this' and 'Yes that' and 'Anything is possible,' you can really screw up."[29]

Others find success after the Black List and then worry about being put in a box with their genre. Josh Zetumer, who wrote *Villain*, which appeared on the Black List in 2006—"a thriller about a guy stuck in a claustrophobic fire-watcher cabin"—said that afterward "the projects they threw me were not only thrillers, they were 'guy-trapped-in-X' movies. 'Would you do a movie about a guy trapped in an elevator?' 'What about a woman trapped in an attic?'"[30] Of course, the fear of being trapped in one role is a relatively good problem to have. It is better than having no role at all.

"Just by its very existence, the Black List makes Hollywood a much better place," Zetumer says. "And that's enough."[31]

How did the Black List become such a powerful document? It is, after all, only a list. Franklin is careful never to overstate the role that it plays in Hollywood, but to me it seems that he gave it an artful setup. A study cannot explain the full story of behavior, but it must be said here briefly—the Black List took away the well-known Asch experiment that occurs in the process of green-lighting scripts. In the 1950s, psychologist Solomon Asch demonstrated how, without knowing it, we tend to abandon our own opinion altogether under two conditions: 1) when we anticipate that our opinion differs from that of a group and 2) when we have to state our dissent aloud. Asch demonstrated this idea with one experiment where he placed a volunteer in a room with seven other people who had all volunteered for a simple test in visual acumen.[32] The volunteer didn't know that the group was made up of actors deliberately giving incorrect answers. Each person in the group would take a turn and state aloud which line is of equal length to the line on the card on the left.

Staring at the page, it looks obvious which one is correct. When asked alone, without this planted group scenario, the person would give the right answer 95 percent of the time on average. Yet in the group experiment, the volunteer would go along with the group of actors and give a correct answer only approximately 25 percent of the time. The larger the number of opponents in the group, the more errors the volunteer made. Yet when each volunteer learned about the influence of the group on their answer after Asch revealed the results of the experiment, they typically expressed little or no awareness of changing their answers in response to group pressure. In other cases,

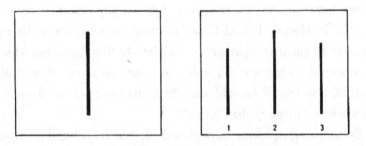

Solomon Asch experiment, *Scientific American*, 1955.
Reproduced with permission. Copyright © 1955
Scientific American, Inc. All rights reserved.

they claimed that they weren't sure of the answer. Not only do we often give up on ourselves when faced with holding a minority opinion. We don't even know that we're doing it.[33]

When we decide not to give up on our dissenting view, the body pays a price. Neuroeconomist Gregory Berns discovered this when updating the Asch experiment in 2005 at Emory University by using fMRI imagery. He wanted to determine what was going on in the brain when individuals shifted their opinion to conform to that of the group. His study found that in instances where a person gave an answer that was different from the group's, there was more activity in the amygdala, initiating the "fight-or-flight" feeling we get in a state of trepidation.[34] Standing your ground in the face of a majority requires courage, the hallmark trait of the iconoclast.

The film industry constantly repeats the Asch test. It's an industry where you have to equate one thing to its closest comparable to approve a script for production and distribution. Determining what will be a commercial success requires judging how well the script in front of you conforms to past films, signaling your opinion in public, and summoning the bravery required for dissent. In the case of uncommon screenplays, this is even more difficult; making a comparison between an unusual work and an existing one is nearly impossible. Producer Michael Uslan, for example, said that *Annie* was the most frequent comparison to the *Batman* film franchise, which he produced. "That was the only other cartoon movie they could think of, you know," he said with lingering exasperation from the years before, "Little orphan Annie!"[35]

By soliciting opinions through a protected e-mail and distribution system, Franklin eliminated this invisible Asch test for film industry executives and the fear associated with public dissent. The anonymity of the Black List created a private space; public adjudication became sequestered exchange. He was not asking what scripts would be most successful commercially. He was just asking which ones they loved. It reduced the relevance of those benchmark comparisons—the sequels, the superheroes, or more formulaic models that allow studios to try to "formalize and repeat success," as filmmaker Stanley Kubrick bemoaned.[36]

Yet as I thought more about the unintended power of the Black List, I couldn't overlook one ironic fact—Franklin had been working for the production company founded by Will Smith, who has become one of the biggest box-office movie stars by applying his acting skills to projects with a clear chance of commercial success. The result is that Smith has remained one of the few golden tickets of Hollywood casting.[37] In the 1990s, he was better known as the Fresh Prince of Bel-Air and has said that he couldn't get a meeting with Hollywood execs, yet his goal was "to be the biggest movie star in the world." Smith and his partner, Lassiter, decided to look at a list of the top-ten-grossing films and assess the trends. Lassiter and Smith, who once longed to be an engineer and almost enrolled at MIT, noticed a pattern. "We realized that 10 out of 10 had special effects. Nine out of 10 had special effects with creatures. Eight out of 10 had special effects with creatures and a love story," the actor revealed to *Time* in 2007. What are Smith's recent movies?

Largely alien movies and creature movies with love stories: *Men In Black II; Bad Boys II; I, Robot; Hitch; The Pursuit of Happyness; I Am Legend; Hancock;* and *Seven Pounds.* They also realized the importance of international box-office receipts. "Being able to get $30 mil in England, 37 in Japan, 15 in Germany is what makes the studio support your movies differently than they support other actors' movies."[38] So for each film, he travels to a new international territory at the time of a major local event—carnival in Rio, Brazil, or South Korea during the World Cup, for example. The argument goes that each movie that Smith has starred in has grossed so much since *Independence Day* and *Men in Black* that a film with him is likely to make at least $150 million. It is a claim no other actor can currently match.[39]

Smith code-broke the film formula. His reliable results underscore why studios are often reluctant to support excellent but unusual scripts. Yet Franklin's Black List shows why studios can also benefit from going formula-free.

The Black List inadvertently identified a weakness in the film industry. In an economic environment where studios may make more conservative decisions when there is more pressure on both the revenue and cost side of the equation, the list allows studios to invest in quality writing instead of relying on trends and historical data. It halts what we could call a Lot's Wife Syndrome, where studios try to move forward by looking back to past films for metrics of success.[40] For financiers, the Black List can offer quantitative evidence to argue for the brilliantly written script that might not seem to have the makings of a huge commercial release, but has a good chance of being a box-office success if the film is well made.

It's a reminder that value is not just associated with superheroes, sequels, or presold properties, but that the quality of a well-told story can justify itself. "Celebrate good work. Good work is not where you think it is all the time." This is the ethic of the Black List.

The examples are legion. *Slumdog Millionaire* was a joke: "Oh, yeah, the Indian who wants to be a millionaire movie? That's gonna be huge," Franklin recalled, "but you know, the script was excellent." Even when *Slumdog Millionaire*'s Oscar-winning director, Danny Boyle, was handed the screenplay, he refused, not wanting to make a film about a game show. After ten minutes of reading the script, he changed his mind. "I knew I was going to make it."[41] The sort of recognition that came with landing on the Black List in 2007 was especially important given the closure of *Slumdog Millionaire*'s production company, Warner Independent Pictures. Warner Brothers considered sending the film straight to DVD. *Slumdog Millionaire* won the People's Choice Award at the Toronto Film Festival in 2008 out of 250 eligible films and received ten Oscar nominations as well. (The year before, *Juno* was the crowd favorite and runner-up for the People's Choice Award.)

The Black List "signals to industry insiders that a given project deserves a second look," Franklin said to Michelle Kung of the *Wall Street Journal*.[42] When the former co-president of production at Sony's Columbia Pictures, Matt Tolmach, started his own production company, and found Oren Uziel's 2010 Black List script *Kitchen Sink*, a *Breakfast Club*-toned story (its title referencing the fact that the writer had given the screenplay his all), he was surprised that no one had picked it up. Spotting it was like spying "the talented kid passed over in the first round of the draft," he said.[43]

By reducing the impact of the Asch experiment, the Black List has made a stance for excellence in writing in a field where there is a tension between art and commercial value. Director Martin Scorsese describes the pressure that pulls apart the twin pillars of merit and popularity, no matter someone's stature: "People say you should do it this way, someone else suggests that, yes, there's financing but maybe you should use this actor. And there are the threats, at the end—*if you don't do it this way, you'll lose your box office; if you don't do it that way, you'll never get financed again.*"[44] As a result, what gets made doesn't always correlate with the best writing. The Black List is one of the rare forums that offers an encomium to writing without it being presented for acquisition through the prism of a director's vision or an actor's performance, which is often a distortion of the original.

It can help to face public evaluation. Screenwriters have to pass the Asch experiment about their own work often on a daily basis. It happens often with the film industry's pitching sweepstakes, where a writer is bidding for a job, goes into an executive's room, sits on their couch with two or three people staring at him or her as the writer tells them an imaginary story that outlines the movie. "Beyond being a little bit awkward, creating a fictional universe sitting on a couch," said Noah Oppenheim, whose script *Jackie* was the second-highest-rated Black List script in 2010, "there's something about it that makes you really vulnerable, especially since, most of the time, someone says to you, we like someone else's version better."[45] Rejection and perseverance requires discounting the voices that say that your work doesn't measure up. To get through it requires what some call tenacity, or others call faith, and it requires more courage than it may seem. It's a constant auto-correct.

The Black List has also become a productive focusing mechanism because of its unexplained nature. It simply, one day, appeared. We tend to ponder mysteries more than incidents that we can explain, particularly ones that start with the headline "Black is the new white."[46] Near failure has become the new success.

——————

Franklin has turned the e-mailed Black List into a customized digital service that constantly churns out lists of unproduced screenplays based on the viewers' preferences. The number of film executives he polls has swelled to around 650. His goal is now to turn the digitized Black List into the conceptual equivalent of Silicon Valley's Angel-List, which connects investors with start-ups, but in this case to introduce studios and investors to scripts they wouldn't have ordinarily found. He has partnered with Dino Sijamic, who went to Tufts University to study programming, and while working for Akamai Technologies by day still took on the role of the chief technology officer for the list. Sijamic built the entire site with a collaborative filter and algorithm for the Hollywood ranking system.

"Is the digital Black List done out of a desire to make it all more scientific, more precise?"

"A little bit, yeah," Franklin confessed. "The inner math nerd in me geeks out over its algorithmic potential. I've been geeking out on algorithmic ratings since I discovered them through Amazon." Before I could dismiss Franklin's repeated insistence that he is, really, a nerd, he told me about the time he was at a birthday party for a manager of screenwriters when he learned that the man who led the move to create Amazon ratings was there. Franklin, a one-time member of Georgia's state team, introduced himself, and doused the man with such praise that he still feels embarrassed over the incident.

Given the large amount of data the server will amass about how information moves and how taste functions in the business, could the Black List change the way that agents connect their clients with quality projects? While Franklin is careful not to overstate the role of the Black List, he has come to embrace its place in his industry. Its potential has him excited.

It may be too early to tell where this Hollywood list will go. But in the first twenty-four hours, over 1,000 professionals were on the wait list to subscribe to the premium digital version. As soon as the site was live, users could filter the scripts by genre, and get recommendations for which scripts they might like after answering a Netflix-like series of survey questions. The site would later allow writers to upload their scripts to the site with or without an agent, and has also become a popular gathering place for the industry, featuring in-depth interviews with screenwriters. The Black List site is a way to exit Franklin's nightmare of the coverless, mammoth library of scripts. Thousands are now catalogued and accessible, sorted based on past ratings.

Late in the summer of 2012, Franklin left Overbrook and focused all of his energy on expanding the Black List's digital reach. One could say that it's the "real time" Black List, "a rolling screenplay competition that grants access instead of a check."[47]

The expanding venture remains about the bravery of the iconoclast. What motivates him is still the writer who potentially won't get her work seen, and finding ways to combat that. It is a way to expand access by offering "a meritocratic way in," one that he admits is not perfect, but still strong.

For some, creating the Black List itself would have been enough, but Franklin still seems to be searching, trying to close a kind of gap—the distance between quality screenplays within a thousand-script-high pile and those executives who should have them in their hands. It is, in part, a curatorial pursuit that I identify with, an interest in scouring the world for what we're failing to see, to proffer it back in the form of a list, a show organized by theme and sequence, splayed out before all. Yet Franklin's work is coupled with another aim—to create a more accessible platform for the works themselves. The result of this goal does something even more: It eliminates some of the dynamic tension between art and commerce such that excellence is not amputated in the process.

Many responses to the Black List's digital expansion were optimistic. The digital Black List proved so popular that it has partnered with the Writers Guild of America, West. Others made clear how much the significance and good intentions of the list's endeavor had endeared Franklin to a coterie of writers whom he's admired from afar, and has never met.[48]

A few have been more circumspect, questioning the depth of the undiscovered talent pool. "At the risk of sounding pessimistic," wrote Amanda Pendolino on her site for aspiring screenwriters, "I'm not sure there are thousands of fantastic scripts floating around out there, just waiting to get read by the right people." Most people think that their problem is not "writ[ing] a great script," but being able to "find someone important who likes it," she said. In her experience, it is the other way around.[49] It is a comment that could apply to the beginning of the Black List itself.

Talking to Franklin just after the digital launch gave me the sense of a man standing apart from a once-familiar creation and assessing it anew. He was witty, but weary. He sounded like many artists I'd spoken to after the public presentation of some hard-won creation, knowing that now it must exist on its own. Out of the slew of press about the digital launch, Franklin mentioned a negative one first, an article that says, "The Black List has jumped the shark." Shrugging it off, he adds, "I've learned that there is absolutely no value in pessimism." It was a lesson he could have learned from the writers on the Black List themselves.

THE DELIBERATE
AMATEUR

To know and then how not to know is the greatest puz-
zle of all . . . So much preparation for a few moments of
innocence—of desperate play. To learn how to unlearn.

—PHILIP GUSTON[1]

"It says, 'No entrance,' but you just enter," physicist Andre Geim
told me as we walked with Ben Saunders at the G8 Innovation /
DNA Summit in London when I was there to interview them onstage. Geim was talking about the graphite mines in the mountains
where he often hikes—his preferred exploit when not researching
in his lab at the University of Manchester, England. It was an echo.
I had heard this from Geim's younger colleague, Konstantin Novoselov, weeks earlier—his precise, pacific voice rising for the first
time in our conversation: "The graphitic mines are completely
unguarded. You can walk right in." Their comments seemed less
about hiking and more like unintended aphorisms, ones that could
explain the insouciance behind their Nobel Prize–winning physics
experiment: the first isolation of a two-dimensional object on the
Earth.

Graphene—as the two-dimensional honeycomb-shaped monolayer of carbon found in graphite is called—has turned out to be
the thinnest, strongest, most conductive material to date on record.[2] The material is finer than silk, two hundred times stronger
than steel, and more inert than even gold. If we made a car out of

graphene, it would be the lightest automobile in existence, but could also drive through walls. Graphene's commercial applications, from solar cells to transistors, have made many think that it will replace silicon. This is a bonus on top of Novoselov and Geim's main feat: identifying a phenomenon that has expanded what we know is possible in the world of physics itself.

The theory was that "Flatland" was a fantasy, just a whimsical invention from author Edwin A. Abbott's mind.[3] Physicists had long thought that objects with length, width, and no depth—meaning that electrons only move on a one-dimensional plane—could not thrive in a three-dimensional world. "It was assumed that they couldn't exist," Geim said, until the two physicists went about finding it by systematically abandoning their expertise.[4] A paradox of innovation and mastery is that breakthroughs often occur when you start down

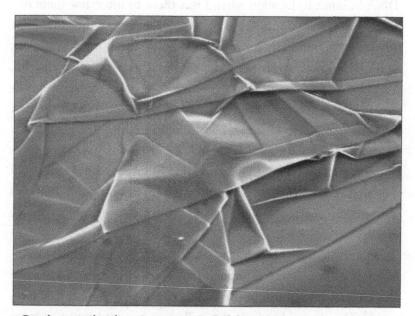

Graphene under the microscope. © Condensed Matter Physics Group, University of Manchester.

a road, but wander off for a ways and pretend as if you have just begun.

Geim knows that, to most, his journey sounds unlikely.

"I tell people if you want to win a Nobel, first get an Ig Nobel," Geim said, deadpan to the laughing audience in London, cued to his sardonic wit. Perhaps the audience knew that Geim is the only scientist to win both a Nobel Prize and Ig Nobel Prize, the reputation-denting award given to scientists for experiments so outlandish that they "first make people laugh, and then make them think."[5] Other Ig Nobel–winning experiments have included an award in chemistry for a wasabi-made alarm clock designed to rouse a sleeping person in an emergency, two prizes in psychology for the study of "why, in everyday life, people sigh," an economics prize for finding that financial strain is a risk indicator for "destructive periodontal disease," and a peace prize "for confirming the widely held belief that swearing relieves pain."[6] Witty, ridiculous, and slyly illuminating, the preeminent journal *Nature* has called the prominent prize announcements organized by the magazine *Annals of Improbable Research*, "arguably the highlight of the scientific calendar."[7]

Geim won the auspicious Ig Nobel in Physics in 2000, ten years before winning the Nobel Prize, for levitating a live frog with magnets.

Geim is proud of his Ig Nobel, he said in his Nobel interview. "In my experience, if people don't have a sense of humour, they are usually not very good scientists either," he reasoned.[8] The image of the flying frog had already made the rounds after its publication in the April 1997 issue of *Physics World*, what many considered just an April Fool's Day prank.[9] Geim didn't care. Most thought that water's magnetism, billions of times weaker than iron, was not strong enough to counter gravity, but the demonstration showed its true force. He had access to some of the strongest electromagnets around when he was working at the Radboud University Nijmegen's High Field Magnet

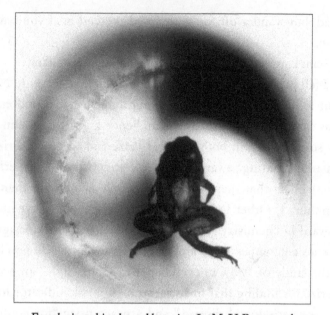

Frog levitated in the stable region. In M. V. Berry and
A. K. Geim, "Of flying frogs and levitrons," *European
Journal of Physics* 18 (June 1997), 312. © IOP Publishing Ltd
and European Physical Society. Reproduced by permission
of IOP Publishing. All rights reserved.

Laboratory in the Netherlands, where he held his first post as professor. The magnets consumed so much power that the lab only operated them at night, when costs were lower.[10] Geim became curious about magnetism when he didn't have the resources to continue his past experiments. If "magnetic water" did exist, he thought he would stand the best chance of demonstrating it with this device.

On a Friday evening, he set the electromagnet to maximum power, then poured water straight into the expensive machine. He still can't remember why he "behaved so 'unprofessionally,'" but through it he saw how descending water "got stuck" within the vertical bore. Balls of water started floating. They were levitating. He

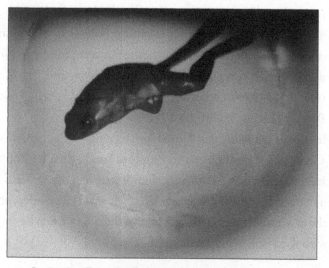

Levitating Frog. © High Field Magnet Laboratory,
Radboud University Nijmegen.

had discovered that a seemingly "feeble magnetic response of water" could act against Earth's gravitational force.

He dropped in all kinds of items containing water—strawberries, tomatoes, anything that would fit—until his lab colleagues, which include his wife, vortex physicist expert Irina Grigorieva, suggested that they levitate an amphibian to emphasize that there is truly diamagnetic force in everything. The frog was a better choice than other animals they considered—lizards, spiders, and even a hamster (too big).[11] The frog may have been too attractive. The discovery made it into so many science textbooks that some mainly know Geim for the flying frog. The popular image also sparked some odd curiosity. A man who claimed to be a pastor from a church in southwest England wrote to Geim asking "very strange questions" about how to acquire his levitation machine and whether it could be concealed under the floor and not interfere with the sound of an organ, "So you can imagine what the application of this experiment would be!" Geim said.[12]

Many of his colleagues warned him that the award might damage his reputation, given its public nature (which is why awardees are given a few weeks to consider whether to accept their Ig Nobel). The raucous prize ceremony, complete with skits and roasts, takes place in a 1,000-person auditorium. Geim asked his colleague, Michael Berry, to accept it with him.

"He often complains that I used him as a fig leaf . . . ah, or whatever," Geim said. He let out an incredulous laugh, then he stopped as if catching himself, his face turning slightly red, leaning forward in his chair, as he recalled it over a decade later.[13] It wasn't a self-deprecating aside about a humble detour. It was part of the direct route he and Novoselov took to isolate graphene itself.

The two acclaimed physicists have acquired the non-expert's advantage through what Geim calls "Friday Night Experiments." On these occasions, their lab works on the "crazy things that probably won't pan out at all," Novoselov told me, "but if they do, it would be really surprising," and could constitute a major breakthrough.[14] From the start of Geim's career, he has devoted 10 percent of his lab time to this kind of research. It was this unique method that first attracted Novoselov to Geim's lab in Holland when he was just a doctoral student. In 2010 when the two men won the Nobel Prize in Physics, Novoselov was thirty-six, the youngest in thirty years to win the award in that category.[15] Just before the award-winning experiments, Novoselov had completed his research but hadn't yet filed the paperwork to officially receive his PhD.

The Friday Night Experiments (FNEs), safe havens for their laboratory, are often so outlandish that they try to limit how long someone works on them—usually just a few months, so as not to hurt the careers of the lab's postdoctoral fellows, undergraduates, or graduate students.

Geim's perspective, blunt as you like, is that it's "better to be wrong than be boring," so he lets those working on the FNEs stay free enough to take risks and, inevitably, fail.[16] This means that the FNEs are, unsurprisingly, unfunded. Due to their nature, they have to be. They are times when "we're entering into someone else's territory, to be frank, and questioning things people who work in that area never bother to ask."

The physicists have become known for the unlikely breakthroughs that have come from these trials. Out of the two dozen or so attempted Friday Night Experiments, many have been near wins, such as one attempting to find the "heartbeats" of unique yeast cells, in which they detected no pulse or electrical signals, but noticed that when threatened, yeast emitted what the physicists jokingly called "the last fart of a living cell." That is, when the cells were treated with excess alcohol, the sensor recorded a large voltage spike as if releasing a "last gasp."[17] Three FNEs have been hits, a success rate of 12.5 percent. The flying frog and the illustration of diamagnetism was the first. The second was the creation of gecko tape, the eponymously titled adhesive that mimics the clinging ability of the gecko's hairy feet.

The third FNE hit was the Nobel Prize–winning isolation of graphene.

––––––––

Friday Night Experiments are a way to live out the wisdom of the deliberate amateur.

"The biggest adventure is to move into an area in which you are not an expert," Geim believes. "Sometimes I joke that I am not interested in doing re-search, only search," he has said about the "unusual" overall career philosophy both men use to "graze shallow." They stay in a field for five years, do some good work, and then get out.[18] The inventiveness and sheer fun of it all can make it look like they're not "doing science in the eyes of other people."[19] Shelving experience to remain open to new possibilities can make an expert look elementary. Yet the gifts from assuming this posture on the unfinished path of mastery can come no other way.

Geim and Novoselov found graphene hiding out in the graphite from an ordinary pencil. They isolated it with a tool that seemed even more rudimentary—a piece of Scotch tape. The physicists had never worked with carbon before. Their team worked long hours to familiarize themselves with the literature. Yet too much reading and research before experimentation can be "truly detrimental," Geim believes. So they were careful not to read so much as to read themselves right out of their own ideas.[20] Concepts are patchworks like centos, an aggregate of ideas from others over time. Graze too much before a new project or experiment and you may conclude that it has all been done.

The graphene FNE began when Geim asked Da Jiang, a doctoral student from China, to polish a piece of graphite an inch across and a few millimeters thick down to ten microns using a specialized machine for an experiment about transistors. Due to their language barrier, and Geim giving him the tougher form of graphite, Da polished the graphite down to "dust," but not the ultimate thinness Geim wanted.[21]

The team salvaged the next step with a lateral move. Their lab also used graphite with scanning tunneling microscopy (STM) experiments, preparing it with adhesive rips to give it a clean, uncontaminated surface. "I knew about the process; it has been used for decades," Novoselov told me, but now, with a low-temperature STM in the lab, he saw up close how they could just discard the Scotch tape after cleaning the samples.

"We took it out of the trash and just used it," Novoselov said.[22] The flakes of graphite on the tape from the waste bin were finer and thinner than what Da had found using the fancy machine. They weren't one layer thick, an achievement that came with successively ripping them with the Scotch tape, but they were closer than any recorded attempt.

The act of writing on a blank page shows how easily graphite, made up of carbon, can be shaved. To write in pencil means putting enough pressure on the tip of graphite such that it peels off onto the paper, leaving a trail of gray—imperceptibly small layers of carbon. Attach graphite to adhesive and it will cleave. Over time, Novoselov perfected a method of using the tape to get the graphite down to one micron thick, pressing it on the graphite and ripping them apart. Their five-, sometimes six-person team then toiled for a year of intensive experiments done during fourteen-hour workdays to measure the monolayer of carbon. They also swapped the adhesive for Japanese Nitto tape, "probably because the whole process is so simple and cheap we wanted to fancy it up a little and use this blue tape."[23] Yet "the method is called the 'Scotch tape technique.' I fought against this name," Geim said, "but lost."[24]

Prior to this discovery, the charge carrier in all known atoms was thought to move through materials like billiard balls knocking into one another, but in graphene atoms the charge carrier mimics massless photons moving with a constant velocity—it appears to move at nearly 1/300th the speed of light. Take a monolayer of carbons out of that three-dimensional home in graphite with repeated Scotch tape rips and it exhibits a list of traits that, in concert, seem impossible. The two men would never call it a "discovery," as much as nonspecialists describe their feat that way. It was there all the while. "We came in one morning with nothing in our hands but a piece of graphite and within a few hours had a device that gave us a non-trivial result."[25] It may have seemed too simple.

The team submitted a paper summarizing their findings to *Nature*. The journal rejected it, such a common fate for historically path-breaking ideas that it could signal an unintended compliment. One of *Nature*'s anonymous referees responded that it was interesting but they would only publish it if the team "measured this, that, and the other thing in addition, and then maybe they'd consider it for publication," Novoselov recalled, skimming over the details.[26] The journal again spurned their resubmitted article. One referee said it did "not constitute a sufficient scientific advance," Geim said in his Nobel Prize speech.[27] *Science* magazine later published an even more polished version.[28] The physicists' second paper on the topic did appear in *Nature*.

"People probably didn't believe that what we had was one-atom thick," Novoselov told me. "It takes a lot of courage from the journal's editor and the referees to put a paper of this proportion through. And at the time, even we didn't understand what the implications might be. We didn't even understand fully how many other people had been working on carbon science. But to this day, I'm not really sure why it was rejected." He said it in a patient voice that held the symphonic contrasts of his own process. Some phrases were straightforward and clear. Others bolted through the phone with the poetry of knowledge crystallized into wisdom.

Their process is so well-known that Geim's colleagues often ask if he'll "move on" now that they've isolated graphene and created a new field of research in custom-designed materials made from two-dimensional objects. They "hope I'll leave the field to them. No chance, guys!" he teased. "You'll have to cope with my sarcastic jokes for longer" as he puts "more stakes in the ground" around what has now become an enormous research area, not the tumbleweeds it was at the start of their experiment.[29] By stakes, though, he doesn't mean filing a patent for the material.[30]

Geim wants to continue the adventure with "exploratory detours" and lateral steps always "away from the stampede."[31] He likens himself to a gold-miner character from a Jack London novel, trying to carry stones through a mountain pass to mark their terrain, a subarea in graphene research.[32] Once he has, then he'll find the next open plain on which to chart a new path.

An ever-onward almost is part of mastery, on the field, in the studio, and in the lab. The wisdom of the deliberate amateur is part of how we endure. Maintaining proficiency is best kept by finding ways to periodically give it up.

It is an old idea for artists, seen in the freedom that comes in a late style or the Zen concept of "beginner's mind," a shift in perspective that comes from trying to see things anew after gaining sufficient expertise.[33] "As you grow older, every book becomes a little more difficult," author Erskine Caldwell told *The Paris Review* about the process of writing, not just "because you're more critical of what you're doing," but because "you reach the point where you know something is wrong but you're incapable of making it any better."[34] Choreographer Twyla Tharp also used the technique. "Experience . . . is what gets you through the door. But experience also closes the door," she said. "You tend to rely on that memory and stick with what has worked before. You don't try anything anew."[35] Without off-road exploration, we have little way of figuring it out.

The amateur's "useful wonder" is what the expert may not realize she has left behind.[36] Psychologists call the unintended routine that comes with expertise the Einstellung effect. It is the cost of success: The bias that creeps in without our notice and can block us from seeing how to do things any other way.[37] Deliberate amateurs are not trying to follow an apprentice's schedule—learn the trade, climb the guild's rungs, train another.

An amateur is unlike the novice bound by lack of experience and the expert trapped by having too much. Driven by impulse and desire, the amateur stays in the place of a "constant now," seeing possibilities to which the expert is blind and which the apprentice may not yet discern. It can lead to playing like there's "no birth certificate on your notes," as Ornette Coleman once said about a trumpeter's sound. It keeps us in the spirit of discovery.[38]

The term *amateur* is now pejorative: to lack in skill or knowledge, to be a dilettante, dabbler, fancier, or hobbyist—all conceptual flirts. Yet centuries ago, the word *amateur* wasn't meant to disparage. It described a person undertaking an activity for sheer pleasure, not solely pursuing a goal for the sake of their profession. The French *amateur* is from the Latin *amator*—a lover, a devotee, a person who adores a particular endeavor.

An amateur's adventure is an embodied feeling of being rapt, utterly absorbed. We sense it after reaching a state of exhaustion, switching tasks to something that has our interest, and feeling refueled, our endurance enhanced by authentic passion. For a moment, we are out of time.[39] It can be the bodily suspension that let Geim pour water down a machine's bore and not be able to explain what possessed him.

German philosopher Arthur Schopenhauer and writer Ludwig Börne both made the case for periodically cultivating this approach. This was an age when arguing for originality had been controversial for centuries. (The term *original* was then a veiled synonym for "crazy," unique in an unenviable way, until René Descartes shifted its valence).[40] Börne argued for "the art of making oneself ignorant" in his controversial 1823 essay, "How to Become an Original Writer in Three Days." Inherited knowledge, he said, was like some "ancient manuscripts where one must scrape away the boring disputes of would-be Church Fathers and the ranting of inflamed monks to catch a glimpse of the Roman classic lying beneath."[41] Schopenhauer developed Börne's idea when he called for an "intellectual Sabbath" from constantly being on "the playground of others' thoughts." Worried that "his age would 'read itself stupid,'" and no longer be able to generate novel ideas, he outlined his logic with an analogy about riding versus walking: If a person only rides and never walks, she will soon lose the ability to walk herself anywhere.[42]

Follow someone else's route too often and soon you lose the ability to map out your own.

Besides, you can't stay interested in your work if "from your scientific cradle to your scientific coffin, you just go along the straight railway line," Geim has said often.[43]

Yet few cultivate this method as a strategy.

"You always can be considered as a fool," Geim said, "inventing the wheel, investing your time into something, which might turn out like a blip."[44] It can turn a walk into a wander. Geim described how hard it was to switch subjects, moving from semiconductor physics to superconductivity. "I went to those conferences as a beginner with having a couple of already prestigious papers, being an associate professor. People looked at me [and said], 'Who is this materials post-doc? What is he doing?' Because I came from a completely different community . . . It's not secure. You're moving in the unknown waters which are not only scientifically unknown but . . . psychologically."[45] The approach means moving forward by backpedaling, running to get up to speed, leaping, then scanning the field midair to find out if you're wasting your time.

This agility takes an inordinate amount of "courage," Geim said. "I suppose," he said, that is where "play comes in."[46] Playfulness lets us withstand enormous uncertainty: The deliberate amateur knows no other way.

"I want to start by discussing the subject of play," said Adam Smith, the editorial director of Nobel Media, who conducted Geim and Novoselov's official interview before the prize ceremony. "People often view science as a very serious exploit, but it's really quite playful, and you in particular keep play at the forefront of your research activities. Can you tell me how play figures in your research?"

It was a reasonable opening question. The same Nobel interviewer had posed the question over the phone a slightly different way two months before. "I guess we could call it the 'Lego Doctrine,'" Geim then said about his philosophy, and described how we build anew based on what "Lego pieces" we have, from "facilities" to "random knowledge."[47] If you tinker enough, if you're curious and industrious enough, he said, "You don't need to be in a Harvard or Cambridge, in one of the universities which collect the smartest people and the best equipment. You can be in the second- or even third-rated universities in terms of facilities and, whatever, prestige, but you still can do something amazing . . . without being at the best place at the best time."[48]

Yet this time, Geim looked down, entwined his fingers, pursed his lips, and looked up at the ceiling. Novoselov started in. "They teach you a lot about physics in the University, but they don't teach you how to do science." Any process that "promotes the freedom of mind" is productive.[49]

As he concluded, Geim was still gazing upward. To talk about play, Smith had to prod.

"And you, Professor Geim?"

He looked to be mid-thought. He is, for all of his wicked humor, serious, even intimidating. The majority of Geim's experiments require extreme focus and care. On the day when he was notified about the Nobel, he had plans to write a paper and answer e-mails and "muddle on as before," but "the Nobel Prize interrupted my work," he said. "I'm not sure that it's a useful interruption, okay. Certainly it's a pleasant one."[50] His Nobel Prize Banquet speech was a reminder about the danger of blurring the line between "opinion" and "evidence."[51] Novoselov values Geim's industriousness and frankness. "It's a great comfort to have someone nearby who is smarter than you are. And Andre is direct enough to also say when he thinks something is bullshit," said Novoselov, even if it's just with a facial reaction. "It won't take much to get a clear answer from him."

But when Geim was asked about the centrality of so-called play to innovation in the formality of the Laureate interview, he deliberated a long time. I would later ask him why he was so reluctant to speak.

When a musician says that someone can *play*, it means they are skilled, responsive, and nimble; the person knows how to harmonize or offer dissonance when it's right. The musician can *play* like Esperanza Spalding, with her hands on the bass and her voice running in a different direction altogether. But it is also the emphasis on the word. Musicians often say it with a downbeat at the end, stretched out like a bass bow, as if the word is as heavy as the talent they've described. Their tone conveys that this skill is serious. We hear the heft inherent in the creative act of play when, for example, author Toni Morrison says that an idea for a book never comes to her "in a flash," but is "a sustained thing I have to play with."[52] Yet outside of the creative process, *play* is a term that can hurt the concept it names. It's nearly axiomatic that play is considered the opposite of much that we value—heft and thoroughness. Use it as a noun, an adverb, or a verb, and most of these words will only skim the surface of what *play* means, and what it can lead to.

We recalled play's importance when Antanas Mockus resigned as president of the National University of Colombia, successfully ran for mayor of Bogotá in 1995 and again in 2001, and became widely credited for transforming one of the world's most chaotic, crime-ridden cities with tactics so playful, so humorous that to some they looked foolish: one policy called for mimes to replace the "notoriously bribable" traffic police. With faces painted white or blue, some dressed in bowties, black pencil on their eyes and eyebrows to exaggerate expression, the mimes would stand at intersections and on streets mocking bad behavior and praising good behavior from pedestrians and drivers. Mockus's theory was that play could help, since people are often more afraid of ridicule than being fined. During his tenure, traffic fatalities dropped by over 50 percent. The homicide rate also decreased by 70 percent. The program was so successful that Mockus fired 3,200 traffic cops. The hundreds of traffic officers that remained were trained as mimes.

"I said to myself, we're six million inhabitants. Those games can't transform behavior," said Rocio Londoño, director of culture and arts in Bogotá, reflecting on Mockus's work.[53] Yet the sprite-like Mockus continued to employ his policies at every turn. To advocate for water conservation, the heavily bearded mayor filmed a (largely cropped) commercial of himself in the shower, turning off the water as he lathered. Water conservation in the city improved by 40 percent during his administration; he was able to provide drinking water to all homes. (Only 79 percent had water in their homes before his tenure.)

Mockus was a deliberate amateur, a university president who intentionally chose a new course. During his two nonconsecutive terms, his policies aimed at fixing the disparity between culture, morality, and the law. Yet, as his colleagues pointed out, he wasn't an expert in political theory. He ran as a true skeptic of traditional politics, the first Independent mayor, with no favors to bind him. Months before his election, he was known only as a mathematician and philosopher. Not yet married to Adriana Córdoba, he ran his 1994 campaign from the house where he lived with his mother, Nijolé, a Lithuanian-born sculptor who disapproved of his entrance into politics. Journalists would come to interview him. His mother would ask the journalists to get out of her house. During his campaign, he literally ran around the city streets, cleaning its "visual pollution" in a self-styled yellow and red "Supercitizen" full-body leotard. The news site *La Silla Vacía* said that Mockus was most like surrealist Salvador Dalí in his relationship to the public: "Even if they don't understand his words, they understand his message." In the country that inspired the magical realism of Gabriel García Márquez, political analysts resorted to artistic analogies to explain Mockus's phenomena in Colombia—the staggering shifts that came through the perception shift of radical play.

We seem to know the centrality of play as we speak through a language of dexterous hands. The symbol for support and approval is a thumbs-up. When we understand a concept, we often say that we grasp it. When a circumstance is under control, we have a grip on it. Even foundational contracts can be signed by a handshake agreement. A gesture or event that moves us is *touching*. We say that we're staying in touch even though we might have no physical contact at all, but communicate regularly. When a show's script needs improvement, it gets a punch up. "The hand is in search of a brain, the brain is in search of a hand, and play is the medium by which those two are linked in the best way," Stuart Brown, founder of The National Institute for Play, summarized.[54]

Perhaps we underestimate its importance because we forget what physical anthropologists know: When we suppress play, danger is often close at hand. Of all the species, humans are the most neotenous; we have great potential to stay supple, flexible, and to retain qualities found in children throughout our lives, one of which is the ability to play. Brown understands its importance from his work in internal medicine, psychiatry, and clinical research. He saw it in a gruesome study on the common theme of play deprivation in homicidal males. After years of taking play histories of individuals, Brown has found that our earliest memories connected to joy and play alter the trajectories of our lives as adults.[55]

Play's importance is also evident in early childhood development and learning. For every fifteen minutes of play, children tend to use a third of that time engaged in learning about mathematical, spatial, and architectural principles. One of my favorite examples comes from a study from the journal *Cognition*, run by MIT professor Laura Schulz, with this setup: In the first group, an experimenter would take a toy with four tubes to a group of four-year-olds, and in one case she would act surprised when she pulled a tube and it squeaked, and then leave them with the toy. Another group of four-year-olds received the same toy, but through directed teaching—"I'm going to show you how this toy works. Watch this!" she said excitedly, and then made the tube squeak. Systematically, when both groups of children were left alone to play with the toy, all made it squeak, but the first group engaged with it for longer than the second group. The group introduced to the toy through play also found out that it had "'hidden features" that the experimenter hadn't hinted at, like the mirror hidden in one of the tubes. The group taught about the toy never discovered all that it could do. Their curiosity was dampened. The research is becoming more and more clear about this counterintuitive fact: directed teaching is important, but learning that comes from play and spontaneous discovery is critical. Endurance is best sustained through periodic play.

"Kids are born scientists," astrophysicist Neil deGrasse Tyson believes. "They're born probing the natural world that surrounds them. They'll lift up a rock . . . They'll experiment with breakable things in your house. It might mean they break a dish someday, because they're experimenting with how dishes roll down the corridor . . . So you buy a new dish. And you say, 'Well, that can be costly.' But as Derek Bok, former president of Harvard, once said, 'If you think education is costly, look at the cost of ignorance.'"[56] Just as C. P. Snow and others argued for the conceptual reunion of art and science, Tyson, Beau Lotto, and others have made the same case for some conceptual blending between what we see as science, discovery, and play, and what constitutes innovation in any field.

The trouble is that the perspective-altering gift of play remains associated with children. "That's been the biggest barrier—people see it as the opposite of work, as something childlike," said Ivy Ross, a pioneering designer and marketing executive who became known for her innovation at firms from Mattel to the Gap by creating new environments that prioritized play.[57] "And that's why it's really a hard thing for people to accept. But play is actually the opposite of depression, since depression is being numb to possibilities."

To work around this, Ross created Project Platypus at Mattel's El Segundo, California, headquarters. The space was informal. She rotated in a team of twelve, stripped of their titles and given positions as mobile as their desks on wheels. They could work with whomever they wanted, however they wanted. Aside from a room for private calls and a room for "sound baths"—a space with chairs with inbuilt speakers, tipped at the angle of an astronaut's shuttle launch chair, that played those rare binaural frequencies meant to stimulate both hemispheres of the brain—their workspace was lined with carpets that looked like grass. It resembled a Montessori environment, with stimuli to satisfy every self-initiated interest: games and even rubber rockets to shoot to give the mind a break. There was no set schedule; the weeks were filled with "mental grazing," the team filling themselves with new ideas, images, and concepts that they knew little about.[58] "Sometimes the ideas gelled, sometimes it wasn't until week seven, but it never disappointed me," Ross said about Project Platypus. They always got more innovative work done than ever before. It was so creative it was fertile. People joked that it was the secret key to pregnancy. After twelve weeks with Ross, women who had been trying to conceive often left somewhere in their first trimester.

"Innovation is an outcome. Play is a state of mind. Innovation is often what we get when we play," Ross believes.

A constellation of voices has begun to argue for the importance of permitting an adventurous approach into the process of innovative, serious work. NASA's Jet Propulsion Lab (JPL) considers play so critical for its engineers' performance that it asks applicants about their hobbies as children. In consultation with Frank Wilson, a neurologist focused on the coevolution of the hand and brain, and Nate Johnson, a mechanic in Long Beach, JPL found that younger engineers were not as good at mechanical problem solving as their retiring engineers. The kind of play that Wilson championed happened so infrequently that NASA experts were then not as comfortable using their hands.[59] JPL then changed its policy to ask candidates about how much they played in their childhood, no matter how stellar their academic pedigree.[60]

Play spaces don't necessarily need anything commodious. The paracosms children often create are a hallmark of innovation of another kind of play: the abstract thinking that produces extended, private meta-worlds. Apparently, MacArthur Fellow "genius" grant winners engage in these magnum daydreams when they are young at a rate twice as high as that found in a sample set of college students. Robert Root-Bernstein of Michigan State University, who pioneered the study that produced this finding with his wife and colleague, Michele, is a MacArthur Fellow recipient himself.[61]

We create because we imagine. Pioneering French polymath Henri Poincaré, who, like Geim, moved from field to field within mathematics and physics, describes how ideas act like objects in motion: "I could almost feel them jostling one another, until two of them coalesced [s'accroachassent], so to speak, to form a stable combination."[62] Perceptions of innovation in science, the arts, or in exploration of any kind can block our view of what is often going on—the constant suspension and multi-sensation of cognitive and physical play.

The slipstream between working and work generated from imagining is also why Novoselov told me that it was impossible to set a true start date for any single experiment. When I asked him when the FNE for graphene began, he mentioned that it began in internal ways—while going to sleep, in the shower—such that making a true start date is inevitably inaccurate.

Yet in the context of scientific research, *play* may never be the right word, at least not publicly.

What Geim wanted, he would later reveal, was a new term, a "slightly different manner of speech," to define what we really mean by play: "curiosity-driven research."[63] He would prefer to call it "adventure."[64] His Nobel Prize Lecture is titled, after all, a "Random Walk to Graphene." That was how he would describe the journey, a hand-connected experiment that is, in fact, not research, but a search.

––––––––––

A process akin to Friday Night Experiments is at work in some of the best science labs in the country, it seems, as Kevin Dunbar discusses his research in four prominent molecular biology labs over the course of a year. Dunbar, now at the University of Maryland, has spent nearly his entire career quantifying just how valuable it is to take mistakes seriously in the lab and how we can overcome the blind spots to them.

"We really know virtually nothing about the scientific process, about how scientists think and reason," he said. After fifteen years of total access to four prominent biochemistry labs, following the scientists at meetings, looking at their lab journals, grants and tests, and watching them interact (what he has termed an "in vivo" research method), Dunbar observed that their experiments were failing 40 to 75 percent of the time, but the best scientists were able to follow up on their unexpected findings. He has found that the most productive labs were the ones where nonspecialist scientists were part of the results review process.[65] In labs where scientists all had the same types of expertise, figuring out what was going wrong was slow and inefficient.[66] When someone thinks they understand something, the mind edits reality so efficiently that errors can be hard to perceive, but when someone observes a scenario that they are unfamiliar with, a part of the brain operates inefficiently, giving us time to see outliers and consider their significance.

Factors such as job security help determine who ultimately sets out to follow the path of the deliberate amateur. Graduate students and postdocs were often the least motivated to go through the laborious process of following up on each failure since "they have short-term goals," Dunbar said. "They want to get a job when they're done and have a good publication, but tenured professors, who have relatively secure career futures, liked the unexpected findings." The more senior the researchers were, he found, the more they could afford to "play."[67]

"How many scientific revolutions have been missed because their potential inaugurators disregarded the whimsical, the incidental, the inconvenient inside the laboratory?"[68] Dunbar offers an answer. The freedom that comes from the context of FNEs can assist the resistance.[69]

These late-night adventures give permission to release ourselves from what can stymie invention—"wrongness," as author Kathryn Schulz calls it. "Recognizing our errors is such a strange experience," she writes: not only is it an unhoned, largely ignored part of our internal lives, but when we do find ourselves confronting our own error "we suddenly find ourselves at odds with *ourselves*."[70] This feeling of wrongness is the sense of recognition that Aristotle described in the *Poetics*, the moment when a character sees his own error in a Greek tragedy. "Error, in that moment, is less an intellectual problem than an existential one—a crisis not in what we know, but in who we are."

Some environments never permit such havens or Friday Night Experiments, and for this we have vacations; time to spend away from our routine to relax and often pursue a passion project. It is the same principle behind the increased efficacy we see when we work with brief intervals of rest during the day.[71] Yet we often see vacations as we do play: a period at odds with productivity when it actually enhances it.

———

The idea of the scientific process as a search, an adventure, is more than a metaphor; Geim has found that research is both his labor and his "hobby." A vacation for him is likely to be a hike or a short walk. I spoke with Geim in London after our panel with Ben Saunders, as both men relaxed in the greenroom of the G8 Innovation / DNA Summit. The physicist was interested in talking with the polar explorer and in getting advice from him. He sensed that their exploits were similar.

"I have these sideways pursuits," he said to Saunders about his explorations when we were offstage, "and because I'll likely never meet another man like you again I'd like to know, what is the most difficult thing you find out in the Arctic? What is it? The perseverance, the stamina—this I know you have, okay—the isolation. It can't be because you talk to your teammates on the phone. It is . . . what?"

"It's being able to withstand it," Saunders said. "Courage," he added, and the surprising ways that we find it within. Geim nodded, looked down, and smiled.

Geim then told me why he had been reluctant to speak about play in his official Nobel interview. He wanted to emphasize the paradox of play. Whimsy is what permits us to endure the gravity of the conditions required for innovation (and exploration). I listened as Saunders talked about his last preparations for the Arctic, and then as Geim laughed, recounting tales of his falls down mountain crevasses. It was as if they had met in the common space between their endeavors. "To strive, to seek, to find . . ."

Trammeled walkways that emerge on the grass and ground are called desire lines—intrepid paths stamped into the ground by the determined impulse of freedom. In the woods and in cities, these footpaths offer more efficient ways to get around than the urban planners have designed with paved streets. In Finland, urban planners often head to parks after snowfall to view how pedestrians would navigate if they followed their own desire.[72] To follow these desire lines is "to respond to an invitation."[73] Someone had to be the first to tread. This is the kind of adventurous search, seeking out roads that, though hidden, are found on open ground, "waiting for our wits to grow sharper."[74]

The graphite mines do lie unguarded. When the trade in graphite fell centuries ago, the mines opened again and the paths to them lay fallow. Hikers discovered them by following the desire lines up the mountainside. Novoselov saw them for himself, surrounded by the higher ranges like Scafell Pike, the tallest mountain in England, near the material's excavation sites. Researching these graphite-lined paths is what he often does when not at work on the next stage of graphene—making custom materials built "layer by layer with atomic precision" that can have predetermined properties and functionality: "We can select one layer to be a sensor, one [could] be photosensitive, act as a solar cell, [and] another layer can act as a transistor."[75] Last I spoke to the physicists, they were able to make custom-designed materials ten microns thick.

The untold story of graphite brought Novoselov home to his lab—the material was originally found, sold, and mined from Britain's Lake District, near his base in Manchester.[76] The veins of the pockmarked mountains, near the wettest part of England, Seathwaite, hold graphite as a pure material, abundant and unmixed with other minerals. Once termed "wad" by locals, graphite was so easy to find that it could be "taken out in lumps sometimes as big as a man's fist."[77] Lake District farmers used it to mark their sheep until the early eighteenth century, while during the Renaissance Flemish traders sold this English graphite to artists—it was perfect for gestural strokes.[78] Graphite was also a valuable material for artillery and protected iron and steel from rust. For a period, an act of Parliament guarded the mines.[79]

Novoselov thinks graphite was used earlier than all of this evidence suggests. He has found graphite pencils and manuscripts that antedate the mines' official history. The material was there all the while.

The entrances to the graphite mines are clearly visible, but only after first scaling its gateway peaks. Otherwise, they remain hidden in plain sight.

To play is a way of climbing and finding hidden mines without serious strain. Those who manage to suspend their disbelief see the threshold—horizontal and often dry—and enter.

THE GRIT OF THE ARTS

The stars we are given. The constellations we make.
—REBECCA SOLNIT

Driving up a New York State highway along the Hudson River to Locust Grove, the house designed for Samuel F. B. Morse, I was just shy of a bridge wall that had recently collapsed when I thought about the line between dogged pursuit and dysfunctional persistence, between knowing when to continue and when to quit and reassess.[1] The difficulty we have in distinguishing between these differences results in the curious fact that somewhere in the world, roughly every thirty years, a major bridge collapses while it is still being erected or soon thereafter.[2] When scientists Paul G. Sibly and Alastair Walker identified the thirty-year cycle, they found that it was not caused by the implementation of any new technology, or because of a lapse in an engineer's rigorous structural analysis, a field with a history of documenting failures dating back to the time of Galileo. It occurred because when engineers are one professional generation removed from the inception of the foundational design, they tend to trust their models too much. If a proven template has no chance of going awry, it is only after an obvious breakdown that the painstaking process of anticipating glitches begins.[3] The ongoing pattern of collapse occurs, in other words, because of the blind spot created by success.

Effective building—of bridges, of concepts, and ideas—comes from a more supple form of grit that knows when development needs to give way to discovery.

When Morse invented the telegraph, he constructed the first model out of cogs, clock springs, and more, and set it into a wooden frame—the abandoned canvas stretcher bars for a painting he would never complete. He longed to be an artist. For twenty-six years, he had worked to become a renowned painter. Then he took what he learned to pioneer the invention of the telegraph.

I wanted to speak with Angela Lee Duckworth about this nimble form of grit. Weeks earlier, as I walked straight down the hall to meet Duckworth in her office at the University of Pennsylvania, and she beat me to it. Casually dressed in a boat-necked striped shirt, pants, and flats, her jet-black hair pulled back in a mid-height ponytail, she was bounding out of her office heading toward me. She was welcoming, warm, and commanding. When she and I were finished talking after that first meeting, her students lined up like ducklings, waiting in the threshold of the open office door, waiting for me to gather my bags. I was in the Positive Psychology Center, which has produced some of the most path-breaking work in the country, and I was talking with the recent MacArthur-winning scholar who humbly knows the limits of what can be studied in the lab.

Her work began in the first few months of her graduate school research, when she and Martin Seligman, head of the Positive Psychology Center, kept thinking about one main question: What are the true barriers to achievement? There are three kinds, as they saw it. The first is adversity, something that happens effectively to you—things implode, break down, or catastrophe strikes. There is also failure, hardship for which you are largely responsible. Then there are plateaus, a more subtle form of stultification where there is no visible movement forward. There may be no progress for decades. During each scenario, the urge to give up is adaptive and reasonable. We need to have that impulse. Yet the urge to hold on could explain how we could sustain ability, capacity for hard labor, and zeal over time. They thought the missing variable was grit.

Duckworth is best known for her research on both self-control and grit—what her studies show is one of the most powerful predictors of achievement, especially in challenging contexts. She has examined grit in a variety of environments from Teach For America to the Scripps National Spelling Bee, and the U.S. Military Academy at West Point. The U.S. Military Academy was so intrigued with the importance of grit that in 2004 she was invited to challenge their "Whole Candidate Score"—a composite score based on GPA, SAT scores, class rank, leadership ability, and physical fitness—against her grit scale derived from a self-report assessment test, comprised of statements such as "I finish whatever I begin" and "new ideas and projects sometimes distract me from previous ones." Which metric was a better longitudinal predictor of the cadets who would last past the grueling summer of Beast Barracks, the punishing training first-year cadets endure at West Point? Whole Candidate Scores were not at all related to the number of cadets who stayed in the program—cadets were equally likely to leave West Point if they were in the top or the bottom of that metric. Grit scores, however, were significant predictors of staying in the program. Grittier cadets were more likely to make it through the summer.[4]

What surprised Duckworth was that grit is not positively correlated with IQ. Grit is connected to how we respond to so-called failure, about whether we see it as a comment on our identity or merely as information that may help us improve.[5]

I wanted to see if she could help me with a riddle, which for now let's call the riddle of Samuel Morse: how to cultivate grit and when to stop before it becomes dysfunctional persistence.

————————

Grit is not just a simple elbow-grease term for rugged persistence. It is an often invisible display of endurance that lets you stay in an uncomfortable place, work hard to improve upon a given interest, and do it again and again. It is not just about resisting the *"hourly temptations,"* as Francis Galton would call them, but toiling *"over years, even decades,"* as Duckworth argues, and even without positive reinforcement.[6] Unlike dysfunctional persistence, a flat-footed posture we ease into through the comfort of success, grit is focused moxie, *aided* by a sustained response in the face of adversity.

Grit and self-control are distinct. Self-control is momentary, exercised by controlling impulses that "bring pleasure in the moment but are immediately regretted," Duckworth said.[7] The most vivid example comes from psychologist Walter Mischel's "marshmallow studies," as they are often called, conducted in the late 1960s, about the predictive power of self-control and delayed gratification. "Do you want one marshmallow now or two marshmallows when I come back?" he had researchers ask each of the children. Some opted for the immediate rush of one treat, while others held out for more. Follow-up studies decades later showed that the trait of self-control endured, and was correlated with high achievement and life outcomes measured by metrics from SAT scores to educational attainment.[8] The time scale is longer for grit.

For the decade before she studied grit, Duckworth looked like its unlikely pioneer. During high school at her family's dinner table in their home in Cherry Hill, New Jersey, her father, a color chemist at DuPont, would ask Duckworth questions such as, "Was Einstein or Newton the greater physicist?" or "Who was the greatest artist who ever lived?" As a teenager, she had been developing this hypothesis that happiness was people's main aim. She asked her father what he wanted out of life. "He said, 'I want to be successful. I want to be accomplished,'" she recalled. "I pushed back on him and said, 'Well, what you mean is that you want to be happy and being accomplished is what makes you happy.' He said, 'No, what I mean is that I want to be accomplished. I don't care if I end up happy or not.'" Habits leading to achievement became a topic that would smolder throughout her life.

Her decade after college is one she summarizes as "how not to be gritty."[9] It is filled with stop-and-start jobs that all required different skills—teaching, speechwriting, and consulting. Then she decided to pursue a doctorate at the age of thirty-two and began studying the psychology of effort.[10] One day she sat in her apartment "doing the hard, depressing math" that she would be "forty years old before I had a real job," and thought about the humiliation of going back to her fifteen-year college reunion still a student. "I realized that working hard is not enough. I needed to work hard consistently on a given path to accomplish anything."

"Angela was fast, about as fast mentally as it is possible for a human being to be," said Martin Seligman.[11] Yet getting her PhD meant curbing her tendencies to flit. She asked for help from her husband, a sustainable real-estate developer. He became her accountability partner to follow through on her decision to complete the degree. There were moments when he had to remind her of their pact, like the time when she complained and wanted to leave the program and go to medical school instead. "You can't do everything," he reminded her. "You have to pick a path. And you've picked a pretty good one."

Duckworth gets up every day to study, research, and teach the psychology of achievement. "I don't play an instrument; I don't study the psychology of eating, for example, although that's kind of cool," she said before a rare pause in her rapid-fire speech style as she looked down and smiled. "I just get up and study the psychology of achievement and effort, why people exert effort and why they don't." In her corner office was some corroborating evidence—a dense pile of white papers stacked and splayed out on her L-shaped desk, on top of file cabinets, at skewed angles with a logic that suggests a personal stratagem, a large mission to achieve, and enough active energy to live it out. My bag was next to the only free space on the floor I could find.

Duckworth wants to understand the psychology of achievement, and not just for "talent at the very high end," but how to cultivate talent that occurs "way further back in the distribution." The conclusion that grit is a critical characteristic for achievement has impacted schools across the country.[12] U.S. Secretary of Education Arne Duncan invited Duckworth to give education policy recommendations; she has worked with charter and private schools like Riverdale Country School, a top-tier New York City private school in the Bronx led by Dominic Randolph, and she is focusing on the portfolio mechanism of grading, one common in creative environments.[13] Her studies and ideas have also become integrated into the pedagogy at the New York City KIPP network of charter schools, where cofounder David Levin has noticed that the alumni who went on to excel in college were the grittiest.[14]

Given the centrality of coping with failure to cultivate grit, it is no surprise that Harvard University president Drew Gilpin Faust recently said that we need to make it safer to fail.[15] "Harvard students are good at performing in areas in which they excel. Learning how to fail is against their understanding of themselves." What book did Faust think that all incoming freshmen should read? *Being Wrong: Adventures in the Margin of Error* by Kathryn Schulz.[16] In her baccalaureate address to seniors, she stood "dressed like a Puritan minister" in the pulpit of Memorial Church, encouraging them to take risks and pursue their Plan A, delivered with a statement of "Veritas" that few expect—to succeed, you have to learn how to handle failure first.[17] Harvard has also initiated the Success-Failure Project, designed to help students cultivate resilience in the face of rejection and setbacks.

Christopher Merrill, director of the International Writing Program at the University of Iowa, a place that is "harder to get into than Harvard," tells me that in every workshop he was ever in, the teacher always thought that someone shouldn't be a writer. "But what they can't tell is how much someone *wants* something," he said, how much a person is willing to work and under what circumstances.[18]

"People ask me all the time, 'Are kids in America working too hard?' Yes, there are privileged kids who are over-programmed, but," Duckworth said, her voice more firm, "I think in life, most people are giving up too early." If we go by the studies, it is not talent, not even self-esteem, but effort that makes the difference in measurable forms of achievement. It leads to the surprising fact that self-esteem increased amongst American children in the 1990s from its 1980s and 1970s levels—a laudable trend, but measurable achievement has not improved along with it.[19] Higher self-esteem without higher levels of achievement means "many American kids, particularly in the last couple of decades, can feel really good about themselves without being good at anything."[20]

In one of our conversations, she told me about Finland's development of *sisu*, a rough cognate for grit. Etymologically, *sisu* denotes a person's viscera, their "intestines (*sisucunda*)." It is defined as "having guts," intentional, stoic, constant bravery in the face of adversity.[21] For Finns, *sisu* is a part of national culture, forged through their history of war with Russia and required by the harsh climate.[22] In this Nordic country, pride is equated with endurance. When Finnish mountain climber Veikka Gustafsson ascended a peak in Antarctica, it was named Mount Sisu. The fortitude to withstand war and foreign occupations is lyrically heralded in the Finnish epic poem, *The Kalevala*.[23] Even the saunas—two million, one for every three Finns in a country of approximately five and a half million— involve fortitude: A sauna roast is often followed by a nude plunge into the ice-cold Baltic Sea. If Iceland is happier than it has any right to be considering the hours the country spends plunged in darkness each year, Finland's past circumstances, climate, and developed culture have turned it into one of the grittiest.

Finland's educational system is also currently ranked first, ahead of South Korea, now at number two.[24] The United States is midway down the list.[25] In Finland, there is no after-school tutoring or training, no "miracle pedagogy" in the classrooms, where students are on a first-name basis with their teachers, all of whom have master's degrees. There is also more "creative play."[26] Perhaps the tradition of *sisu* and play, I suspect, are part of the larger, unstated reason for its success.[27]

"Wouldn't it be great if you heard people talking about how they were going to do something to build their grit?" Duckworth asked.

Gritty people often sound, says Duckworth, like one of her favorite actors, Will Smith. He once said, "The only thing that I see that is distinctly different about me is I'm not afraid to die on a treadmill. I will not be outworked. Period. You might have more talent than me, you might be smarter than me, you might be sexier than me; you might be all of those things—you got it on me in nine categories. But if we get on the treadmill together, there's two things: You're getting off first, or I'm gonna die. It's really that simple, right? . . . You're not going to outwork me."[28]

They can even sound like James Watson, co-discoverer of the structure of DNA. "When I was a boy, I had to reconcile the fact that I didn't have a good IQ, but I still wanted to do something important," Watson told me, recalling the reasons for his path-breaking discoveries from his office at Cold Spring Harbor one July afternoon. "I knew it would take grit, no question about it," he said. He remains gritty about his avocations, too. "I want one hour with Roger Federer," the octogenarian scientist said, explaining that he had started to get serious about tennis in his fifties and sixties. He volleys with the same tennis racquet Federer does. "I want to see if I could get even just one point on him."[29]

Gritty people also sound like Morse.

Morse stated his decades-long ambition in even more lofty terms: "To be among those who shall revive the splendor of the fifteenth century; to rival the genius of a Raphael, a Michael Angelo [*sic*], or a Titian; my ambition is to be enlisted in the constellation of genius now rising in this country."[30] By his early forties, Morse considered destroying every canvas on which he'd ever laid his brush. Encountering every imaginable type of criticism about his work, failing repeatedly to receive painting commissions, and unable to support himself and his family, he felt "jilted," his ardor returned with dust.[31]

Yet Morse would go on to build the nation a network; an invented trace of dots and dashes that ultimately bridged the extent of the globe. The telegraph, from the Greek *tele* and *graph* (to write at a distance), "annihilated space and time."[32] Its unprecedented communication speed seemed to have "chained the very lightning of heaven." Its "almost supernatural agency" as one newspaper said, astonished. It left people "wonder-stricken and confused." News of the signing of the Declaration of Independence once took two weeks to travel on horse or by foot from Philadelphia to Virginia. With the telegraph, news moved within minutes. A circuit that controlled recording keys—a lever, a magnet, a stylus, and scrolling paper—would create its signal dots and dashes, lines fashioned by electric current. While it would take decades to finalize the code and the relay, this principle was correct from the start. An exemplar of Yankee ingenuity, the telegraph model on loan from the Smithsonian now sits in the Oval Office. Many considered "the lightning line," as the telegraph was often called, to be "the greatest triumph of the human mind."[33]

Kenneth Silverman's biography of the painter and inventor has an appropriate title: *Lightning Man: The Accursed Life of Samuel F. B. Morse.*

Morse had achieved stature as cofounder and president of the National Academy of Design in New York helping to nurture American artistic identity during the post-revolutionary era, and as an associate of the American Academy of the Fine Arts, but couldn't eke out a living with his "migratory wanderings" in New England, painting portraits for fifteen dollars per head when he could find the work. He settled his family in New Haven while he painted and slept in his New York City studio, concluding, "If I am to live in poverty it will be as well there as any where." He received a few prestigious commissions. Exhibiting them put him in debt. After the painting career that Morse considered, largely, a failure and the personal catastrophes it later created for his family, there was a nearly two-decade-long trial to create a transatlantic telegraph model—one filled with setbacks, prohibitive debt, social defections, public controversies, and feuds. At the end of his life, he felt that he had endured enough to drive anyone "into exile or to the insane hospital or to the grave."[34]

Sometime after 1832, in Washington Square—his lodgings at the University of the City of New York (now New York University), where he was the school's first professor of Painting—he nailed the wooden backing of the canvas firmly to a table to hold the telegraph model together. The battery wires and the frame of the first device were to him "so rude," so coarse, that apart from relatives and trusted students, "he was reluctant to have it seen."[35]

Morse devised the idea on the ship *Sully* on his way back from a two-and-a-half-year trip spent in Europe to study painting. He splayed out his concept for electrical telegraphy on three pages of his pocket sketchbook, constructing its "system of signs and the apparatus" underneath a list of countries, what could have been a model for a listed message sent over his imagined telegraph wires that read:

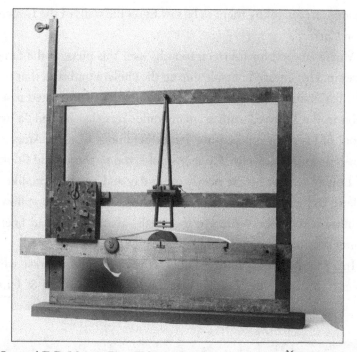

Samuel F. B. Morse, First Telegraph Instrument, 1837.[36] Division of
Work and Industry, National Museum of American History,
Smithsonian Institution.

"War. Holland. Belgium. Alliance. France. England. Against. Russia.
Prussia. Austria."[37]

In 1837, he applied for a patent for his model, having heard that
Boston physician Dr. Charles Jackson might have done so first. Fear
of a near win forced his hand.[38]

Morse would not live to see one of his paintings, completed just
before quitting the profession to work on the telegraph, garner international acclaim. This was his six-feet by nine-feet canvas *Gallery of the Louvre* (1831–33), for which Morse replicated thirty-eight
largely Italian masterpieces, including the *Mona Lisa* by Leonardo da
Vinci and multiple works by Titian, Veronese, Poussin, Rubens, and

Claude Lorrain, piling them as he saw fit on the walls of the Louvre's Salon Carré.[39]

Morse labored for fourteen months over this piece at the famed museum. He ventured outside during the cholera outbreak that took lives, maintaining such ascetic work habits that he "created a sensation in the Louvre," with so many onlookers that he had "a little school of his own," said author James Fenimore Cooper, America's then-best-known novelist. Cooper would stop by the second floor of the Louvre to visit Morse nearly every day and egg him on, like an athletic fan in the stands: "Lay it on here, Samuel—more yellow—the nose is too short—the eye too small—damn it if I had been a painter what a picture I should have painted."[40]

In 1833, Morse's painting failed to ignite public interest when it went on display in New York at the bookstore Carvill & Com-

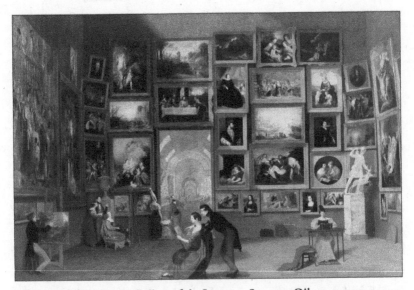

Samuel F. B. Morse, *Gallery of the Louvre*, 1831–33. Oil on canvas, 73¾ x 108 in. Daniel J. Terra Collection, 1992.51. Terra Foundation for American Art, Chicago / Art Resource, NY.

pany on Broadway and Pine Street. The store charged twenty-five cents to see the work on display. The reviews were warm, but the public didn't show. Financial valuation is hardly the same as artistic value, but the painting then sold for barely half of the asking price. "My profession . . . ," he said, "exists on charity."[41] In 1982 the Terra Foundation for American Art purchased Morse's *Gallery of the Louvre* for $3.25 million. It was a record for the sale of an early American painting at that time.[42]

Morse considered *Gallery* his chef d'oeuvre. The painting emblematizes a way of seeing that predates the modern age. It showed the once ritual space of the salon, where some large works were "skied," or hung near the ceiling, before the gallery space would be reconsidered as the antiseptic white cube, where, as artist and critic Brian O'Doherty put it, even the body can feel like an intrusion.[43]

Morse's eventual level of acclaim compared with his litany of failures seemed so improbable that the public speculated about his personal characteristics. Some thought it a wonder that he "succeeded at all, that he did not sink under the manifold discouragements and hardships."[44] The *Home Journal* conducted an unofficial phrenological exam on Morse and concluded that he was "forcible, persevering, almost headstrong, self-relying, independent, aspiring, good-hearted, and eminently social, though sufficiently selfish to look well to his own interests."[45] To be sure, he might have been all of those things. Yet Morse thought the answer lay elsewhere.

———

Grit is a portable skill that moves across seemingly varied interests. Grit can be expressed in your chosen pursuit and appear in multiple domains over time. It can be expressed through the pursuit of painting, and then through the invention of the telegraph. "It is possible to switch course, and still be gritty underneath it all," Duckworth said.[46]

Morse documented his process in his letters home through his many decades as an itinerant painter and art student in Europe, and eventually as a professor at New York University. He started studying how others responded to defeat. When he found out that getting into the Royal Academy of Arts in London had recently become "a much harder task" given the new requirement to know anatomy, he wrote to his parents that he felt "rather encouraged from this circumstance, since the harder it is to gain admittance, the greater honor it will be should I enter."[47] When he studied with acclaimed painter Washington Allston in London, he wrote to his family: "It is a mortifying thing . . . when I have been painting all day very hard and begin to be pleased with what I have done, and on showing it to Mr. Allston, with the expectation of praise, and not only of praise but a score of 'excellents,' 'well dones,' and 'admirables,' I say it is mortifying to hear him after a long silence say, *"very bad, Sir, that is not flesh, it is 'mud,' Sir, it is painted with 'brick dust and clay.'"*[48] The comments at first made Morse want to "dash" his "palette knife through" his work, but later made him "see that Mr. Allston is not a flatterer but a friend, and that really to improve I must see my faults."[49]

As if understanding the color theory all painters know: to create shadow, to give an object depth and volume, you blend its color with one least like it (yellow blends with purple to create a shadow, orange with blue, red with green), and so Morse would study how his icons thrived through adversity. He had studied with legendary president of the Royal Academy and painter Benjamin West, and wanted to know how West had been able to withstand "so much abuse" and "virulence" with a "nobleness of spirit," remaining "heedless of the sneers, the ridicule, or the detraction of his enemies."[50] He began to look to past artists such as Giotto and Ghirlandaio, whose works some considered "rude, and stiff, and dry," for their concordant strengths in their quality of expression.[51] For decades, Morse's letters show that he extended this perspective into other fields. On his way to Florence and Rome, he stopped at the island of Elba and lingered in the room that the defeated emperor Napoleon had occupied, and laid on the bed as he "endeavored to conceive for the moment how he, who had in that very situation seen the same objects when he woke, then viewed the reverses of life, to which he had apparently hitherto believed himself superior."[52]

Around the same time of his reflections on Jackson's and Pope Gregory's responses to defeats, Morse felt his painting began to improve. He started teaching a few students, and settled into a studio on Broadway in New York. "My storms are partly over," he said, as if previsioning his life.[53] Soon after, he would file the patent for the model for the electromagnetic telegraph.

Despite all of the false alarms and setbacks with the telegraph, Morse's perspective remained. He could respond to his friend that his telegraph "trials" were the things that "accompany the most valuable enterprises," and, also, that "they are often compensated by important experience, the lessons of which will be profitable for the future."[54]

His tenacity is apparent in his attempt to send a message in 1842 through the cable of his recently invented telegraph device from Manhattan to Governors Island, submerged under water over the mile distance. The *Herald* advertised the event as a chance to witness the device "destined to work a complete revolution in the mode of transmitting intelligence throughout the civilized world." A few letters went through successfully, then the transmission came to an abrupt end. What looked like failure was, in fact, an accident; a ship crossing the river had entangled the cable in its anchor. The crowd scattered. Morse could barely sleep after what looked like yet another "mortifying" failure. He spent that night considering how the failed trial had mapped his solution. What would happen if he eliminated the wire altogether? Electricity could pass through water itself.[55] It led to the breakthrough that let the telegraph cross oceans, one that would take decades to complete.

"I have been told several times since my return that I was born one hundred years too soon for the arts in our country," Morse once wrote to his friend, Fenimore Cooper. If he was to be a "Pioneer," he said, he was "fitted for it."[56]

Grit gives the impression that it is a straight line, as if we just drill down in ways that may feel uncomfortable, and then improve. "Gritty people have a pattern of staying with one path," Duckworth has said. "Grit is choosing to show up again and again."[57]

Yet, she clarified: "Whatever you're doing, you have to figure out when to give out effort and when to withdraw it. The really high-functioning people are able to do both; somehow have an eye [for] asking whether they are in the game too long. They have to be willing to commit to higher-level goals by shifting lower-level tactics. The higher level it is, the more you should be tenacious. The lower level it is, the more concrete or particular it is, the more you should be willing to give it up. I think it's a good rule of thumb."

I asked her for her thoughts on how we escape the dark side of grit. "I'm not sure we know exactly," she told me. What makes someone pull back and change course when they're focused is a hard thing to measure, but, she revealed, "It's actually on our list to study in the next few years."

Yet it may be more art than science. It seems to be the riddle of Morse—that true grit is not made up of just grit at all.

Reverberating under the surface of some of these grit pioneers and policymakers—Duckworth, Mischel, Duncan, and Dominic

Randolph—seemed to be an interest in how the processes at work in art and design can help cultivate this nimble form of grit, and how central they are for the work and play of innovation. I heard it first from Randolph, the headmaster of Riverdale, which has implemented Duckworth's ideas about fostering grit into its pedagogy. We barely ate our breakfast one day in June as he interlaced comments about making, spatial and visual thinking, and the pedagogy of art and design that can aid in cultivating this important trait. Most schools are structured around "mono-modal work," Randolph said, drilling down on one thing without seeing its interrelated connections to other ideas. To teach students about grit, he realized that he would have to have them understand that there is no linear path.

In most public schools in America, the main way to do that is through the arts, and in the United States, the arts have been virtually eliminated since the 1970s. Since 1990, creativity scores have declined in general, but creativity scores for children from kindergarten to the sixth grade, as measured by Torrance Tests of Creative Thinking between 1968 and 2008, have dropped for the first time since its testing began. During the same period, IQ scores have increased each decade.[58]

As the arts are eliminated, so is the avenue to one of their irreplaceable gifts: the agency to withstand ambiguity long enough to discern whether to pursue a problem or to quit and reassess—when to see, as Morse did, that the painting could also be part of a telegraph. Agency comes from the convergent and divergent thinking that the creative process requires. With the recent decline in our investment in the arts and education, we are smarter, yet less equipped to find novel approaches to problems (as Duncan, too, has noted). If we are low in grit, as well, we are less able to stay with these problems long enough to resolve them.

Randolph had Riverdale begin working with Imagination Playground, a massive block set in weather-resistant blue material with no instructions, developed by architect and designer David Rockwell of the Rockwell Group. It lets "kids build things, and inherent in that process is that they're going to build things that don't quite work out," Randolph says. A third-grade group he observed couldn't start playing at first. They were stymied with no instructions, no set path. It was "free play with a purpose."[59] It neutralized the negative connotations of setbacks in a developmentally appropriate way.

"The idea of building grit and building self-control is that you get that through failure, and in most highly academic environments in the United States, no one fails anything," Randolph says.[60] Instead, we have a culture where everyone, particularly those in little league athletic competitions, wins some form of a trophy, regardless of how they perform. This form of play, of building, of creating made "having a setback okay."

What inspired Randolph was an experience he had after college when he wanted to pursue a specific interest—studying copper-plate etching. He traveled to Florence, Italy, and sought out a press that used to cater to Robert Motherwell and Pablo Picasso. There was little instruction in this largely studio-based environment, until one teacher came in and gave him Allston-style feedback. Randolph didn't know Italian, but said, "I did know what it meant to have my work thrown on the floor. . . . Wood is a very good teacher."

As Randolph spoke, I realized he was echoing Morse's comments after his painting critique sessions in Europe. Randolph described the critique as "the strongest experience I've ever had in my life."

———

When Morse transformed the stretcher bars of the canvas into the telegraph, he was still, in essence, making things. He was no scientist. He was no Lord Kelvin. He was still pioneering through intelligent facture. The telegraph was not his first invention. Years earlier, he had come up with a machine to reproduce marble sculpture that he couldn't patent, along with a leather piston.[61] He had studied developments in electricity with Professor James Freeman Dana of Columbia College. He was also one of the first in America to experiment with the early form of photography, the daguerreotype, having learned the technique in Paris from Louis Daguerre. Morse was still innovating through making, playing, using what art historian Henri Focillon called "the mind in the hand."[62]

As Morse invented the telegraph, he had spent over twenty years in a field where grit and reframing are prerequisites. In the arts, to persist regardless of public opinion is a matter of survival. This skill, nearly as important as talent, means focusing as much on process as outcome.

———

The "crit." This is the creative environment where Morse's letters reveal that he experienced this limber form of grit. Short for critique, the crit process remains the core activity in arts programs around the country such as the Yale School of Art, centuries after Morse walked the school's campus as an undergraduate. In Yale's Photography Department, the crit process happens in "the pool," and in the Painting and Printmaking Department, they take place in "the pit"—both rectangular rooms below the main floor of their respective buildings that heighten a sense of inspection. A student often sits on a stool or chair for forty-five minutes as the faculty and, at times, other MFA students discuss his or her work displayed on the surrounding walls. To hear Yale MFA graduate and painter Lisa Yuskavage reflect on it, a crit can feel like "the general nightmare of standing nude in public," but with the added dimension of "something else you fear, like standing nude on a scale."[63] Perhaps it feels this way because constructive honesty has long remained its ethic.

"Art comes out of failure," said legendary conceptual artist John Baldessari, who set up the "Post Studio" crit sessions at California Institute of the Arts (CalArts) in 1970, the school's inaugural year. He famously incinerated an entire body of acclaimed work he had made from 1953 to 1966 that didn't meet his own standards—his *Cremation Project* (1970). "You have to try things out. You can't sit around, terrified of being incorrect, saying, 'I won't do anything until I do a masterpiece.'"[64]

The goal of the crit is to help the student close the gap between their intentions and the work's effect. It can mean withstanding, as Morse said, a brutal, "mortifying" comment. To hear conceptual artist Mel Bochner, a highly respected former Yale faculty member, say to a student in this audience-filled group crit, "Go back to the library and start with A," as he once did to an MFA student with a wispy grasp of art history, is not uncommon.[65] Of course, external and internal criticism can become too much and can crush the creative spirit, launching attacks that no defense mechanism can withstand, yet the grit that polished Morse's own practice in Europe with Allston is still the essence of this crit.

Crits are part of how artists learn the paradox of creative balance.[66] Part of it means learning the wisdom that painter Elizabeth Murray knew, that "to be right doesn't mean that everyone else has to be wrong." It is a benevolent approach to art-making paths that photographer Gregory Crewdson understands as head of the Photography Department at the Yale School of Art, encouraging artists to "find that 1 percent that really helps you" and just "forget 99 percent of what [you] hear."[67] The constant reframing these crits require helps artists sort out the riddle of the blank review, figuring out what feedback to ignore and what 1 percent is crucial to absorb.

The crit embodies the wisdom of the circle. It is at the heart of the myth of the trickster deity Eshu-Elegba, the West African

Yoruba legend I learned from the legendary art historian Robert Farris Thompson.[68] Disguised as a man, Eshu-Elegba strolled through a town in a cap topped with a crimson parrot feather, half painted white and the other half red, bisected by a line from the middle of his forehead to the top of his spine. Some in the town thought that they saw him walk by in a red cap. Others thought it was white. One person who had swept through the entire town knew that the cap was both colors. Chinua Achebe described the lesson of the myth in reference to an Igbo festival masquerade: "If you want to see it well, you must not stand in one place . . . If you're rooted to a spot, you miss a lot of the grace."[69] This is the meaning at the heart of the legend about the crossroads, and the crit—you can't know a subject until you've walked its circumference, seen it from as many perspectives as possible, then taken its full measure.

We reframe when we consider not only what subject the artist has made his or her own, but what self-defined problem their body of work is trying to solve, like Cézanne's aim of realizing nature in paint, or Morse trying to make the genre of history painting extend to a quotidian scene in the Louvre. "Every important work of art can be regarded both as a historical event and as a hard-won solution to some problem," art historian George Kubler said about the entire arc of artistic production in *The Shape of Time*, his seminal text describing what he sees as the generative force behind artistic development across the ages.[70] Some artists, he argued, were dealing with foundational questions, what he calls "prime objects"—questions that can't be divided or nuanced further and thus lead to an unending chain of potential answers, the query is so essential and irreducible. "The important clue is that any solution points to the existence of some problem," he said. "As the solutions accumulate," he continued, "the problem alters."[71]

Many artists speak about their work in this unexpected way.

Among them is Frank Gehry, who considers architecture to be about "bringing an informed aesethetic point of view to a visual problem."[72] Miró, who wrote to J. F. Ràfols Montroig about his excitement in "discovering new problems!!," felt that would carry him from "deadly *momentarily interesting* work to really *good painting*." Baldessari created a piece about how addressing problems is a tenet of art-making itself[73]:

"Often people miss insights because they are not looking at it as a problem. It's important to ask 'Why,' not 'what,' said James Watson. A shift between focused sight and peripheral vision comes when you consider your work in progress as an issue for which you aim

SOLVING EACH PROBLEM AS IT ARISES

IT CAN BE SUBJECT MATTER OF A RELIGIOUS NATURE, A SCENE IN A FOREIGN COUNTRY. WHATEVER THE SUBJECT, THE PROFESSIONAL ARTIST MAKES EXHAUSTIVE STUDIES OF IT. WHEN HE FEELS THAT HE HAS INTERPRETED THE SUBJECT TO THE EXTENT OF HIS CAPABILITIES HE MAY HAVE A ONE-MAN EXHIBITION WHOSE THEME IS THE SOLUTION OF THE PROBLEM. IT IS SURPRISING HOW FEW PEOPLE WHO VIEW THE PAINTINGS REALIZE THIS.

John Baldessari, *Solving Each Problem As It Arises*, 1966–68. Acrylic on canvas 172.1 x 143.5 cm (67 3/4 x 56 1/2 in.). Yale University Art Gallery. Janet and Simeon Braguin Fund, 2001.3.1.

to find a solution. It's why dancer and choreographer Twyla Tharp advocates picking a fight as a way to find out what issue you're trying to deal with, what you're willing to fight to express.[74] For at the heart of every innovator is a rebel, someone dissatisfied with the status quo. Yet the rebel's affirmative cause often remains undefined. Determining what you're fighting for helps to discern it.

"It's important to be able to move beyond someone or something," Watson told me. Framing ideas as a problem puts us on the quest to pursue what seems incomplete.

"Fields die just because no one thinks they can outdo what has been done."[75]

Reframing our projects as a problem to solve happens through creating a series of amended pictures. This inner pictorial process helps us adjust our goals. It occurs not just with artistic practice, but also through visual thinking.

Reframing can turn an artist's studio into a laboratory, combining things never before considered. Perhaps not all are as obvious as Morse's. His students recalled seeing galvanic batteries, wires, and wooden materials strewn about his Washington Square space and the "sketch upon the canvas untouched."[76] One student, Daniel Huntington, remembers Morse's studio with details about his teacher mixing colors with milk, at times with beer, as if having observed an experiment.[77] On September 2, 1837, at NYU, Morse debuted the telegraph device, a tracing of dots and dashes. He had learned to sketch another way.

Many have argued that there is a need to bring the arts and sciences together. A clarion call to connect art and science came after C. P. Snow's 1959 lecture "The Two Cultures and the Scientific Revolution" made the claim that we needed to better perceive the connections between science and literary intellectuals in Western culture.[78] Sociobiologist Edward O. Wilson later said that there should be a "consilience" between art and science.[79] Former NASA astronaut Mae Jemison took selected images with her on her first trip to space, including a poster of dancer and former artistic director of the Alvin Ailey American Dance Theater Judith Jamison performing the dance *Cry*, and a Bundu statue from Sierra Leone, because, as she said, "the creativity that allowed us . . . to conceive and build and launch the space shuttle, springs from the same source as the imagination and analysis it took to carve a Bundu statue, or the ingenuity it took to design, choreograph, and stage 'Cry.' . . . That's what we have to reconcile in our minds, how these things fit together."[80] As a jazz musician once told me, musicians are mathematicians as well as artists.

Morse's story suggests that the argument started not because of the need to bring art and science together, but because they were once not so far apart.[81] When Frank Jewett Mather Jr. of *The Nation* stated that Morse "was an inventor superimposed upon an artist," it was factually true.[82] Equally true is that Morse could become an inventor because he was an artist all the while.

In one of the final paintings that laid him flat, the painting that failed to secure his last attempt at a commission, one he had worked fifteen years to achieve, Morse may have left a clue about his shift from art to invention, and the fact that the skills required for both are the same. He painted *The House of Representatives* (1822–23) as evidence of his suitability for a commission from Congress to complete a suite of paintings that still adorn the U.S. Capitol building. The painting has an odd compositional focus. In the center is a man screwing in an oil chandelier, preoccupied with currents.

Morse was "rejected beyond hope of appeal" by the congressional commission led by John Quincy Adams. When he toured the picture for seven weeks—displayed in a coffee house in Salem, Mas-

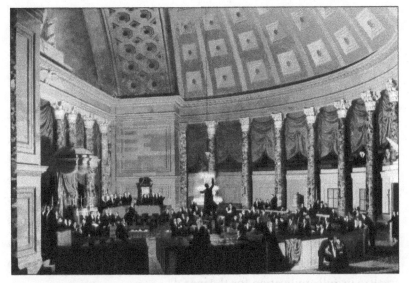

Samuel F. B. Morse, *The House of Representatives*, 1822–23. Oil on canvas. 86 7/8 × 130 5/8 in. Corcoran Gallery of Art, Washington D. C. Museum purchase, Gallery Fund.

sachusetts, and at exhibitions in New York, Boston, Middleton, and Hartford, Connecticut—it lost twenty dollars in the first two weeks. Compounded by a litany of embarrassing, near-soul-stealing artistic failures, he took to his bed for weeks, "more seriously depressed than ever." This final rejection forced him to shift his energies to his telegraph invention.[83] By 1844 Morse went to the Capitol focused on a current that would occupy the work of Congress—obtaining a patent for the telegraph.

In 1932, during the centennial celebration of Morse's telegraph innovation, his work as a painter came to much of the public as a shock. A student of Morse's, Samuel Isham, seemed to sense that his teacher's invention might become disconnected from its artistic foundation. Yet Isham hoped we would all remember how "the qualities of mind which led to" his painting professor's "world-wide fame" were, in fact, "developed in the progress of his art studies."[84] Morse, too, felt that the had always kept "an Artist's heart."[85]

If we fail to cultivate grit, it is also because we often grant little importance to the practice of making and the process that it can teach us throughout our lives.

Inventions come from those who can view a familiar set of variables from a radical perspective and see new possibilities. Creative practice is one of the most effective teachers of the spry movement of this perspective shift. It offers agency, required for supple, nimble endurance that helps us to sense when the bridge is about to collapse. It lets us shift our frame, like a painter who stared at a set of canvas stretcher bars for years and one day saw its potential to be an original communication device. And then persisted for decades to realize its full application for the world.

———

When I arrived at Locust Grove, Morse's Italianate villa in Poughkeepsie, I strained to see it. His main request of the architect's redesign was that there be no direct line of sight from his garden to his house. Seeing it fully should require a series of moves and turns. He only wanted the approach to be of bits of the house "peeping through the verdure."[86] Landscaping traditions at the time made that style au courant. It was a fitting conceptual approach to a house for a man who once wanted to be as pioneering as Rembrandt, but was then an American hero entering the same league as Benjamin Franklin, so well known that he simply wanted, as he wrote to a friend, "*Obscurity*."[87] This jagged path also mimed the agile darting that led to his feats. It was an example of what this deft form of grit can look like in action.

Our stories constitute their own human science—felt-facts long before studies could confirm them, our earliest form of psychology.[88] Perhaps this is why there is a myth about inventors and artists of all kinds, such as there was about Morse when he lived. He never entirely gave up on his first ambition. "I sometimes indulge a vague dream that I may paint again," he confessed to Fenimore Cooper.[89] The man who once spent each working day for months in the Louvre would later visit countries and never venture into a single museum. Yet he would later call his telegraph invention part of "the Arts" of this country.[90] It is, too, the art of how we create out of seeming ruin.

After World War II, the telephone took the path laid down by the telegraph; "sounders" and clicking devices would replace paper tape recordings; fiber optic cables replaced the insulated copper conducting wires along oceans—yet the telegraph remains a foundational bridge that connects continents, built around the globe.[91]

———

Decoding how to cultivate grit would be "akin to discovering the semiconductor," Duckworth said.[92] She is currently collaborating with Walter Mischel of Columbia University, the pioneer of self-control studies, to see how people develop this pliant trait.

What are the inner resources required for grit, and are they truly all within, I wondered, as I thought about the mentorship Duckworth found in her husband, Randolph found in his Italian instructor, Morse found in Allston, and many artists find in the crits they receive from others.

It seemed like the right time to describe Morse's nimble path. She smiled and within a second recalled Mischel's answer to a question posed to him by *New York Times* reporter David Brooks during a public interview at the Association for Psychological Science. What might Mischel choose to become if he had to do it all over again? He paused, reflected on it, and said, "I might become a painter."[93]

EPILOGUE: THE STARS

We are here for what amounts to a few hours,

> *a day at most.*

We feel around making sense of the terrain,

> *our own new limbs,*

Bumping up against a herd of bodies

> *until one becomes home.*

Moments sweep past. The grass bends

> *then learns again to stand.*
>
> —TRACY K. SMITH, "US & CO.,"
> FROM *LIFE ON MARS*

Out on the salt flats, in high mountain ranges, and on the Arctic, sky-glow doesn't compete with stellar light. There we may see isolated radiance and not mislabel it as an outlier, but nodes within a larger narrative. We once looked to our stars, not simply to seek a story of how we came to be, but to etch out the contours of tales about what we have done since. Each society mapped constellations and aster-isms differently over the centuries. Chinese culture looked at the sky and saw celestial light as they did in terrestrial society, assigning the stars names of rulers and soldiers, not the figures of myth, as did the ancient Greeks. Nearly all the stars we can now see are carved out into discrete territories, codified based on seventeenth- and eigh-teenth-century models, and the information about them kept by the International Astronomical Union. For the unaided eye, this mod-ern sky, it seems, has mapped mystery so thoroughly that in the mid-twentieth century, some thought it would take no less than an explosion on the moon itself to turn our attention above.[1] We now peg our dreams to stars of other kinds.

So on a night of teasing warmth, the kind that cleaves summer from autumn, I responded to a curious invitation to come to Bryant Park—to the lawn Paul Holdengräber once showed me lies above the underground archive of the New York Public Library—to celebrate the launch of a capsule of humanity into geosynchronous orbit for billions of years, nestled in the Clarke Belt. My interest in what would actually happen at such an event brought me out. I darted needle-like through the crowd for yards, trying to find one of the metal seats on the grass where hundreds sprawled to sit and listen. Telescopes to view the gloaming sky—an alternative set up by members of the Amateur Astronomers Association of New York—piqued my interest. I stood there instead to have a closer look at the transition into night.

Vision that evening was bodily. To look up, people craned. When rapt, people were still in dense silence. When scanning the sky, heads swiveled, as panoramic vision is never resolved, not static, but constant. In the gloaming, interest seen in gestures and isometric poses never seemed to wane.

The program didn't emphasize the logistics of how this communications satellite with an image-containing silicon disc, as small as a piece of microfiche affixed to its anti-earth deck, would be launched from a remote part of Kazakhstan later that fall, and the crowd that filled the tightly packed lawn the size of half a city block didn't seem to be there to hear it. Central to the run of the show instead was a reading by Pulitzer Prize–winning poet Tracy K. Smith, a talk by Trevor Paglen, an artist and geographer at the University of California–Berkeley, remarks by the chief curator of Creative Time, Nato Thompson, who, along with Anne Pasternak, invited Paglen to conceive the time capsule project, and a dialogue moderated by Holdengräber, director of public programs at the New York Public Library, featuring filmmaker Werner Herzog on how Paglen had selected the pictures that would go into the capsule—all meditations on how we would record our endeavors here on Earth, a cave painting for the future.

Paglen admitted that the project's conceit was ambitious and fanciful, even "absurd." It was not done in the hopes that ancient aliens might come across the satellite, and miraculously see the many pictures and photographs. "Do the aliens have eyes? Do they care about art? I wouldn't overburden them with art," Herzog teased, as he began to turn the talk into a roast.

Yet opacity is what gives the project poignancy. We could never convey what we have done on, to, and through the Earth with our lives.

"It's meant for us," Herzog later admitted, his antics subsided, his taunts turning to thoughtful meditations.

What one hundred images did Paglen elect? They included HeLa cells culled from Henrietta Lacks in 1951 without her knowledge; the monster math function by cognitive scientist Rafael Núñez which had no real-world applications, a fact that Henri Poincaré lamented in 1899 as a failing, but Núñez saw as a sign of human agency; a detail of the painting the *Tower of Babel* by Pieter Bruegel the Elder—an emblem of communication breakdown; an image of a bug in the computer (the Mark II Aiken Relay Calculator at Harvard, where a moth in the computer's paper created circuit failures); a picture of Babylonian math tablet YBC 4713 filled with word problems; a detail of a list from a book of a million numbers; and the longest pattern-free list produced by the RAND Corporation to show the limits of mathematics. There is, too, orbiting around us a captured moment of astonishment: the NASA image *Earthrise*, taken from a lunar landscape; a transcription of the "Wow!" sequence—a frequency detected and seen as a potential sign of life in other realms—and a photo of the first time we put sharks behind glass in aquariums just as we put mannequins clothed behind display windows.

The accent was on an atlas of experiences of a particular kind—

the lines between our feats and our failures, the one planetary story of which we are all a part, "a perpetual crumbling and renewing" as Virginia Woolf called it, on a global scale.[2] The project's potentially inert nature (no one may ever come to view these works) is an allegory for the centrality of failure to the society which created it.[3] On the lawn, I watched as we talked about hurling into orbit—the widest horizon we have—images of triumphs, folds, and how we managed to meet the mountain that hovered in our sights.

I wrote this book, too, as a time capsule, a way to gather seemingly disparate stories to show their common themes and as evidence of the capacity of the human spirit that often has to be seen to be believed.

The moment we designate the used or maligned as a state with generative capacity, our reality expands. President John F. Kennedy once mentioned an old saying that success has many fathers, but failure is an orphan.[4] Failure is an orphan until we give it a narrative. Then it is palatable because it comes in the context of story, as stars within a beloved constellation.

Once we reach a certain height we see how a rise often starts on a seemingly outworn foundation. The gift of failure *is* a riddle. Like the number zero, it will always be both the void and the start of infinite possibility. The arc is one for which there are few perfect words. Its most succinct summary may come from the wisdom in seventeenth-century poet and samurai Mizuta Masahide's haiku: "My barn having burned down / I can now see the moon."

When we take the long view, we value the arc of a rise not because of what we have achieved at that height, but because of what it tells us about our capacity, due to how improbable, indefinable, and imperceptible the rise remains. There are advantages to certain opportunities, including their seeming opposite, that make our path as curved and as precise as an arrow's course.

APPRECIATION

I would open a journal, follow an impulse to attend an event, have a conversation with a friend, hear a lecture, and from these experiences a new story for this book would appear, expanding the scope of the project. For this, I no doubt have assistance in other realms to first thank.

My incredible parents, Ted and Diane Lewis, could not have been more committed throughout my life to ensuring that I had every possible opportunity to excel. I thank them for their love and sacrifice, and for suppressing the confusion they must have had about why, during years committed to excellence, I would take out so much time to write about its seeming opposite.

I am fortunate to have a wise, astute, and kind literary agent in Eric Simonoff, who dedicated time to help shape countless drafts of my manuscript proposal. I am grateful that Ben Loehnen and Jonathan Karp understood my vision from the start. Without Ben's acumen, counsel, and patience, I have no idea how I would have ever found the space and encouragement to put that vision on the page. Without Brit Hvide and Jonathan Evans's professionalism and patience, my words never would have made it to the page. Working with this team, along with Richard Rhorer, Meg Cassidy, Cary Goldstein, Marie Kent, and Tracy Fisher and Simon Trewin at WME has been a true gift.

At Yale, I have learned a great deal from my advisors, colleagues, and students. I wanted to thank a few in particular: Robert Farris Thompson, Alexander Nemerov, Kobena Mercer, John MacKay, Matthew Frye Jacobson, Laura Wexler, Elizabeth Alexander, Timothy Barringer, David Blight, Gregory Crewdson, John Pilson, Collier Schorr, Taryn Simon, Deborah Kass, Rochelle Feinstein, William Villalongo, Didier William, Sarah Oppenheimer, David Humphries, Robert Storr, and Sam Messer.

Alongside my colleagues, I often look to and am inspired by the exemplary work of authors, scholars, and artists, such as Deborah Willis, Junot Díaz, Rebecca Solnit, John Jeremiah Sullivan, and Edwidge Danticat. I remain inspired by the rigor and imaginative richness of scholarship by Drew Gilpin Faust, Deborah Willis, Farah Griffin, Bob O'Meally, and Daphne Brooks, Salamishah Tillet, Richard Powell, and Patricia Williams, among others. From this set of brilliant minds, I have found exemplary fellowship when I needed it most.

Much of the research for *The Rise* was the result of near-Talmudic study, questioning the many potential meanings behind any given statement, done with some research assistance from producer Christine An, Courtney Fiske, Carla Giugale, Folake Ologunja, Yasmeen Qureshi, and Sarah Zhang. I'd like to thank Courtney in particular for her fortitude and insights at times when I needed it most.

Nearly one hundred fifty individuals gave of their time to be interviewed for this book, and I thank them all, particularly the following: Liz Diller, Ben Saunders, Ivy Ross, Wendy Palmer, Konstantin Novoselov, Franklin Leonard, Mike Bonifer, Jim Dawson, Angela Lee Duckworth, Dominic Randolph, Peter Gombeski, Ellen Harvey, Jeanne C. Finley, Bashir Salahuddin, Aileen Passloff, David Seidler, Noah Oppenheim, Megan Tulac, Daniel Lerner, William Powhida, Jennifer Dalton, Kamau Patton, and Ashley Good, Paul Louis Iske, Parker Mitchell, and George Roter of Engineers Without Borders, Alden Hadwen, and Cass Philips and Diane Loviglio of FailCon.

There were a few moments of unexpected fellowship about this topic that spurred me on at important times. One came thanks to

Ari Emanuel, Patrick Whitesell, Eric Simonoff, and Jennifer Rudolf Walsh, who invited me to interview former vice president Al Gore at a William Morris Endeavor (WME) conference. I am enormously appreciative of my colleagues at Yale University, both in the History of Art Department and at the School of Art, and those at the Sundance Institute, Creative Time, the Rare Book Manuscript Library, the New York Public Library, the CUNY Graduate Center, the Ford Foundation, and The Opportunity Agenda. A large influence on my work also came from a set of formidable, confidential conversations about the importance of freedom of expression with fellow board members at the Andy Warhol Foundation for the Visual Arts. The courage I found to write about aesthetic force and its connection to justice stems, in large part, from interactions found there.

Midway through writing this book, Marion Boulton Stroud generously granted me a place in Mount Desert Island, Maine during the summer where I found the peace that let me access a sense of knowing, a surety that let me finish this daunting book. I still have no way to possibly thank her. With a number of chapters in progress on the arts and pedagogy, The Brearley School community—Paula Campbell, Georgia Levenson Keohane, Alan Jones, Deborah Berke, Deborah Ascheim, Jane Fried, Jaime Nicholls, Wilhelmina Eakin, Sharese Bullock-Bailey, Sayuri Ganepola, Jessica Jenkins, and Cherise Fisher—played a more constitutive role than they know in listening to works in progress and offering helpful feedback.

I am also extraordinarily grateful to those friends who took precious time and particular care to read the manuscript, in part or in full, and offer me feedback at a crucial period during my manuscript revisions: Wynton Marsalis, Agnes Gund, Drew Gilpin Faust, Nell Irvin Painter, Darren Walker, Dream Hampton, Dodie Kazanjian, Samantha Boardman, Annie Leibowitz, Anne Pasternak, Adam Weinberg, David Adjaye, Blair Miller, Joel Wachs, Sara Menker, Liz Kabler, RoseLee Goldberg, Benjamin Bronfman, Latham Thomas,

Mehret Mandefro, Daniel Belasco, Michelle Coffey, April Yvonne Garrett, Binta Brown, Miles Adcox, Julian Breece, Stanley Crouch, Therese Workman, Gabriella De Ferrari, Shirin Neshat, Sharese Bullock-Bailey, Jennie Tarr Coyne, Andrew Tsai, Tanya Ryk Friedman, Folake Ologunja, Chai Vasarhelyi, and Isca Greenfield-Sanders. Especially prescient insights form Garnette Cadogan and Hank Willis Thomas helped me to see past my own blind spots in my work. Damian Woetzel's keen eye aided me in making my writing on dance and Paul Taylor as true to the spirit of 7 *New Dances* as possible. Two divinely timed conversations with Carrie Mae Weems, who also generously read this book, helped me to see what this book was meant to be.

"Arctic Summer: Surrender," the most difficult chapter for me to write, was borne of reflection on a decade spent healing from a compound grief, a period aided by care from a blessed set of sprites: Chelsea Clinton, Deepak Abraham, Sarah Melvoin Bridich, Amma Ghartey-Tagoe Kootin, Mehret Mandefro, Salamishah Tillet, Jessica Schwartz, Monique Robinson, Alexandra Dean, and Careina Williams. The time I took reflecting on this period in my life on Lake Clear in the Adirondacks, courtesy of Nell Irvin Painter, helped me to clarify the meaning of this journey, and to reflect on the gratitude I feel for so many whose conversation, care, writing, or scholarship have encouraged me along the way, not least of whom is dear Nell herself.

Writing is its own ever onward almost, one that requires constant care and support. For love and inspiration, I have one man here on earth in particular to thank, and he knows who he is. The other is the soulful Shadrach Emmanuel Lee, still all around and, as I would like to believe, smiling down.

NOTES

Epigraph

1. Lincoln, quoted in Michael Burlingame, *Abraham Lincoln: A Life*, vol. 1 (Baltimore, Maryland: Johns Hopkins University Press, 2008), 358.

Archer's Paradox

1. The varsity archery team is made up of women from both Barnard and Columbia.
2. Sarah Chai, quoted in Corey Kilgannon, "Keeping Titles, and Targets, in Sight," *New York Times*, February 18, 2011.
3. T. S. Eliot, "Burnt Norton," *Four Quartets* (Orlando, FL: Harcourt Books, 1971), 15.
4. Aynsley Smith, interview with the author, August 2011; Terry Wunderle, interview with the author, 2011; Frank Thomas, interview with the author, 2011; Katie Thomas, "The Secret Curse of Expert Archers," *New York Times*, August 1, 2008 (last accessed March 4, 2013), http://www.nytimes.com/2008/08/01/sports/olympics/01archery.html?pagewanted=all&_r=0.
5. Duke Ellington, quoted in John Edward Hasse, *Beyond Category: The Life and Genius of Duke Ellington* (New York: Simon & Schuster, 1993), 218.
6. Thomas Edison, quoted in *The World Book Encyclopedia*, vol. E (Chicago: World Book, 1993), 78.
7. Arthur Fifield, letter to Gertrude Stein, quoted in Gertrude Stein, *Three Lives* (New York: Vintage Books, 1909).
8. Lewis Hyde, *The Gift: Creativity and the Artist in the Modern World* (New York: Vintage Books, 2007), 63–64.
9. Eric Weiner's wonderful book *The Geography of Bliss: One Grump's Search for the Happiest Places in the World* introduced me to this bizarre material, francium, the most unstable of the first 101 elements on the periodic table. For more on francium, named after France, where Marie Curie's former student Marguerite Perey discovered it in the early twentieth century, see C. R. Hammond, "Francium," in *CRC Handbook of Chemis-*

try and Physics 2012–2013, ed. W. M. Haynes (Boca Raton, Florida: CRC Press, 2012), 4–14.

10. See Scott A. Sandage, *Born Losers: A History of Failure in America* (Cambridge, MA: Harvard University Press, 2005).

11. A blank, too, was how the analogous number zero was once described, from China to Babylonia, before the eighth century, before cultures found a way to denote it with a symbol. It was just a blank space. The result was that things not at all congruent looked very much alike and when zero was on its own and no positional context could help identify it, there was no marking whatsoever. Zero never appears in a terminal position on these ancient tablets. There was initially no term to suggest what we ultimately discovered, that zero was never the end. No one is quite sure where the symbol, the cipher, came from: As Charles Seife has eloquently described, perhaps it came from Greece via Alexandria and was then transmitted to India where we have its first extant description in 876, but eventually it became a symbol of the mystery of creation itself—"a round goose egg" was used to denote it, which, in time, became a symbol of its riddle, a seeming void, and a circle, a line without end. For more, see Uta C. Merzbach and Carl B. Boyer, *A History of Mathematics*, 3rd ed. (New Jersey: John Wiley & Sons, 2011), 24–25, 192–93. The symbol for zero did not represent the Greek letter omicron as formerly suspected. In the Byzantine Empire, it looked like a small letter *h* or a dot. Also see Charles Seife, *Zero: The Biography of a Dangerous Idea* (New York: Penguin Books, 2000).

12. Christopher Fry, *Thor, with Angels*, in *The Plays of Christopher Fry: Three* (London: Oberon Books, 2007), 191.

The Unfinished Masterpiece

1. See Chris Taylor, "Dissolving between Land and Sky: Mapping Wendover," *Rhizomes* 18 (Winter 2008), last accessed February 13, 2012, http://www.rhizomes.net/issue18/taylor/index.html.

2. Jan Sousman, a research scientist at the Max Planck Institute for Biological Cybernetics, found that having a landmark is the one thing that prevents us from walking in circles without a perspective-granting sign. See Matt Soniak, "Do People Really Walk in Circles When They're Lost?" *mental_floss*, last accessed October 29, 2012, http://mentalfloss.com/article/12892/do-people-really-walk-circles-when-they%E2%80%9A%C3%84%C3%B4re-lost.

3. Meredith James, interview with the author, November 2012.

4. Here, I use the term *classic* as Italo Calvino meant it in his itemized list of definitions, but centrally, as I see it, through these two: "a book which has never exhausted all it has to say to its readers" and "a work which

constantly generates a pulviscular cloud of critical discourse around it, but which always shakes the particles off," Italo Calvino, *Why Read the Classics?*, trans. Jonathan Cape (New York: Pantheon Books, 1999), 5–6. My thanks to Maria Popova's work for bringing this text to my attention.

5. William Faulkner, "The Art of Fiction No. 12," *The Paris Review*, no. 12 (Spring 1956), 39.

6. Cézanne, as relayed by Émile Bernard, on his *Trois Crânes Sur un Tapis d'Orient (Three Skulls on an Oriental Rug)*, 1904, in Bernard, "Memories of Paul Cézanne" in *Conversations with Cézanne*, ed. Michael Doran, trans. Julie Lawrence Cochran (Berkeley: University of California Press, 2001), 58. First published in the *Mercure de France* in October 1907.

7. The first version of the story was published in the newspaper *L'Artiste* under the title "Maître Frenhofer" in 1831. A later version was included in Honoré de Balzac's *Études philosophiques* in 1837.

8. Balzac, *The Unknown Masterpiece*, trans. Richard Howard (New York: New York Review of Books, 2001), 27. Balzac published multiple versions of this manuscript, but the 1837 version is considered the definitive text.

9. Cézanne, as relayed by Émile Bernard, on his *Trois Crânes Sur un Tapis d'Orient (Three Skulls on an Oriental Rug)*, 1904, in Bernard, "Memories of Paul Cézanne," *Conversations with Cézanne*, ed. Michael Doran, trans. Julie Lawrence Cochran (Berkeley: University of California Press, 2001), 65.

10. Ambroise Vollard, *Cézanne*, trans. Harold L. Van Doren (New York: Dover Publications, 1984), 86. "That's the terrible thing," Alberto Giacometti said about Cézanne with sympathy, "the more one works on a picture, the more impossible it becomes to finish it." Giacometti began by saying, "It's impossible to paint a portrait . . . [Cézanne] never finished them. After Vollard had posed a hundred times, the most Cézanne would say was that the shirt front wasn't so bad. And he was right. It's the best part of the picture. Cézanne never really finished anything. He went as far as he could, then abandoned the job." *Cézanne & Giacometti: Paths of Doubt*, eds. Felix A. Baumann and Poul Erik Tøjner (Ostfildern: Hatje Cantz, 2008), 163.

11. See John Rewald, *Paul Cézanne: A Biography*, trans. Margaret H. Liebman (New York: Simon & Schuster, 1948), and see David W. Galenson, *Old Masters and Young Geniuses: The Two Life Cycles of Artistic Creativity* (Princeton: Princeton University Press, 2006), 14.

12. Czeslaw Milosz, "The Art of Poetry No. 70," *The Paris Review*, no. 133 (Winter 1994), 265.

13. Benjamin Blech and Roy Doliner, *The Sistine Secrets: Michelangelo's Forbidden Messages in the Heart of the Vatican* (New York: HarperOne, 2008), 293.

14. There are many other translations of Michelangelo's sonnet, "To Giovanni da Pistoia When the Author Was Painting the Vault of the Sistine Chapel," 1509. Below is the full translation of the one I have cited, from Gail Mazur's *Zeppo's First Wife: New and Selected Poems* (Chicago: University of Chicago Press, 2005), 116–17. The sonnet reads in full:

> I've already grown a goiter from this torture,
> hunched up here like a cat in Lombardy
> (or anywhere where the stagnant water's poison).
> My stomach's squashed under my chin, my beard's
> pointing at heaven, my brain's crushed in a casket,
> my breast twists like a harpy's. My brush,
> above me all the time, dribbles paint
> so my face makes a fine floor for droppings!
> My haunches are grinding into my guts,
> my poor ass strains to work as a counterweight,
> every gesture I make is blind and aimless.
> My skin hangs loose below me, my spine's
> all knotted from folding over itself,
> I'm bent taut as a Syrian bow.
> Because I'm stuck like this, my thoughts
> are crazy perfidious tripe:
> anyone shoots badly through a crooked blowpipe.
> My painting is dead.
> Defend it for me, Giovanni, protect my honor.
> I am not in the right place—I am not a painter.

The other translations of this sonnet can be found in the following texts: George Bull, *Michelangelo: A Biography* (New York: St. Martin's Griffin, 1998), 427; George Bull and Peter Porter, trans. *Michelangelo: Life, Letters, and Poetry* (Oxford: Oxford University Press, 1987), 139; Robert N. Liscott, ed. *Complete Poems and Selected Letters of Michelangelo*, Creighton Gilbert, trans. (Princeton: Princeton University Press, 1980), 5–6; Elizabeth Jennings, trans. *The Sonnets of Michelangelo.* (London: Allison & Busby, 1969), 14–15; Christopher Ryan, ed. and trans. *Michelangelo: The Poems* (London: J. M. Dent & Sons, 1996), 5; Anthony Mortimer, trans. *Michelangelo: Poems and Letters* (London: Penguin Classics, 2007), 3–4; John Addington Symonds, trans. *The Sonnets of Michelangelo* (Plymouth, UK: Vision Press Ltd., 1989), 25; James M. Saslow, trans. *The Poetry of Michelangelo: An Annotated Translation* (New Haven: Yale University Press, 1991), 70; Joseph Tusiani, trans. *The Complete Poems of Michelangelo* (London: Peter Owen Publishers, 1960), 24; John Frederick Nims, trans. *The Complete Poems of Michelangelo* (Chicago: University of Chicago Press, 1998), 10–11.

15. Ascanio Condivi, *The Life of Michelangelo*, trans. Alice Sedgwick Wohl, ed. Hellmut Wohl (University Park: Pennsylvania State University Press, 1999), 57. Part of the reason for the mold was that Michelangelo was not used to working with Roman lime, a material composed of travertine that does not dry quickly. It was a mixture that art historian Antonio Forcellino reminds us was different from the kind Michelangelo was used to in Florence, which was derived from marl and sand from the Arno. Michelangelo had hired assistants from Florence (Francesco Granacci, Giuliano Bugiardini, Aristotile da Sangallo, and Agnolo di Donnino) and they mixed the Roman materials in the same proportion that they had those from Florence, which contributed to the trouble. Architect Giuliano da Sangallo helped Michelangelo make corrections with the measurements so that he could continue. See Antonio Forcellino, *Michelangelo: A Tormented Life*, trans. Allan Cameron (Cambridge: Polity Press, 2009), 96–97; Giorgio Vasari, *Life of Michelangelo*, trans. Gaston du C. de Vere, ed. Frank Sadowski (New York: Alba House, 2003), 34. Michael Hirst, *Michelangelo: The Achievement of Fame, 1475–1534*, vol. 1 (New Haven: Yale University Press, 2011), 96.

16. Such as *St. Matthew* (1505–6) and *Battle of the Centaurs* (1490–2). For more on this topic, see John T. Spike, *Young Michelangelo: The Path to the Sistine: A Biography* (New York: Vendome Press, 2010), 204, 209.

17. Michelangelo quoted in Spike, 222.

18. Other examples include: Puccini's opera *Turandot*, Mahler's *Tenth Symphony*, Jimi Hendrix's last album, *First Rays of the New Rising Sun*.

19. Elif Batuman, "Kafka's Last Trial," *New York Times Magazine*, September 26, 2010, 36. I say purportedly because only Brod has seen this letter with Kafka's last wishes.

20. *New York Times Magazine* reports that Kafka had already told Brod about this in 1921. Ibid, 38.

21. Ibid.

22. Semir Zeki, *Splendors and Miseries of the Brain: Love, Creativity, and the Quest for Human Happiness* (London: Wiley-Blackwell, 2008), 109.

23. Romare Bearden, quoted in "Painting: Touching at the Core," *Time*, October 27, 1967.

24. James Baldwin to Jordan Elgrably in "The Art of Fiction No. 78," *The Paris Review*, no. 91 (Spring 1984), 69.

25. This concept that came to us from the design and engineering world is explained through the phenomenon of the Dunning–Kruger effect. Social psychologist and Cornell professor David Dunning and then-graduate student Justin Kruger described this paradox with four simple self-assessment studies after they noticed that participants who had scored in the bottom quartile on these tests of humor, grammar, and logic, putting them in the twelfth percentile, had grossly overestimated

their test performance and ability and considered themselves to be in the sixty-second percentile instead. See Kruger and Dunning; "Unskilled and Unaware of It: How Difficulties in Recognizing One's Own Incompetence Lead to Inflated Self-Assessments," *Journal of Personality and Social Psychology* 77, no. 6 (1999): 1121–34.

26. Albert Einstein, quoted in *Dear Professor Einstein: Albert Einstein's Letters to and from Children*, ed. Alice Calaprice (New York: Promethus Books, 2002), 140.

27. I have Richard Stanton's book *The Forgotten Olympic Art Competitions* (Victoria, B.C.: Trafford, 2000) to thank for this new information, and the brilliantly curated magazine of interesting arcana, *mental_floss*, for bringing this forgotten history to my attention.

28. It is as if second place finishers can tell that the metal alloys in gold and silver medals are nearly the same. 93 percent of an Olympic gold medal is made up of silver, just .5 percent less than the percent of silver in an Olympic silver medal itself. Actual gold medals were only given out at three Olympics. See Melonyce McAfee, "Why Olympians bite their medals," CNN, August 10, 2012 (last accessed March 15, 2013), www.cnn.com/2012/08/09/living/olympians-bite-medals.

29. These reactions are innate, found in congenitally blind and sighted athletes, psychologists from the University of British Columbia, Jessica Tracy, and San Francisco State University, David Matsumoto, have argued. They studied it by asking an official of the International Judo Federation to use high-speed film to take before and after photographs of athletes at match time at the 2004 Olympic and Paralympic Games, capturing their behavioral responses from moment to moment. They did not tell the official what the study was about. Tracy and Matsumoto then compared the images of the athletes without knowing the outcome of the match. They found that both blind and sighted athletes did the same thing after winning—raise their arms, stick out their chest. The non-finalists' slumped-shoulder posture of shame after a match was consistent among the blind from country to country. Their research study of sighted and congenitally blind athletes from over thirty countries from the United States to North Korea, Taiwan, Algeria, and the Ukraine showed that nonverbal expressions of pride and shame were learned or innate human biological responses. See Tracy and Matsumoto, "The spontaneous expression of pride and shame: Evidence for biologically innate nonverbal displays," *Proceedings of the National Academy of Sciences of the United States of America* 105, no. 33 (2008): 11655–60. Victoria Husted Medvec, Scott F. Madey, and Thomas Gilovich, "When Less is More: Counterfactual thinking and satisfaction among Olympic medalists," *Journal of Personality and Social Psychology* 69, no. 4 (1995): 603–10.

30. Daniel Kahneman and Amos Tversky, "The simulation heuristic," in

Notes

Judgment under Uncertainty: Heuristics and Biases, ed. Daniel Kahneman, Paul Slovic, and Amos Tversky (Cambridge and New York: Cambridge University Press, 1982), 201–8.

31. R. L. Reid, "The Psychology of the Near Miss," *Journal of Gambling Behavior* 2, no. 1 (Spring/Summer 1986): 34. And see Michael J. A. Wohl and Michael E. Enzle, "The Effects of Near Wins and Near Losses on Self-Perceived Perspectives on a Fundamental Human Capacity," *European Journal of Social Psychology* 42, no. 3 (2012): 269–75.

32. Bob Kersee, quoted in Sharon Robb, "First Lady of Hope Predicted for Stardom, Jackie-Joyner Kersee Aims to Impress Us Again," *Sun Sentinel*, July 23, 1992.

33. Andrea Kremer, interview with the author, May 2012. All quotes from Kremer come from this interview.

34. Australian artist Tracey Moffatt slowed down footage of vanquished athletes who came seconds, minutes, and inches shy of winning a medal in Olympic competitions, just long enough to capture it with a camera lens. She printed twenty-six photographs of different individuals, each with a similar expression, registering the frozen, rigid, initial shock of loss as they comprehend the horror of exactly what has occurred. For images of Moffatt's *Fourth* series, 2001 (last accessed April 8, 2012) see http://www.roslynoxley9.com.au/artists/26/Tracey_Moffatt/12/.

35. James Dawson, interview with the author, June 13, 2012.

36. *Werner Herzog Eats His Shoe*, dir. Les Blank, 1980.

37. Gilovich's Cornell study did not attempt to track a durational set of data to assess when the phenomenon might stop.

38. I first heard this quote attributed to Winston Churchill, but after trying to source it precisely I learned from Michael Shelden that this quote has never been sourced in Churchill's speeches, letters, or even in remarks from those in conversation with him. Richard Langworth's *Churchill by Himself: The Definitive Collection of Quotations* (New York: PublicAffairs, 2008) lists the quote in an appendix titled "Red Herrings: False Attributions": "Broadly attributed to Churchill, but found nowhere in his canon. An almost equal number of sources credit this saying to Abraham Lincoln; but none of them provides any attribution," 580. I am grateful to Michael for also pointing out to me that Langworth put this quote in his blog under the section "Among the Things Churchill *Never* Said," http://richardlangworth.com/success. My thanks to Priscilla Painton as well for helping me learn the definitive word on this.

39. APQC, "Mayo Clinic," *Innovation: Putting Ideas into Action* (Houston: American Productivity & Quality Center, 2006), 139.

40. Nira Liberman, Michael Sagristano, and Yaacov Trope, "The Effect of temporal distance on level of mental construal," *Journal of Experimental Social Psychology* 38 (2002): 523–34.

41. Julie Moss, "The Most Famous Finish in *Ironman* History: Julie Moss Takes You Through Her Race," *Ironman*, February 26, 2003 (last accessed February 28, 2013), www.ironman.com/triathlon-news /articles/2003/02/the-most-famous-finish-in-ironman-history-julie-moss-takes-you-through-her-race.aspx#axzz2KhArsEOo.

42. Jad Abumrad and Robert Krulwich with Julie Moss and Wendy Ingraham, "Limits of the Body," *Radiolab*, Season 7, episode 3, April 5, 2010, www.radiolab.org/2010/apr/05/limits-of-the-body/.

43. Julie Moss, "The Most Famous Finish in Ironman History: Julie Moss Takes You Through Her Race," *Ironman*, February 26, 2003 (last accessed February 28, 2013), www.ironman.com/triathlon-news /articles/2003/02/the-most-famous-finish-in-ironman-history-julie-moss-takes-you-through-her-race.aspx#axzz2KhArsEOo.

44. Ibid.

45. T. J. Murphy, "How Triathlon Got Hot," *Experience Life*, July–August 2004 (last accessed February 13, 2013), http://experiencelife.com/article /how-triathlon-got-hot/.

46. Vincent M. Mallozzi, "TRIATHLON; Winner Who Didn't Finish First," *New York Times*, October 18, 2003, 7.

47. Rebeccca Solnit, *Wanderlust: A History of Walking* (New York: Viking Penguin, 2000), 73.

48. "Mark Bradford: Paper," prod. Susan Sollins and Nick Ravich, ed. Monte Matteotti, *Art21* video short, 2006, www.art21.org/videos/short-mark-bradford-paper.

49. Wynton Marsalis, quoted in Leslie Gourse, *Wynton Marsalis: Skain's Domain: A Biography* (New York: Schirmer Books, 1999), 265–66.

50. Michelangelo had learned his lesson from an early commission of the *Bacchus* sculpture, which clearly shows the imperfection in the rock chosen. The patron of the work, Cardinal Raffaele Riario, did not ultimately acquire it; Jacopo Gallo did instead. Michelangelo's first trip to Carrara was in 1497, where he acquired marble for the *Pietà*. See Condivi, *The Life of Michelangelo*, 30; Spike, *Young Michelangelo*, 188–89; and Michael Hirst, *Michelangelo: The Achievement of Fame, 1475–1534*, vol. 1, 30–31, 34–35. Also see Jamie Katz, "The Measure of Genius: Michelangelo's Sistine Chapel at 500," Smithsonian.com, April 10, 2009, www.smithsonianmag.com/arts-culture/The-Measure-of-Genius -Michelangelos-Sistine-Chapel-at-500.html.

51. Hirst, *Michelangelo: The Achievement of Fame, 1475–1534*, 35. Hirst claims, "The pattern of such intense personal involvement in his supply of marble seems to have been without precedent and would remain a life-long one." Spike discusses Michelangelo's search for quality stone in high quarries in 1505. See Spike, *Young Michelangelo*, 191.

52. See Condivi, *The Life of Michelangelo*, 29–30. Hirst writes: "There are no

Notes

records of Michelangelo's initial stay in Carrara in the autumn of 1497; indeed, his presence there in this period has even been questioned. But there can be little doubt that it was in this period, undocumented as it is, that he sought and found the marble of the quality he required and, before leaving for Florence, made arrangements for its quarrying." See Hirst, *Michelangelo: The Achievement of Fame*, 35.

53. Eric Scigliano, *Michelangelo's Mountain: The Quest for Perfection in the Marble Quarries of Carrara* (New York: Free Press, 2005), 136. The quote in Italian is: "Questa era, disse una pazzia venutami per detta. Ma s'io fusse sicuro di vivere 4 volte quanto son vissuto, sare'vi entrato." Condivi, *Vita di Michelangolo Buonarroti* (Firenze, Italy: Studio per edizioni scelte, 1998), 42.

54. The original Italian reads "Davicte cholla Fromba / e io collarcho / Michelangolo," Spike, *Young Michelangelo*, 145.

55. Galeano quoted in *We Are Everywhere: The Irresistible Rise of Global Anti-Capitalism*, ed. Notes from Nowhere (London: Verso, 2003), 499. Umberto Eco's essay collection, *Inventing the Enemy*, has a beautiful passage about the fleeting, never-found nature of utopias as islands in his piece, "Why the Island Is Never Found." He describes utopia as "moving about like one of Edwin Abbott's characters in *Flatland*, where there is only one dimension and we see things only from the front, like lines with no thickness—with no height and no depth—and only someone from outside flatland could see them from above." Umberto Eco, *Inventing the Enemy: Essays* (Boston: Houghton Mifflin Harcourt, 2012), 192.

Blankness

1. Gia Kourlas, "Ailey's Torch Bearer Honors Another of His Inspirations," *New York Times*, December 4, 2011, AR.6.

2. Paul Taylor, *Private Domain: An Autobiography* (New York: Knopf, 1987), 362. Taylor was elected as Chevalier de l'Ordre des Arts et des Lettres.

3. Taylor, 53. Also see Calvin Tomkins, *Off the Wall: A Portrait of Robert Rauschenberg* (New York: Picador, 2005), 94.

4. Taylor, 79.

5. Jennifer Dunning, "Paul Taylor—Looking Back and Ahead," *New York Times*, April 11, 1982, A26.

6. Taylor, 76–77.

7. Dunning, "Looking Back and Ahead."

8. Taylor, 77.

9. Taylor, "The Choreographer on Why He Makes Dances: A 'Reticent Guy' Speaks Candidly About What Motivates His Works," *The Wall Street Journal*, February 23, 2008, W14. The full quote reads: "I don't

make dances for the masses—I make them for myself. That is, even though they are meant to be seen in public (otherwise, what's the point?), I make dances I think *I'd* like to see."

10. Taylor, 76. Also see Taylor's comment in Dunning, "Looking Back and Ahead": "I began to feel a nagging discontent with Merce's and Martha's dances and my own. My dances were nice, but they were not nice enough. What was their movement base, I wondered? Their structure? What, indeed, was a dance?"

11. "Inwardly, I'm sinking; outwardly, tics of my neck are betraying nervousness," Taylor wrote about that moment. Ibid, 79. Also see Lincoln Kirstein's review of *Private Domains*, "The Monstrous Itch," *New York Review of Books*, June 11, 1987, http://www.nybooks.com/articles/archives/1987/jun/11/the-monstrous-itch/?pagination=false.

12. Ibid., 79–80.

13. Ibid., 80.

14. Ibid.

15. "Guide to the Horst, Louis, 1884–1964. Louis Horst Collection." Jerome Robbins Dance Division, New York Public Library.

16. Taylor, 59.

17. Walter Terry, "Experiment? Joke? Or War of Nerves?," *New York Herald Tribune*, October 27, 1957.

18. Taylor, 51. Also see Kay Larson, *Where the Heart Beats: John Cage, Zen Buddhism, and the Inner Life of Artists* (New York: Penguin, 2012).

19. Ibid., 47.

20. Ibid., 54.

21. Ibid., 80.

22. Taylor quoted in Dunning.

23. Ibid., 80.

24. Aileen Passloff, interview with the author, September 5, 2012.

25. Taylor, 99–100.

26. Ibid., 80. Also see Paul Taylor interviewed by Rose Eichenbaum, *Masters of Movement: Portraits of America's Great Choreographers* (Washington, DC: Smithsonian Books, 2004), 175.

27. Twyla Tharp with Mark Reiter, *The Creative Habit: Learn It and Use It for Life* (New York: Simon & Schuster, 2005), 22.

28. Taylor, 61.

29. Ibid, 49.

30. Ibid.

31. Ibid, 58.

32. Ibid, 50.

33. Taylor later lists Toby Glanternik (not Anita Dencks) as his partner for *Duet*.

34. Taylor, 58.

35. Ibid., 88–9.
36. Leonardo da Vinci, quoted in Jean Paul Richter, *The Notebooks of Leonardo Da Vinci*, vol. 1, ed. Jean Paul Richter (New York: Dover Publications, 1970), 291. Ira Glass has also described this gap between ambition and ability. Diane Arbus has, too, which she called the "gap between intention and effect." See *Diane Arbus: An Aperture Monograph*, ed. Marvin Israel (New York: Aperture, 1972), 1–2. Marcel Duchamp also spoke about this gap in a lecture in April 1957 at the convention of the American Federation of Arts in Houston, Texas. He called it "the difference between the intention and its realization," but felt that this "gap" was one that "the artist is not aware of." See Duchamp quoted in "The Creative Act," in Robert Lebel, *Marcel Duchamp*, trans. George Heard (New York: Grove Press, 1959), 77–78.
37. August Wilson, "The Art of Theater No. 14," *The Paris Review*, no. 153 (Winter 1999), 69–72.
38. Ezra Pound, "The Art of Poetry No. 5," *The Paris Review*, no. 28 (Summer/Fall 1962), 33.
39. My thanks to visual artist and filmmaker Mary Reid Kelley for mentioning this fantastic exchange. Here is a transcript of Hammer speaking about this exchange: "In the Beinecke, there's a little letter, a handwritten pencil letter from Pound to Hart Crane, which Hart Crane received when he was eighteen, I think, around your age, after he had sent his poems to *The Little Review*. And this is a letter from Pound which says about Crane's poems: 'It is all very egg. There is perhaps better egg. But you haven't the ghost of a setting hen or an incubator about you.' I'm not sure what that means. But this was a rejection slip, and Crane kept it all his life, like a kind of diploma that in some way he was a member of modern poetry because he had gotten a rejection from Ezra Pound. In fact, Crane's first book, if you go over to the Beinecke, and you turn it over, it has a picture. It has a portrait, not of Hart Crane but of Ezra Pound, because it has an ad for Pound and his book, *Personae*. And I like this fact because it's representative, I think, of Pound's importance and dominance and prominence in the poetic culture of the 1920s and '30s. He was part of the world that a younger poet like Hart Crane had to get to know and make his place in. One of the famous books about modern poetry, one by Hugh Kenner, is called simply *The Pound Era*, as if modern poetry was all about Ezra Pound." See YCAL 37 Series No. III, Box 8, Folder 310, Correspondence between Hart Crane and Ezra Pound, letter undated, Beinecke Rare Book and Manuscript Library, Yale University.
40. Roy F. Baumeister and John Tierney, *Willpower: Rediscovering the Greatest Human Strength* (New York: Penguin Books, 2011), 76, 81–84.
41. Baumeister and Tierney, 83–84. Also see Lassi A. Liikkanen, "Music in Everymind: Commonality of Involuntary Musical Imagery" in K.

Miyazaki, Y. Hiraga, M. Adachi, Y. Nakajima, & M. Tsuzaki (eds.), Proceedings of the 10th International Conference on Music Perception and Cognition (ICMPC10) (2008), 408–12.

42. Taylor, *Private Domain*, 54.

43. Ibid., 55.

44. Ibid., 95.

45. Ibid., 169.

46. I've heard this saying from musicians, but have heard it attributed to author Max Lucado, and also to the nineteenth-century Scottish-born Canadian politician James Crook.

47. Alastair Macaulay, "Jumps, Turns and Breathtaking Feats, Aligned With Dense Structures," *New York Times*, March 23, 2012, C3.

48. Rainer Maria Rilke, "*Viareggio*, near Pisa (Italy), April 23, 1903," in *Letters to a Young Poet*, trans. Stephen Mitchell (New York: Vintage Books, 1986), 23–24.

49. Wood considers this story "probably apocryphal." See James Wood, *The Broken Estate: Essays on Literature and Belief* (New York: Picador, 2010), 89.

50. Renée Fleming, quoted in *Renée Fleming: A YoungArts Masterclass*, HBO, 2012.

51. Umberto Eco, quoted in Mukund Padmanabhan, "I am a professor who writes novels on Sundays," *The Hindu*, October 23, 2005.

52. Charles Limb, "Your Brain on Improv," TEDxMidAtlantic, November 2010.

53. Wynton Marsalis, interview with the author, May 2012.

54. Nick Zagorski, "Music on the Mind," *Hopkins Medicine* (Spring /Summer 2008), last accessed February 28, 2013, http://www.hopkins medicine.org/hmn/so8/feature4.cfm.

55. Wynton Marsalis with Geoffrey C. Ward, *Moving to Higher Ground: How Jazz Can Change Your Life* (New York: Random House, 2008), 3.

56. August Wilson, "The Art of Theater, No. 14," *The Paris Review*, no. 153, (Winter 1999), 79–80.

57. Shane Aslan Selzer, interview with the author, March 31, 2011.

58. Clarissa Pinkola Estés, *The Creative Fire: Myths and Stories on the Cycles of Creativity*, Sounds True, Incorporated; Unabridged edition (October 2005). (See Session 2.)

59. Giorgio Vasari, *The Lives of the Most Excellent Painters, Sculptors, and Architects*, trans. Gaston du C. de Vere, ed. Philip Jacks (New York: Modern Library, 2006), 336.

60. Ralph Waldo Emerson, "Self-Reliance," *Essays: First Series* (Boston: Houghton Mifflin, 1883), 48.

61. Taylor, quoted in Rose Eichenbaum, *Masters of Movement: Portraits of America's Great Choreographers* (Washington, DC: Smithsonian Books, 2004), 175.

62. Taylor, *Private Domain*, 141.

63. Taylor, 75.

64. Neil Ellis Orts, "Louis Horst," *Dance Teacher* magazine.

65. Ibid.

66. Taylor, 81.

67. Ibid., 136.

68. Harold Bloom, *The Anxiety of Influence: A Theory of Poetry*, 2nd ed. (New York: Oxford University Press, 1997), 5.

69. Taylor, 127–29, 132.

70. Ibid., 135–37.

71. To clarify, Skowhegan in Maine is a unique residency and with the word "school in the title" (its full name is Skowhegan School of Painting & Sculpture), you could easily not realize that it's not exactly a school at all. It has a resident faculty of experienced mid- to late-career artists, visiting faculty, and sixty-five selected participants from a highly competitive pool of applicants who stay for a nine-week session in the summer.

72. Liz Lerman, "What Happens on a Residency?" in *Hiking the Horizontal: Field Notes from a Choreographer* (Middleton, CT: Wesleyan University Press, 2011), 151.

73. Oliver Sacks, quoted in "Me, Myself, and The Muse," *Radiolab*, Season 9, Episode 3, March 8, 2011. Sina Najafi, editor of *Cabinet*, went through a similar process on December 11, 2011, when he published a book created from a twenty-four-hour period of writing. The critical responses to it were published in an anthology entitled *Reception Rooms*. The French movement Oulipo and the Surrealists' practice of automatic writing, were some of the inspirations for this project.

74. The connection between creativity has been shown in studies conducted by Harvard psychologist Ellen Langer, known for her pioneering work on "the psychology of possibility" long before there was a positive psychology movement, and on the power of "mindfulness" on behavior at a time when the mind-body connection was only discussed in the arena of spiritualism. See Ellen Langer, *Mindfulness* (New York: Da Capo Press, 1990), 121.

75. Karl Weick, "The Collapse of Sensemaking in Organizations: The Mann Gulch Disaster," *Administrative Science Quarterly*, vol. 38, December 1993, 628–52.

76. Jobs, quoted in Walter Isaacson, *Steve Jobs* (New York: Simon & Schuster, 2011), 155.

77. Jason Horowitz, "Does a Moleskine notebook tell the truth?" *New York Times*, October 16, 2004. Also see Emine Saner, "The joy of Moleskine notebooks," *The Guardian*, Shortcuts blog, June 19, 2012, http://www.theguardian.com/lifeandstyle/shortcuts/2012/jun/19/joy-moleskine-notebooks.

Notes

78. Taylor, quoted in Nancy Dalva, "PAUL TAYLOR with Nancy Dalva," *The Brooklyn Rail*, March 2, 2012, http://www.brooklynrail.org/2012/03/dance/paul-taylor-dance-company.

79. The work is "about pieces lost, then found again. And probably lost again," Taylor quoted in Dunning, "Paul Taylor—Looking Back and Ahead."

80. Gia Kourlas, "Looking Back With Darkness And Insects," *New York Times*, March 11, 2012, AR5.

Artic Summer

1. David Crane, *Scott of the Antarctic: A Life of Courage and Tragedy* (New York: Knopf, 2006), 4.

2. Edward J. Larson, *An Empire of Ice: Scott, Shackleton, and the Heroic Age of Antarctic Science* (New Haven: Yale University Press, 2011), 137, 158.

3. Ibid, 205. The four men who reached the South Pole with Scott were Lawrence "Titus" Oates, Edward Wilson, H. R. "Birdie" Bowers, and Edgar Evans.

4. Ibid.

5. Ibid, 139. Edward Wilson, *Diary of the "Terra Nova" Expedition to the Antarctic, 1910–1912* (New York: Humanities Press, 1967), 146–47; Apsley Cherry-Garrard, *The Worst Journey in the World: Antarctic, 1910–1913* (New York: George H. Doran; London: Constable & Company, 1922), 238.

6. Larson, 128, 206.

7. Fergus Fleming, "The World's Most Famous Failure," *Literary Review*, no. 333 (November 2005), 31. The term "Golden Age" is used to refer to nineteenth-century expeditions, but also to fourteenth- and fifteenth-century ventures.

8. Ben Saunders, interview with the author, July 2011. All quotes from Saunders are from this interview, or ones that took place in March and May 2012, and again in June 2013, unless otherwise indicated.

9. Jean-Louis Etienne is often considered the fourth person to travel to the North Pole, but he used dogsleds. The other two who have completed the journey solo and on foot are Borge Ousland and Pen Hadow. See Ginny Dougary, "The man with polar vision," *The Times*, March 15, 2003: "If Pen Hadow makes it to the North Pole alone and unaided, without supplies dropped by aircraft, he will be the first to do so by his chosen route from the Canadian side of the Arctic Ocean. This is generally considered to be the hardest route, though in 1994 a Norwegian, Borge Ousland, made an unsupported expedition via the longer but smoother Russian route. Nobody has since repeated that success. In 1978 a Japanese man, Naomi Uemura, crossed on the Canadian route

with seven resupplies and a dog team, and in 1986, a Frenchman, Jean-Louis Etienne, made it with five resupplies."

10. Saunders, "Ben Saunders: Why did I ski to the North Pole?", TED Talk, February 2005.
11. Saunders, quoted in "Ben Saunders, Arctic Explorer," *Intelligent Life*, December 2007 (last accessed March 8, 2012), http://moreintelligentlife.com/story/ben-saunders-arctic-explorer.
12. Saunders, "Ben Saunders: Why did I ski to the North Pole?", TED Talk, February 2005.
13. Ibid.
14. "The objects of Arctic exploration, in these days, must be to obtain valuable scientific results," explained Clements Markham, once president of the Royal Geographical Society, Britain's amateur gentleman's association, which largely funded the journeys that would become the stuff of legend. Markham, quoted in Larson, 75.
15. Saunders, "Why bother leaving the house?" TEDSalon London, November 2012, http://www.ted.com/talks/ben_saunders_why_bother_leaving_the_house.html.
16. Robert Stafford, Royal Geographical Society historian, quoted in Larson, 74.
17. Saunders, statement in interview article by Mark Quart, "Exploring the Limit," *PORT*, iss. 5, Spring 2012. Also see Ed Moses in Alanna Martinez, " 'I Just Wait Until It Goes Pow!': Abstract Painter Ed Moses on His Methodical and Intuitive Process," *Modern Painters*, September 2012.
18. As I wrote this, the only person I met through casual conversation who knew about Ben Saunders was the Norwegian explorer Inge Solheim.
19. Ben Saunders kindly provided me with the files he kept of this no longer active website. For the sake of context, Saunders showed me the question that he received on his site, which prompted his terse response to the "Random Person on the Internet." The question was: "I think it is about time you decided what to do with the money you raised when you offered each mile on your failed South expedition for sponsorship. You have done nothing for a long time, save talk and train. You have failed in your attempts because you are attempting the impossible. You need to recognize this failure and do the hardest thing of all: accept that you are not a hero or a god. Get a job, Ben. And come clean on that money." (To be clear, Saunders had not been accused of any fund-raising irregularities.)
20. Subhankar Banerjee, *Arctic Voices: Resistance at the Tipping Point* (New York: Seven Stories Press, 2012), 1.
21. For more on this study about Arctic sea ice melting, see Gunnar Spreen, Ron Kwok, Dimitris Menemenlis, "Trends in Arctic sea ice drift and role of wind forcing: 1992–2009," *Geophysical Research Letters* 38, no. 19 (October 2011).

22. Tennyson's words were selected for a 1906 Royal Geographical Society ceremony honoring polar explorer Roald Amundsen. Larson, 248.

23. Saunders is now focused on his Antarctic expeditions, but at the time, he was making another trip to the Arctic.

24. Yann Martel, *The Life of Pi* (New York: Harcourt, 2001), 79, 217.

25. Saunders, "Ben Saunders: Why did I ski to the North Pole?"

26. Ibid.

27. The quote is from Joseph Campbell, describing Nietzsche's idea: "If you say no to a single factor in your life, you have unraveled the whole thing," in Joseph Campbell with Bill Moyers, *The Power of Myth* (New York: Doubleday, 1988), 202. Nietzsche's idea was connected to his sense of *"Verhängnis,"* the "hanging together" of things. "One is a piece of fate, one belongs to the whole, one *is* in the whole." See Friedrich Nietzsche, *Twilight of the Idols and The Anti-Christ*, trans. R. J. Hollingdale (London: Penguin, 1990), 65.

28. Jearl Walker, quoted in George Leonard, *The Way of Aikido: Life Lessons from an American Sensei* (New York: Plume, 2000), 48–49.

29. Wendy Palmer, *The Practice of Freedom: Aikido Principles as a Spiritual Guide* (Berkeley: Rodmell Press, 2002), 113. Palmer is the founder of Aikido of Tamalpais in California with George Leonard and Richard Heckler. She developed a way of taking aikido training off the mat and into everyday life with her "Conscious Embodiment" principles.

30. Palmer, *The Practice of Freedom*, 113, 117.

31. Peter Gombeski, interview with the author, July 8, 2012.

32. Palmer, interview with the author, October 26, 2012. All quotes from Palmer are from this interview unless otherwise indicated.

33. Leonard, *The Way of Aikido*, 176. Palmer also owned this dojo with Richard Heckler.

34. Palmer, *The Practice of Freedom*, 111.

35. James Baldwin, "The Artist's Struggle for Integrity," in *The Cross of Redemption: Uncollected Writings*, ed. Randall Kenan, 1st ed. (New York: Pantheon Books, 2010), 46.

36. It is the wisdom that a clinical psychologist left me with when I first began writing about this topic. She hoped I would mention this fact, one that psychologists Jacquelyn Raftery and George Bizer's research findings show. If we suppress our emotions after negative feedback, it takes cognitive resources that could be used for new tasks, they argue, and this often leads to poorer follow-up performance. Yet when we don't hold back our natural response to failure, it's possible for negative feedback to enhance the performance. See Jacquelyn Raftery and George Bizer, "Negative feedback and performance: The moderating effect of emotion regulation," *Personality and Individual Differences* 47, no. 5 (October 2009): 481–86. Also see Jane M. Richards and James J. Gross, "Emotion

regulation and memory: The cognitive costs of keeping one's cool," *Journal of Personality and Social Psychology* 79, no. 3 (Sept. 2000): 410–24.

37. Eric Weiner, *The Geography of Bliss: One Grump's Search for the Happiest Places in the World* (New York: Twelve, 2008), 147.

38. William Shakespeare, *King Lear*, ed. R. A. Foakes (Walton-on-Thames, Surrey: Thomas Nelson and Sons, 1997—3rd Series, The Arden Shakespeare), 305–6.

39. Harry Belafonte, interview with Elvis Mitchell, Sundance Film Festival, Feb 2011. Also see "King 'Had a Tic,' " The History Channel (last accessed February 14, 2013), http://dev.history.com/shows/king/videos/harry-belafonte-king-had-a-tic#harry-belafonte-king-had-a-tic.

40. Kathleen Kennedy Townsend quoted in *Ethel*, dir. Rory Kennedy. HBO Documentary Films. Los Angeles: Moxie Firecracker Films, 2012.

41. Scott A. Sandage, *Born Losers: A History of Failure in America* (Cambridge, MA: Harvard University Press, 2005), 271.

42. "Money is a singular thing. It ranks with love as man's greatest source of joy. And it ranks with death as his greatest source of anxiety." John Kenneth Galbraith, *The Age of Uncertainty* (Boston: Houghton Mifflin, 1977), 161.

43. Karen Armstrong, *A Short History of Myth* (New York: Canongate, 2005), 51, 52, 54–56, 79–81.

44. A recent experiment has created conditions where gas reaches negative temperatures. However, the behavior of these molecules operates as if they are, in fact, hotter than zero. In short, the way that we think about temperature and kinetic energy is too elementary to describe what is really at work in quantum physics. For all those who want to know more about this concept of below absolute zero, see S. Braun et. al, "Negative Absolute Temperature for Motional Degrees of Freedom," *Science* 339, no. 6115 (2013): 52–55. Also see Zeeya Merali, "Quantum gas goes below absolute zero: Ultracold atoms pave way for negative-Kelvin materials." *Nature*, January 3, 2013 (last accessed March 23, 2013), www.nature.com/news/quantum-gas-goes-below-absolute-zero-1.12146.

45. Tom Shachtman, "The Coldest Place in the Universe," *Smithsonian* 38, no. 10, January 2008, 20–21.

46. For more on the history of zero, see Charles Seife, *Zero: The Biography of a Dangerous Idea* (New York: Penguin, 2000).

47. The rich history of the term *duende* is more abundant than this chapter on surrender will allow. Yet for more on the resonance between the idea of surrender and *duende*, first see Tracy K. Smith's collection of poetry, *Duende: Poems* (Saint Paul: Graywolf Press, 2007) and her beautiful interview with poet Elizabeth Alexander, "The Line Between Two Worlds," *American Poet* 32, no. 16 (Spring 2007), www.poets.org/viewmedia.php/prmMID/19726. As Alexander notes, other writers and scholars such as

poet Edward Hirsch and Terrance Hayes have expounded on it in later years. Also see work on *duende* by Federico García Lorca, who first popularized the term in his 1933 essay, "Play and Theory of the Duende," in *In Search of Duende* (New York: New Directions, 1998—6th printing): 48–62.

48. Jerry Colonna, interview with the author, March 23, 2012. All other quotes by Colonna are from this interview unless otherwise indicated.

49. See Pema Chödrön, *When Things Fall Apart: Heart Advice for Difficult Times* (Boston: Shambhala, 1997), 12.

50. Also see Jan Ullrich with Hagen Boßdorf, *Ganz oder gar nicht: Meine Geschichte* (Berlin: Econ, 2004), 91–92.

51. George Moore, *The Brook Kerith: A Syrian Story* (New York: Macmillan, 1916), 123.

52. Saunders, "Ben Saunders: Why did I ski to the North Pole?"

53. Lopez, *Arctic Dreams*, xxii.

54. This sentence appears in an essay I wrote, "Unfinished Masterpieces," in *Garage* magazine, no. 3, Fall/Winter 2012. I retain the copyright in this work.

55. Larson, *An Empire of Ice*, 143.

56. A variant on this sentence is from my essay "Unfinished Masterpieces."

57. Saunders said this in the transcript of an interview with Mark Quart for Quart's article "Exploring the Limit," *PORT*, no. 5, Spring 2012.

58. Ibid.

59. Paul Binding, "Into the Darkness," *The Guardian*, October 10, 2003, Review Section, 36.

60. Henry Wadsworth Longfellow, "The Poet's Tale; The Birds of Killingworth," in *The Complete Poetical Works of Henry Wadsworth Longfellow* (Boston, New York: Houghton Mifflin, 1893), 243.

61. The term "broken open" is mentioned often in spiritual contexts. Of the two with which I am familiar, one is from Omega Institute cofounder Elizabeth Lesser, who features the idea as the title of her book, *Broken Open: How Difficult Times Can Help Us Grow* (New York: Villard, 2005), and the other is Clarissa Pinkola Estés, who mentions the same term on her album *Seeing in the Dark: Myths and Stories to Reclaim the Buried, Knowing Woman*, in the track on the sorceress Medea, in connection with the seemingly impossible idea of a broken-open vessel containing more than it did before.

Beauty, Error, and Justice

1. Elaine Scarry, in her keynote address "Beauty and Social Justice" to the conference "Pain in Performance and 'Moving Beauty,'" Cambridge University, May 21–22, 2010, (stated around 32:00). (This is one of two

keynotes.) A video of the entire lecture is available on the website of the Centre for Research in the Arts, Social Sciences and Humanities, Cambridge University, http://www.crassh.cam.ac.uk/events/1232/27.

2. See Jefferson, letter to Madame de Tott, February 28, 1787, in *The Papers of Thomas Jefferson*, vol. 11, ed. Julian P. Boyd (Princeton: Princeton University Press, 1955), 187. Jefferson considered beauty to induce morality, which is not my argument here. Also see Mihaly Csikszentmihalyi and Rick Robinson, *The Art of Seeing: An Interpretation of the Aesthetic Encounter* (Malibu, CA: J. P. Getty Museum and the Getty Center for Education in the Arts, 1990), vii. Haidt and Patrick Seder argue that awe occurs "when we encounter something vast (usually physically vast, but sometimes small things reveal vast power, genius, or complexity) that cannot be comprehended using existing mental structures." See Haidt and J. Patrick Seder, "Admiration and Awe," in *The Oxford Companion to Emotion and the Affective Sciences*, ed. David Sander and Klaus Scherer (New York: Oxford University Press, 2009), 4–5.

3. No work of scholarship does more for our understanding of the impact of the lives lost during the Civil War than Drew Gilpin Faust, *This Republic of Suffering: Death and the American Civil War* (New York: Vintage, 2009). I owe a great debt to her work for helping me to have a powerful enough sense of this time to sense exactly why Frederick Douglass's argument about pictures would have seemed both so unusual and so profound. In the context of such loss, pictures took on more than a sense of a memento mori. They were a way to see what could not even be imagined—wartime loss depicted on a grand scale.

4. "Douglass was a magazine of divine judgments; he was volcanic—a veritable bomb of human dynamite." Rev. A. A. Miner, "A Bomb of Human Dynamite: Memorial to the Late Hon. Frederick Douglass," *The Monthly Review: An Illustrated Independent Magazine Devoted to the Interests of the American People Throughout the United States and the World* 3, no. 1 (March 1895): 9. Also see the scrapbook created by Charles Douglass, Douglass Family Scrapbook, 1875, 29, Collection of Walter O. Evans, Savannah, Georgia.

5. *The Life and Writings of Frederick Douglass*, ed. Philip S. Foner, 5 vols. (New York: International Publishers, 1950–1975), 48. See John Stauffer, *Giants: The Parallel Lives of Frederick Douglass and Abraham Lincoln* (New York: Twelve, 2008), 85–86, 200. Also see David W. Blight, *Frederick Douglass' Civil War: Keeping Faith in Jubilee* (Baton Rouge: Louisiana State University Press, 1989).

6. For more on Lincoln's three meetings with Douglass in the White House and their significance, see James Oakes, *The Radical and the Republican: Frederick Douglass, Abraham Lincoln, and the Triumph of Antislavery Politics* (New York: W. W. Norton & Co., 2007). See Elizabeth Cady

Stanton, quoted in Frederick S. Voss, *Majestic in His Wrath: A Pictorial Life of Frederick Douglass* (Washington, DC: Smithsonian Institution Press, 1995), Also see Scott A. Sandage, *Born Losers: A History of Failure in America* (Cambridge, MA: Harvard University Press, 2005), 218.

7. Douglass spoke of "pictures" in this lecture redrafted four times, though I am expanding the category to art in general.

8. Frederick Douglass, "Pictures and Progress," in John W. Blassingame, ed., *The Frederick Douglass Papers* [hereafter *FDP*], series 1, vol. 3, (New Haven: Yale University Press, 1985), 461. This volume contains the transcript of his 1861 speech.

9. Ibid. For "ideal contrasted," see Douglass, "Pictures and Progress" (1865), 18, ms. speech file, reel 18, frames 142–54, Library of Congress. For more on Douglass see Celeste-Marie Bernier, *Characters of Blood: Black Heroism In the Transatlantic Imagination* (Charlottesville and London: University of Virginia Press, 2012), 251–98.

10. Stauffer, 246. "On the wires," see Benjamin Quarles, *The Negro in the Civil War* (New York: Russell & Russell, 1968), 173.

11. William McFeely, *Frederick Douglass* (New York: W. W. Norton, 1991), 100, 383.

12. Frederick Douglass, "Pictures and Progress," in Blassingame, ed., *FDP*.

13. Douglass, "Pictures and Progress," *FDP*, 459. Martin Heidegger would later go on to describe this as a "world picture." See "The Age of the World Picture" in *The Question Concerning Technology, and Other Essays*, trans. William Lovitt (New York and London: Garland, 1977), 130. Also see Nicholas Mirzoeff, *An Introduction to Visual Culture* (New York: Routledge, 1999), 5. W. J. T. Mitchell considered the focus of philosophy in the West to be on images, on pictures, rather than text. See W. J. T. Mitchell, *What Do Pictures Want? The Lives and Loves of Images* (Chicago: University of Chicago Press, 2005). If Mitchell makes the case for what he calls a "metapicture," pictures that do not embody one message, but inspire a meditation on how it produces meaning, Douglass took the argument further, showing how pictures produce our actual world. Since Douglass's speeches on the importance of pictures have only been studied quite recently, I want to cite the work of a few other scholars who have pioneered this work: Laura Wexler, " 'A More Perfect Likeness': Frederick Douglass and the Image of the Nation," and Ginger Hill, " 'Rightly Viewed': Theorizations of Self in Frederick Douglass's Lectures on Pictures," in *Pictures and Progress: Early Photography and the Making of African American Identity*, ed. Maurice O. Wallace and Shawn Michelle Smith (Durham and London: Duke University Press, 2012), 18–40 and 41–82.

14. John Eaton, quoted in *In Memoriam: Frederick Douglass*, ed. Helen Douglass (Philadelphia: John C. Yorston & Co., 1897; reprint, Freeport, NY:

Books for Libraries Press, 1971), 71. Douglass may have said nearly the same about Lincoln. In his most famous speech, "Self-Made Men," so highly in demand it was given over fifty times, he dwelled on the improbable ascents of "self-made" men and women—Milton as blind. See "Self-Made Men: An Address Delivered in Carlisle, Pennsylvania, in March 1893," *FDP*, ser. 1, vol. 5, ed. John Blassingame and John McKivigan (New Haven: Yale University Press, 1992), 562: "Vast acquirements and splendid achievements stand to the credit of men and feeble frames and slender constitutions. Channing was physically weak. Milton was blind. Montgomery was small and effeminate. But these men were more to the world than a thousand Sampsons." The speech ended with Lincoln, whom he emphasized in his speech in all caps.

15. "If slavery was a kind of living death, as Douglass had sometimes suggested, he now demanded Old Testament retribution . . ." Stauffer, 148–49.

16. Henry Mayer, *All on Fire: William Lloyd Garrison and the Abolition of Slavery* (New York: W. W. Norton, 1998), epigraph.

17. Douglass, "What To the Slave Is The Fourth of July?: An Address Delivered in Rochester, New York, on July 5, 1852," *FDP*, ser. 1, vol. 2, ed. John Blassingame (New Haven: Yale University Press, 1982), 371.

18. Stauffer, 244.

19. Sandage, 223.

20. Ibid., 221–22. Of course, all of mankind depends on one another, Douglass clarified from the start. Being wholly "self-made" cannot fully exist. All that we value "have been obtained either from our contemporaries or from those who have preceded us in the field of thought and discovery. We have all either begged, borrowed, or stolen." He might have revised the term to include both sexes. He was, after all, off to give a speech for women's suffrage the day he died, working up until his end. But in those days, he argued that by "self-made" he meant people who demonstrate the "grandest possibilities of human nature, of whatever variety of race or color" through their ordered, constant industriousness. None were ever fully "self-made." It was, Douglass thought, a riddle that these rises occur "unheralded and from unexpected quarters." See Douglass, "Self-Made Men: An Address Delivered in Carlisle, Pennsylvania, in March 1893," *FDP*, ser. 1, vol. 5, ed. John Blassingame and John McKivigan (New Haven: Yale University Press, 1992), 549, 550.

21. Ibid., 223. At this point after the Civil War, when the inspirational novel was popular in the American market, failure and success both became unhooked from their origins in finance. As Francis Clark described it, "Every rich man is not, by any means, truly successful; every poor man is not, by any means, unsuccessful." Francis E. Clark, *Our Business Boys* (Boston: D. Lathrop and Co., 1884), 14. This fact, in part, had to do with

how much more common wealth became in the Gilded Age. There were a handful of wealthy millionaires during the Civil War and four thousand millionaires in the United States by 1892. The much-criticized but widely significant "New Thought" or neo-Transcendental movement had emerged in the nineteeth-century and central to it was the idea of, as Weiss describes it, an "individual's power for self-direction." See Richard Weiss, *The American Myth of Success: From Horatio Alger to Norman Vincent Peale* (Urbana: University of Illinois Press, 1988), 99, 130.

22. Douglass, "Self-Made Men," *FDP*, 545–75.

23. Aristotle described it more fully this way: "Now, if theories were sufficient of themselves to make men good, they would deserve to receive any number of handsome rewards, as Theognis said, and it would have been our duty to provide them. But it appears in fact that, although they are strong enough to encourage and stimulate youths who are already liberally minded, although they are capable of bringing a soul which is generous and enamoured of nobleness under the spell of virtue, they are impotent to inspire the mass of men to chivalrous action. . . . It is difficult to change by argument the settled features of character." *The Nicomachean Ethics of Aristotle*, trans. J. E. C. Welldon (London: Macmillan, 1920), 343–44.

24. Tamar Gendler, "Censorship," Philosophy 181, Lecture 24, Yale University, New Haven, April 14, 2011.

25. Junot Díaz, keynote speech, "Facing Race: A National Conference," November 2012, Baltimore, MD (last accessed February 15, 2013), http://colorlines.com/archives/2012/12/watch_junot_diaz_keynote _speech_from_facing_race_2012_video.html.

26. I want to clarify that I am here speaking about aesthetic force, not making a moral argument about how pictures function. I acknowledge that pictures are marshaled as propaganda for all sorts of purposes that run counter to supporting humanity. There is ample scholarship on the subject, but what I want to do in this chapter is not spill more ink on those examples, but offer a ballast to the many negative examples we can find of that sort to remind us of the galvanizing force that aesthetic force can, has, and will continue to have on us all. This idea of aesthetic force also has a cognate in spiritual discourse in Zen Buddhism's idea of "sudden enlightenment" teachings.

27. Robert Legato, "The art of creating awe," TEDGlobal, June 2012.

28. Daniel Schacter to Taylor Beck, "Making sense of memory: Harvard's Schacter examines links between past and future," *Harvard Gazette*, August 16, 2012, (last accessed August 18, 2013), http://news.harvard .edu/gazette/story/2012/08/making-sense-of-memory/.

29. The theory borrows its philosophy from Thomas Jefferson, who said that such images in either "sight or imagination" had a catalytic effect

after he viewed Jean-Germain Drouais's *Marius Imprisoned at Minturnae* (1786) in Paris. Perhaps the most well-known and often derided study is about Florence syndrome, also known as Stendhal syndrome. Coined by Graziella Magherini, it references Stendhal's (Marie-Henri Beyle) feeling of being overcome at the Basilica of Santa Croce in 1817, which he describes in *Naples and Florence: A Journey from Milan to Reggio.* Magherini wondered if there is a measureable response to aesthetic overwhelment, outlining her study of it in *La sindrome di Stendhal* (1989). See Francine Prose, "What Makes Us Cry?" *New York Review of Books* (last accessed February 14, 2013), www.nybooks.com/blogs/nyrblog/2012/sep/06/marina-abramovic-when-art-makes-us-cry/ and Melinda Guy, "The Shock of the Old," *Frieze,* no. 72 (January–February2003), 50–51. See Sara B. Algoe and Jonathan Haidt, "Witnessing excellence in action: the 'other-praising' emotions of elevation, gratitude, and admiration," *The Journal of Positive Psychology* 4, no. 2, 105–27. My thanks go to Samantha Boardman for bringing Haidt's work on this topic to my attention.

30. *Longinus on the Sublime: The Greek Text edited after the Paris Manuscript,* trans. W. Rhys Roberts (Cambridge: Cambridge University Press, 2011), 43. The full quote reads: "The effect of elevated language upon an audience is not persuasion but transport." But Longinus, like Plato, was interested in distinguishing between higher and lower pleasures. There were others like Plotinus who had a spectrum-based sense of beauty, the sense that aesthetic beauty allowed us to move on to enjoy beauty in other areas of life. Christopher Peterson and Martin Seligman, *Character Strengths and Virtues: A Handbook and Classification* (Washington, DC: American Psychological Association; New York: Oxford University Press, 2004), 540–41. Abraham Maslow has also considered the paths to awe in his studies of peak experiences, found in Peterson and Seligman, 543. William James equated this capacity for awe with health itself, though he confined awe to religion. See William James, *The Varieties of Religious Experience* (New York: Macmillan, 1961).

31. Leo Tolstoy, *What is Art?* trans. Aylmer Maude (London: Funk & Wagnalls, 1904), 210. John Keats, "Letter to George and Tom Keats," December 21, 27 (?), 1817, in *Selected Letters of John Keats,* ed. Grant F. Scott (Cambridge, MA: Harvard University Press, 2002), 61.

32. Michael Brenson, "Art Criticism and the Aesthetic Response," *Acts of Engagement: Writings on Art, Criticism, and Institutions, 1993–2002* (Lanham, Maryland: Rowman & Littlefield Publishers, 2004), 66. My thanks to Deborah Kass for letting me know about Brenson's soulful piece.

33. Charles L. Black Jr., "My World with Louis Armstrong," *Yale Law School Faculty Scholarship Series,* Paper 2532 (1986): 1595–1600.

34. *Beauty Matters,* ed. Peg Zeglin Brand (Bloomington: Indiana University Press, 2000), 7.

35. It is fitting, too, that it was Armstrong, a man who became synonymous with diplomacy and justice on a national scale. For more see Fred Kaplan, "When Ambassadors Had Rhythm," *New York Times*, June 29, 2008, AR17.

36. Douglass, "Pictures and Progress," *FDP*, 456. Here he was paraphrasing Andrew Fletcher, a Scottish essayist. See *The Political Works of Andrew Fletcher, Esq; of Saltoun* (Glasgow: Printed by R. Urie, for G. Hamilton and J. Balfour, 1749), 266.

37. Abolitionist Thomas Clarkson made this print based on a hypothetical projection of a slave ship plan. The legal limit accommodated by the regulations of the Regulated Slave Trade Act of 1788 was 454 persons. See Marcus Rediker, *The Slave Ship: A Human History* (New York: Viking, 2007). Also see Marcus Wood, *Blind Memory: Visual Representations of Slavery in England and America 1780–1865*, (New York: Routledge, in association with Manchester University Press, 2000).

38. Malia Wollan, "Recipe for a Perfect Photo: Clear Sky, Sunset and Water," *New York Times*, February 26, 2013, A12.

39. Here I am thinking of poets from Reza Baraheni in Iran, dedicating his five decades of work to human rights after torture by the shah's regime for his writing, to those in the Generation of '27 in Spain imprisoned and exiled during the Spanish Civil War and Franco's regime, to Wole Soyinka and Ngugi wa Thiong'o.

40. Elaine Scarry, *On Beauty and Being Just* (Princeton: Princeton University Press, 2001), 48.

41. Douglass, *Narrative of the Life of Frederick Douglass: An American Slave* (New York: Modern Library, 2000), 68–69. There was, of course, the dignity he gained from daring to fight and not to submit to his overseer when he was just sixteen years old, but he credits this image with giving him the vision of freedom.

42. Stauffer, 137.

43. Historian Brent Edwards notes that scholars such as John Blassingame, Eric Sundquist, and John David Smith have only recently focused on the literary feats that Douglass's more mature writings convey and their impact at the time of publication. See Brent Edwards, "Introduction," in *My Bondage and My Freedom* (New York: Barnes & Noble, 2005), xviii.

44. *Under the Sky of My Africa: Alexander Pushkin and Blackness*, ed. Catharine Nepomnyashchy, Nicole Svobodny, and Ludmilla Trigos (Evanston, IL: Northwestern University Press, 2006), xii.

45. See John Stauffer, *The Black Hearts of Men: Radical Abolitionists and the Transformation of Race* (Cambridge, MA: Harvard University Press, 2002), 51–52, 54. Here, Stauffer is quoting an 1864 version of Douglass's speech in Stauffer's epigraph to the chapter. The quote is from *FDP*, Library of Congress (and on microfilm), a version of the speech distinct

from the 1861 version cited in John Blassingame's edited series of Douglass's work in which the 1861 version appears.

46. John William Draper made a daguerreotype of the moon less than a year
    after Daguerre's invention was announced to the Academy. My thanks
    to Laura Wexler, Professor of American Studies & Women's, Gender,
    & Sexuality Studies at Yale University, for giving a lecture in April 2012
    about these attempts to photograph the moon in the nineteenth century.
    While I knew about these events from previous study, she presented it in
    a way that captivated me so, I never forgot it.

47. Michael Leja, *Looking Askance: Skepticism and American Art from Eakins to
    Duchamp* (Berkeley: University of California Press, 2004), 12.

48. Painter Rosa Bonheur's work was praised because people thought it
    offered a truthful depiction of horses in motion, the rapid action that
    surpassed the ability of the camera or the eye as seen in her work *The
    Horse Fair* (1853–55), given to the Metropolitan Museum in 1887. Muy-
    bridge made Bonheur the example of failure in the arts in his 1878 lec-
    tures "Motion of the trotting horse" in San Francisco, and later at the
    Royal Society of Arts on April 4, 1882.

49. The result of this visit is the artist's famous serial photograph *The Horse
    in Motion*, 1878.

50. Leja also describes that the power of this moment was also in showing
    what the eye was failing to see, setting up a relationship of mild distrust
    about the limits of the human body. Étienne-Jules Marey gave the name
    chronophotography to the new stop-action photography Muybridge
    pioneered. See Nancy Mowll Mathews with Charles Musser, *Moving Pic-
    tures: American Art and Early Film, 1880–1910* (Manchester, VT: Hud-
    son Hills Press, in association with Williams College Museum of Art,
    2005), 16, 20, and Rebecca Solnit, *Motion Studies: Time, Space and Ead-
    weard Muybridge* (New York: Bloomsbury, 2003). I am grateful to Alex-
    ander Nemerov's teaching for helping me to understand this particular
    moment in time.

51. "There is something in the extreme of minuteness, which is no less won-
    derful,—might it not almost be said, no less majestic?—than the extreme
    of vastness." See William Carpenter, *The Microscope and its Revelations*
    (London: John Churchill, 1856), 37.

52. "Lay bare a world of enchantments," see Fitz-James O'Brien, "The Dia-
    mond Lens," *Atlantic Monthly*, January 1858, 354–67. "Astounding," see
    Jabez Hogg, *The Microscope: its history, construction, and applications, being
    a Familiar Introduction to the use of the Instrument and the study of microscop-
    ical science*, 5th ed. (London: Routledge, Warne, and Routledge, 1861),
    597. Also see Martin Willis, *Vision, Science and Literature, 1870–1920:
    Ocular Horizons*, no. 15 (London: Pickering & Chatto, 2011).

53. Theodore Dreiser "Reflections," *Ev'ry Month* (March 1896); reprinted in

Theodore Dreiser's *Ev'ry Month*, ed. Nancy Warner Barrineau (Athens: University of Georgia Press, 1996), 56.

54. Leja, 13.

55. Charles Seife, *Zero: The Biography of a Dangerous Idea* (New York: Penguin Books, 2000), 87. Perspective was developed in the fifteenth century after Italian architect Filippo Brunelleschi (1377–1446) created his drawings.

56. Sarah Luria, *Capital Speculations: Writing and Building Washington, D.C.* (Durham, NH: University of New Hampshire Press, 2006), 78.

57. "In the United States Senate a resolution was offered reciting that in the person of the late Frederick Douglass death had borne away a most illustrious citizen, and permitting the body to lie in state in the rotunda of the Capitol on Sunday." Charles Chesnutt, *Frederick Douglass* (Boston: Small, Maynard, 1899), 130.

58. Douglass, "Pictures and Progress," *FDP*, 458.

The Blind Spot

1. El Anatsui, explaining the meaning of the title of his piece, *They Finally Broke the Pot of Wisdom* (2011). Andrew Russeth, "Light Metal: El Anatsui Weaves Delicate Tapestries From Rough Material," *New York Observer*, December 11, 2012 (last accessed, February 23, 2013), http://galleristny.com/2012/12/light-metal-el-anatsui-weaves-delicate -tapestries-from-rough-material/.

2. Liz Diller, interview with the author, June 2012. All quotes from Diller are from this interview unless otherwise indicated.

3. Joshua David, quoted in Joshua David and Robert Hammond, *High Line: The Inside Story of New York City's Park in the Sky* (New York: Farrar, Straus and Giroux, 2011), 6.

4. Ibid., 18.

5. Joel Sternfeld, quoted in Adam Gopnik, "A Walk on the High Line," *New Yorker*, May 21, 2001, 49.

6. Gopnik, "A Walk on the High Line," 41, 47.

7. Hammond quoted in David and Hammond, *High Line: The Inside Story*, 12.

8. John Stilgoe, "Steganography Photographed," in *Joel Sternfeld: Walking the High Line* (Göttingen: Steidl; New York: Pace/MacGill Gallery, 2001), 37. As Stilgoe kindly explained, *ortsbewüstung* is a cognate of *Ortswüstung*, which conveys a more static kind of wilding. Neither word has an equivalent term in English to convey something more "topographical" than moral as it does in German, more about nature than human behavior, as a "wilding" state.

9. David, quoted in Ibid., 12.

10. Sternfeld quoted in Gopnik, 45, 47.

11. Jun'ichirō Tanizaki, *In Praise of Shadows* (Sedgwick, ME: Leete's Island Books, 1977). Or see the edition translated by Thomas J. Harper and Edward G. Seidensticker (London: Jonathan Cape, 1991), 22.

12. Margherita Long's translation of Tanizaki's essay "In Praise of Shadows" includes these words in her book, *This Perversion Called Love: Reading Tanizaki, Feminist Theory, and Freud* (Palo Alto, CA: Stanford University Press, 2009), 18.

13. Jean Verdon, *Night in the Middle Ages*, trans. George Holoch (Notre Dame: University of Notre Dame Press, 2002), 111, and Jane Brox, *Brilliant: The Evolution of Artificial Light* (New York: Houghton Mifflin Harcourt, 2010), 17–18.

14. Keith Gessen, "Loser Wins," *The Review of Contemporary Fiction* 31, no. 1 (Spring 2011): 13–14.

15. Melville, quoted in James Wood, "The All and the If: God and Metaphor in Melville," *The Broken Estate: Essays on Literature and Belief* (New York: Picador, 2010), 49.

16. Norman Mailer, interviewed in *When We Were Kings*, dir. Leon Gast (1996; Gramercy Pictures).

17. *ABC World News with Diane Sawyer*, Season 3, Episode 52, http://abc news.go.com/WNT/video/spanx-entrepreneur-shares-advice-15889928.

18. See also Hugo Lindgren, "Be Wrong as Fast as you Can," *New York Times Magazine*, January 6, 2013, 45.

19. Tim Brodhead, interview with the author, 2011. Shortly after our interview, in February 2011, Brodhead announced his resignation and the board named his successor, Stephen Huddart, as the foundation's next president and CEO.

20. Henry Petroski, *To Forgive Design: Understanding Failure* (Cambridge, MA: Belknap Press, 2012), 36–37.

21. Robin Finn, "Two Friends, and the Dream of a Lofty Park Realized," *The New York Times*, July 11, 2008, http://www.nytimes.com/2008/07 /11/nyregion/11lives.html?_r=0.

22. Robert Hammond quoting Doug Sarini, *High Line: The Inside Story*, 7.

23. Christine Quinn, quoted in David and Hammond, *High Line: The Inside Story*, 15.

24. Technically, the tracks are an adaptive reuse or a renovation, but from the start, Diller knew that the High Line was "neither a park, nor a piece of architecture. It was something else." The team's aim was to let it all through as a legible "transcription, or a translation of what was already there in a way that it could be appreciated."

25. *Designing the High Line: Gansevoort Street to 30th Street*, ed. Friends of the High Line, (New York: Friends of the High Line, 2008), 31.

26. El Anatsui, quoted in Russeth "Light Metal."

27. Robert Macfarlane, *The Old Ways: A Journey on Foot* (New York: Viking, 2012), 95.

The Iconoclast

1. Umberto Eco, quoted in Susanne Beyer and Lothar Gorris, "SPIE-GEL Interview with Umberto Eco: 'We Like Lists Because We Don't Want to Die' " *Spiegel*, November 11, 2009, http://www.spiegel.de /international/zeitgeist/spiegel-interview-with-umberto-eco-we-like-lists-because-we-don-t-want-to-die-a-659577.html.

2. See James Joyce's *Finnegan's Wake*, Dante's *Paradiso*, Homer's endless list of ships to describe the strength of the Greek army in the *Iliad*, and Walt Whitman's seemingly limitless lists in "Song of Myself."

3. Meryl Streep, "Hope Springs," *Charlie Rose*, August 6, 2012.

4. Vanessa Taylor wrote *Hope Springs*, a film about an attempt to save a tepid thirty-one-year-old marriage, as a spec script when she was in between jobs as an exercise of sorts "without any hope of getting it read, let alone made." Vanessa Taylor to Colin Bertram, "'Hope Springs' for Spec Screenwriter" NBC, August 7, 2012.

5. Vanessa Taylor, Interview with Jenna Milly, http://screenwritingu.com/ blog/screenwriter-vanessa-taylor-sexy-romantic-comedy-hope-springs.

6. Kevin Maher, "Hollywood's secret movie Black List revealed," *The Times*, June 10, 2011.

7. Scott Meslow, "How Hollywood Chooses Scripts: The Insider List That Led to *Abduction*," *The Atlantic*, September 23, 2011 (last accessed February 25, 2013), www.theatlantic.com/entertainment/archive/2011/09/ how-hollywood-chooses-scripts-the-insider-list-that-led-to-abduction /245541/.

8. Franklin Leonard, interview with the author, July 9, 2011. All comments by Leonard were stated directly to the author unless otherwise indicated.

9. Leonard, interview with the author, but it was also a quote he gave to the *New York Times*: "Mr. Leonard created the list casually, slapping 'a vaguely subversive name on it,' and e-mailed it around to friends and associates." Amy Chozick, "Hollywood's Black List Gets an Upgrade," *New York Times*, Media Decoder, October 12, 2011.

10. The Hollywood blacklist led to protests in support of a group that became known as the Hollywood Ten: Alvah Bessie, Herbert Biberman, Lester Cole, Edward Dmytryk, Ring Lardner Jr., John Howard Lawson, Albert Maltz, Samuel Ornitz, Robert Adrian Scott, and Dalton Trumbo—a group of artists fired by studio executives acting under the aegis of the Motion Pictures Association of America, with pressure from HUAC. This group refused to answer the question: "Are you now or have you

ever been a member of the Communist Party?" The list is not a reference to the film and photographic project *The Black List* directed by Timothy Greenfield-Sanders, a compilation of interviews with African Americans in a range of industries speaking about their experiences of race in America. *"Un-American" Hollywood: Politics and Film in the Blacklist Era*, ed. Frank Krutnik et al. (Rutgers: Rutgers University Press, 2007).

11. See James Baldwin, "Everybody's Protest Novel," in *The Price of the Ticket: Collected Nonfiction, 1948–1985* (New York: St. Martin's Press, 1985), 30. There he faults *Uncle Tom's Cabin* for its use of color symbolism that "black equates with evil and white with grace." Also see James Baldwin, "Color," Ibid., 319–24. In this essay, Baldwin argues that the idea of "color" should be considered differently, and tries to reclaim the "color" of blackness from its negative connotation. For more on color symbolism in film noir, see Manthia Diawara, "Noir by Noirs: Towards a New Realism in Black Cinema," *African American Review* 27, no. 4 (Winter 1993): 525–37. See Rebecca Walker, ed., *Black Cool: One Thousand Streams of Blackness* (Berkeley, CA: Soft Skull Press, 2012).

12. Lisa Cortes, interview with the author, February 17, 2012.

13. Cliff Roberts, quoted in Nicole Sperling, "The Black List: How Hollywood's Buzziest Scripts Get Their Juice," *Entertainment Weekly*, December 10, 2008 (last accessed February 25, 2013), www.ew.com/ew/article/0,,20245388,00.html.

14. Maher, "Hollywood's secret movie Black List revealed," 4.

15. Over a seven-year period, scripts on the Black List grossed $11 billion in box-office sales worldwide and have resulted in 125 distributed feature films.

16. Leonard quoted in Meslow, "How Hollywood Chooses Scripts."

17. Franklin has also told a compressed version of this episode in a speech for *Fast Company*. See Austin Carr, "Superstorm: The Worst Leonardo DiCaprio Movie Never Made," *Fast Company*, July 8, 2010 (last accessed February 25, 2013), www.fastcompany.com/1667970/superstorm-worst-leonardo-dicaprio-movie-never-made.

18. Nathan Adams, "Selena Gomez is a 'Hot Mess,' " *FilmSchoolRejects*, October 18, 2011 (last accessed June 23, 2012), http://www.filmschoolrejects.com/news/selena-gomez-hot-mess-nadam.php.

19. Oliver, quoted in Nicole Sperling, "The Black List: How Hollywood's Buzziest Scripts Get Their Juice."

20. Margy Rochlin, "Guy and Doll, and the Woman Behind Them," *New York Times*, October 7, 2007, 2.19. Also on the first Black List was Allan Loeb, who was anonymous in Hollywood and was about to leave altogether before two of his scripts landed in the top five of the Black List in 2005 and launched his career as one of Hollywood's most-prolific screenwriters. Just before this happened he thought he should just go

back and work at the Chicago Board of Trade. Loeb was "the baby writer at the lowest rung within the system," the one that he ghoulishly said had "just enough rope to hang himself." His agent had dropped him as a client in 2004. Before leaving, Loeb decided to give writing one more attempt. He wrote the screenplay *Things We Lost in the Fire*. It landed on the Black List in the number-one slot. The visibility that it gained from the Black List helped it to be produced and released in 2007 with Halle Berry and Benicio Del Toro as the leads. Another one of his scripts, *The Only Living Boy in New York*, was also voted into the number-four slot of the 2005 Black List. As I write, his name is on a sizeable chunk of the movies distributed either as a writer or a rewriter. Loeb is one of Hollywood's highest-paid screenwriters, earning over a million dollars per screenplay.

21. Mike Goodridge, "Inaugural Brit List highlights most liked unproduced screenplays," *Screen Daily*, November 1, 2007 (last accessed March 14, 2013), www.screendaily.com/inaugural-brit-list-highlights-most-liked-unproduced-screenplays/4035610.article.

22. Alexandra Arlango, interview with the author, June 7, 2012. The original Brit List was created by London-based agent Rachel Holroyd, who polled forty of her British and Irish colleagues, tallied the results, and circulated the vote-based list to the British film industry. The Brit List has also morphed into a term for rabid Anglophilia—spotlighting anything or anyone British and underappreciated. The term "Brit List," as of late, has become the title for a program that launched in 2012 on BBC America, scrolling out a weekly list of any unsung British thing from unusual foods to unsung national treasures, all of which should "be carried around the world at shoulder height," but are currently ignored. See Fraser McAlpine, "The Brit List: 10 Internationally Unsung UK National Treasures," BBC America, April 17, 2012 (last accessed June 2, 2012), http://www.bbcamerica.com/anglophenia/2012/04/the-brit-list-10-internationally-unsung-british-national-treasures/.

23. David Seidler, interview with the author, June 2, 2012. All comments by Seidler are from this interview unless otherwise indicated.

24. Some of Seidler's own recollections, such as his success with the "expletive cure," made it into the script. So does the Freudian "talking cure" approach that Seidler discovered Logue had used on his own uncle. But the intensity—every day for an hour, including weekends—and structure of the visits and frequency of their communication was all corroborated from letters between the king and Logue. Some of the dialogue and details about how the king had to be dressed, comported (standing only), and more were all taken directly from diaries that Logue kept.

25. Marc Seidler quoted in Carolyne Meng-Yee, "Proud of his Dad's Work," *The New Zealand Herald*, February 20, 2011, (last accessed August 18,

2013), http://www.nzherald.co.nz/entertainment/news/article.cfm?c _id=1501119&objectid=10707497

26. Michael Bodey, "David Seidler, a writer who found his voice," *The Australian*, March 7, 2011 (last accessed June 2, 2012), http://www .theaustralian.com.au/news/features/david-seidler-a-writer-who-found-his-voice/story-e6frg6z6-1226016762328.

27. Comment by Writer A on Nikki Finke's "The Black List 2009: Full Roster," *Deadline Hollywood*, December 11, 2009 (last accessed February 25, 2013), www.deadline.com/2009/12/the-black-list-to-be-posted-here-in-entirety/.

28. S. T. VanAirsdale, "What's Left to Discover on the Black List?" *Movieline*, December 13, 2010 (last accessed February 25, 2013), http://www .movieline.com/2010/12/13/whats-left-to-discover-on-the-black-list/.

29. Diablo Cody, video interview with Scott Myers, The Black List, December 11, 2011 (last accessed February 25, 2013), http://blog.blcklst .com/category/diablo-cody/.

30. Margaux Froley Outhred, "Writers to Watch: Joshua Zetumer," *Just Effing Entertain Me*, June 27, 2008 (last accessed June 23, 2012), http:// www.justeffing.com/2008/06/27/writers-to-watch-joshua-zetumer/.

31. Zetumer quoted in Maher, 4.

32. See Solomon E. Asch, "Effects of group pressure upon the modification and distortion of judgments," in *Groups, Leadership and Men: Research in Human Relations*, ed. Harold Guetzkow (Pittsburgh: Carnegie Press, 1951): 177–90 and Asch, *Social Psychology* (New York: Prentice-Hall, 1952).

33. Asch, "Opinions and Social Pressure," *Scientific American* 193, no. 5 (November 1955): 31–35. Gregory S. Berns et al., "Neurobiological Correlates of Social Conformity and Independence During Mental Rotation," *Biological Psychiatry* 58, no. 3 (2005): 247 [with permission from Elsevier]. Also see Gregory Berns, *Iconoclast: A Neuroscientist Reveals How to Think Differently* (Boston: Harvard Business Review Press, 2008), 88–104.

34. Ibid.

35. Michael Uslan, keynote lecture, Summit Series, Squaw Valley, California, February 2012.

36. Kubrick, quoted in Michel Ciment, *Kubrick*, trans. Gibert Adair (New York: Holt, Rinehart and Winston, 1983), 177. At issue isn't the efficacy of these strategies for box-office hits. There is no commercial reason why a studio shouldn't capitalize on an established brand, like action figure-based films. If a country such as Brazil is currently one of the fastest-growing markets, it is logical that setting a film there might result in high-grossing sales. *Fast Five* and *Rio* could become two of the highest-grossing films in recent years. A movie can generate nearly seventy percent of its revenue abroad, so perhaps it is no surprise that two of

Hollywood's most successful films at the box office, *Avatar* and *The Lord of the Rings*, are set in lands of make-believe, dodging associations with one country at the expense of another. Nicole Allan, "How to Make a Hollywood Hit," *The Atlantic*, May 2012, 70–71.

37. Bill Simmons, "The Movie Star: Perceived success is the name of the game in Hollywood," Grantland, June 29, 2011 (last accessed February 25, 2013), www.grantland.com/story/_/id/6716942/the-movie-star.

38. Rebecca Winters Keegan, "The Legend of Will Smith," *Time* 170.24, December 10, 2007, 85.

39. Simmons, "The Movie Star."

40. Ahmir Thompson, also known as the drummer Questlove, quoted in *Philadelphia* magazine. When asked about his greatest achievement, he said: "The downfall of any artist is to pull a 'Lot's wife' and start reflecting and basking in their career achievements. That is the true secret to my success—I never bask in the glory. I do a job, and the next day I'm on to the next challenge with the energy of a freshman with something to prove." "One of Us: ?uestlove [*sic*]," *Philadelphia*, April 2011 (last accessed February 25, 2013), www.phillymag.com/articles/one-of-us-uestlove.

41. Boyle, interview with Nic Harcourt, "Turn it Up," *Los Angeles Times Magazine*, February 2009 (last accessed June 23, 2012), http://www.latimesmagazine.com/2009/02/turn-it-up-february-2009.html.

42. Michelle Kung, "In Search of a Movie Gem," *The Wall Street Journal*, October 13, 2011 B10.

43. Tolmach quoted in Mike Fleming Jr., "Matt Tolmach Options Black List Topper 'The Kitchen Sink,'" *Deadline Hollywood*, January 13, 2011 (last accessed June 22, 2012), http://www.deadline.com/tag/matt-tolmach-producer/.

44. Scorsese quoted in Rick Tetzeli, "The Vision Thing: How Marty Scorsese risked it all and lived to risk again in Hollywood," *Fast Company* 162 (December 2011/January 2012), 103.

45. Noah Oppenheim, interview with the author, March 2012.

46. Daniel Gilbert, *Stumbling on Happiness* (New York: A. A. Knopf, 2006), 207–8.

47. Leonard, video interview with The Bitter Script Reader, posted October 16, 2012 (last accessed February 25, 2013), http://thebitterscriptreader.blogspot.com/2012/10/exclusive-interview-with-franklin.html.

48. There were some, like screenwriters John August and Ol Parker of *The Best Exotic Marigold Hotel*, a film that landed on the Brit List, who tweeted a note when the list expanded its services calling Franklin "a remarkable man," and saying that "if anyone can make this work, he can." Ol Parker, Twitter post, October 16, 2012, https://twitter.com/olparker1.

49. Amanda Pendolino, "The Black List Launches Service For Aspiring Writers," *The Aspiring TV Writer and Screenwriter Blog*, October 15, 2012 (last accessed February 25, 2013), http://aspiringtvwriter.blogspot.com/2012/10/the-black-list-launches-service-for.html?m=1.

The Deliberate Amateur

1. Philip Guston, quoted in Musa Mayer, *Night Studio: A Memoir of Philip Guston* (New York: Da Capo Press, 1997).
2. Scientists used to think this honor went to carbon nanotubes, but what was considered one-dimensional turned out to be three, as they are made up of cylinders. *Science Watch* newsletter interview with Andre Geim, "U. Manchester's Andre Geim: Sticking with Graphene—For Now," *Science Watch*, August 2008 (last accessed February 11, 2013), sciencewatch.com /inter/aut/2008/08-aug/08augSWGeim/.
3. Konstantin Novoselov begins his Nobel Lecture with an epigraph by mathematician, theologian, and novelist Edwin Abbott Abbott, author of the satirical novella, *Flatland: A Romance of Many Dimensions* (1884). Novoselov likens graphene to this idea, while explaining how the discovery was about more than finding a flat crystal. Novoselov, "Materials in Flatland," Nobel lecture, December 8, 2010, www.nobelprize.org/mediaplayer/index.php?id=1420.
4. Geim, "U. Manchester's Andre Geim: Sticking with Graphene—For Now," *Science Watch*.
5. "About The Ig Nobel Prizes," *Improbable Research* (last accessed February 18, 2013), www.improbable.com/ig/.
6. The full list of those awards is available here: http://www.improbable.com/ig/winners/. The very small list I have cited is as follows: "The 2011 Chemistry Prize to Makoto Imai, Naoki Urushihata, Hideki Tanemura, Yukinobu Tajima, Hideaki Goto, Koichiro Mizoguchi, and Junichi Murakami of Japan, for determining the ideal density of airborne wasabi (pungent horseradish) to awaken sleeping people in case of a fire or other emergency, and for applying this knowledge to invent the wasabi alarm"; the 2011 Psychology Prize to Karl Halvor Teigen of Norway "for trying to understand why, in everyday life, people sigh"; the 1996 Economics Prize to Dr. Robert J. Genco of the University of Buffalo for his study linking financial strain and periodontal disease; and the 2010 Peace Prize to Richard Stephens, John Atkins, and Andrew Kingston of Keele University "for confirming the widely held belief that swearing relieves pain."
7. Helen Pilcher, "Laughter in the lab," *Nature*, October 1, 2004, http://www.nature.com/news/2004/040927/full/news040927-20.html.
8. Ibid.

9. Edwin Cartlidge, "A Physicist of Many Talents," *Physics World* 19, no. 2 (February 2006): 8–9.
10. Geim, "Random Walk to Graphene," Nobel lecture, December 8, 2010, 73. www.nobelprize.org/nobel_prizes/physics/laureates/2010/geim _lecture.pdf.
11. Sean O'Neill, "Words from the wise: Andre Geim," *New Scientist* 2847 (January 14, 2012): 10.
12. Geim, quoted in his Nobel Prize interview with Adam Smith, December 6, 2010. See "Video Player." *Nobelprize.org*. Nobel Media AB 2013. Web. 28 Aug 2013. http://www.nobelprize.org/mediaplayer/index .php?id=1408.
13. Ibid.
14. Novoselov, quoted in Nobel Interview with Andre Geim and Konstantin Novoselov. See "Video Player." *Nobelprize.org*. Nobel Media AB 2013. Web. 28 Aug 2013. Nobelprize.org. November 27, 2012. http://www. nobelprize.org/mediaplayer/index.php?id=1408&view=1.
15. Konstantin Novoselov, interview with the author, December 20, 2012. All quotes from Novoselov are from this interview unless otherwise indicated.
16. Geim, "Random Walk to Graphene," Nobel lecture. *Nobelprize.org*.
17. Ibid.
18. Geim, "U. Manchester's Andre Geim: Sticking with Graphene—For Now," *Science Watch*, August 2008.
19. Novoselov, quoted in Geim and Novoselov, Nobel Prize interview with Adam Smith, December 6, 2010. "Video Player." *Nobelprize.org*. Nobel Media AB 2013. Web. 28 Aug 2013.
20. Geim, "Random Walk to Graphene," Nobel lecture.
21. Ibid.
22. Another colleague, senior fellow Oleg Shklyarevskii from Kharkov, Ukraine, pulled out a piece of adhesive tape with some graphite that stuck to it from the waste bin to find more for another attempt.
23. Novoselov, quoted in Novoselov, Interview with Gary Taubes, *Science Watch*, February 2009.
24. Geim, "U. Manchester's Andre Geim: Sticking with Graphene—For Now," *Science Watch*.
25. Ibid.
26. Novoselov, Interview with Gary Taubes, *Science Watch*.
27. Geim, "Random Walk to Graphene," Nobel lecture, 82.
28. See K. S. Novoselov, et al., "Electric Field Effect in Atomically Thin Carbon Films," *Science*, 306, no. 5296 (October 2004): 666–69; K. S. Novoselov, et al., "Two-dimensional gas of massless Dirac fermions in graphene," *Nature* 438, no. 7065 (November 2005): 197–200, doi:10.1038/nature04233.

29. Geim, "U. Manchester's Andre Geim: Sticking with Graphene—For Now," *Science Watch*.

30. He did consider a patent after they published the first paper on graphene and was about to file—the papers were still with the lawyers—when Geim was at a conference and approached an executive at a "major electronics company," one that makes "billions and billions of dollars," Geim coyly offers as the only clue, to see if they might collaborate, given how expensive holding a coveted patent can be at filing and in its defense, and how little Geim was interested in royalties. The response? The company had planned to only make it harder for Geim to keep the patent. They were already looking at graphene, and didn't think anything would come of it in the first ten years, so it wasn't worth it to them. Yet, if graphene delivered on its promise in the eleventh year and Geim had a patent, the executive said the company would "put hundreds of lawyers" on the case and file so many patents per day that the man said Geim would have to spend his entire life, "and the GDP of your little island . . . trying to sue us," to prevent Geim from having a monopoly on the material. Rudeness aside, Geim appreciated the useful point. He had patented earlier discoveries, like his gecko tape, but with graphene he had no commercial use in mind to make it worth the financial and administrative onslaught. Geoff Brumfiel, "Andre Geim: in praise of graphene," *Nature*, October 7, 2010, http://www.nature.com/news/2010/101007/full/news.2010.525.html, doi:10.1038/news.2010.525. He also realized that "there is no point in patenting whole areas of visionary ideas." Geim, quoted in Geim and Novoselov, Nobel Prize interview with Adam Smith, December 6, 2010. Besides, he has come to see scientists' patents as often just an "expensive memorial to your vanity." Patents are about pride, not about remuneration, as Geim pointed out in an article for the *Financial Times* Andre Geim, "Most patents serve only as a memorial to a professor's pride," *Financial Times*, July 3, 2012, 11.

31. Geim, "Random Walk to Graphene," Nobel lecture, 79.

32. Geim, telephone interview with Adam Smith, October 5, 2010, http://www.nobelprize.org/mediaplayer/index.php?id=1380.

33. For more on the Zen idea of "Beginner's Mind," see Shunryu Suzuki, *Zen Mind, Beginner's Mind: Informal Talks on Zen Meditation and Practice* (Boston: Shambala, 2006). For more on the freedom of late style, see Theodor Adorno's 1930 piece on Beethoven and subsequent essays on the topic by Edward Said in the posthumously published collection of his essays. Edward W. Said's *On Late Style: Music and Literature against the Grain* (New York: Pantheon, 2006) as well as Theodor W. Adorno, *Beethoven: The Philosophy of Music: Fragments and Texts*, ed. Rolf Tiedemann, trans. Edmund Jephcott (Cambridge: Polity Press, 1998), and Karen Painter, "On Creativity and Lateness," in *Late Thoughts: Reflections*

on Artists and Composers at Work, ed. Karen Painter and Thomas Crow (Los Angeles: Getty Research Institute, 2006).

34. Erskine Caldwell, "The Art of Fiction No. 62," *The Paris Review,* no. 86 (Winter 1982), 141.

35. Tharp, 167.

36. Philip Ball uses this term to describe how Descartes saw the function of wonder. "Why science needs wonder," *New Statesman,* May 2, 2012 (last accessed February 28, 2013), www.newstatesman.com/sci-tech/sci-tech /2012/05/sublime-intervention.

37. The effect is systematic. When Karim Lakhani and Lars Bo Jeppesen of Harvard Business School went to study its efficacy at InnoCentive, a company founded to work around complex challenges that fall into the blind spot of a Fortune 500 company's expertise, they found that the solutions came from the nonexperts further away from the domain of the problem.

38. Stanley Crouch, interview with the author, December 10, 2012.

39. See Mary Baine Campbell, *Wonder and Science: Imagining Worlds in Early Modern Europe* (Ithaca, NY: Cornell University Press, 1999).

40. Descartes enacted this shift with *Discours de la méthode* (1637). See Leland de la Durantaye, " 'The Art of Ignorance': An Afterword to Ludwig Börne," *Harvard Review* 31 (2006), 79. Börne became a writer perforce (it was the one profession available to the German Jewish civil servant after the repeal of Napoleonic liberal laws in Frankfurt). Börne's essay is controversial for the potentially mindless haste that it encourages, since it was a time, at the start of the Industrial Revolution, when many were teaching others how to mechanize their production. He, too, advocated automatic writing, a technique later adopted by the Surrealists. However, Börne's core insight about the art of ignorance remains. See Leland de la Durantaye, " 'The Art of Ignorance,' " 77–80.

41. Ludwig Börne, "How to Become an Original Writer in Three Days," trans. Leland de la Durantaye, *Harvard Review* 31 (2006), 64, 68.

42. Schopenhauer, quoted in de la Durantaye, 77.

43. Geim, quoted in Geim and Novoselov, Nobel Prize interview with Adam Smith, December 6, 2010.

44. Geim, telephone interview with Adam Smith, Nobel Prize, October 5, 2010.

45. Geim, quoted in Geim and Novoselov, Nobel Prize interview with Adam Smith, December 6, 2010.

46. Ibid.

47. Geim, "U. Manchester's Andre Geim: Sticking with Graphene—For Now," *Science Watch.*

48. Geim, telephone interview with Adam Smith, Nobel Prize, October 5, 2010.

49. Novoselov, quoted in Geim and Novoselov, Nobel Prize interview with Adam Smith, December 6, 2010.
50. Geim, telephone interview with Adam Smith, Nobel Prize, October 5, 2010.
51. Geim, "Banquet Speech," December 10, 2010 (last accessed February 20, 2013), www.nobelprize.org/nobel_prizes/physics/laureates/2010/geim-speech_en.html.
52. Toni Morrison, "The Art of Fiction No. 134," *The Paris Review*, no. 128 (Fall 1993), 92.
53. Rocio Londoño, interviewed in the documentary on Antanas Mockus, *Bogotá Cambió*, http://www.youtube.com/watch?v=mR5p1ckXGoM&list=TLJv5PV52GLFk.
54. Stuart Brown, "Play is more than just fun," TED Talk, May 2008 (last accessed February 11, 2013), http://www.ted.com/talks/stuart_brown_says_play_is_more_than_fun_it_s_vital.html. Also see Brown and Christopher Vaughan, *Play: How it Shapes the Brain, Opens the Imagination, and Invigorates the Soul* (New York: Penguin, 2009).
55. Ibid.
56. Neil deGrasse Tyson, quoted in "Neil deGrasse Tyson: Learning how to think is empowerment," Interview with Deborah Byrd, *EarthSky*, December 15, 2011 (last accessed, February 11, 2013), http://earthsky.org/human-world/neil-degrasse-tyson.
57. When Ivy Ross was at Coach, her team found an idea for how to make a handbag close in a unique way from the hardware on a bathroom door. Ivy Ross, Interview with the Author, November 11, 2012. All quotes from this interview unless otherwise indicated.
58. Ross, quoted in Roger Thompson, "A Life by Design," *Harvard Business School Alumni Bulletin*, December 2004, www.alumni.hbs.edu/bulletin/2004/december/profile.html.
59. Frank Wilson, *The Hand: How its Use Shapes the Brain, Language, and Human Culture* (New York: Pantheon Books, 1998).
60. Brown, "Play is more than just fun," TED Talk, May 2008.
61. The MacArthur Fellows sampled were from the period 1981 to 2001. See the study: Michele Root-Bernstein, "Imaginary Worldplay as an Indicator of Creative Giftedness," in Larisa Shavinina, ed., *International Handbook on Giftedness* (New York: Springer, 2009) 599–616. Also see Michele and Robert Root-Bernstein, *Sparks of Genius: The Thirteen Thinking Tools of the World's Most Creative People* (New York: Houghton Mifflin, 1999).
62. The quote from the original French text is: "Un soir, je pris du café noir, contrairement à mon habitude, je ne pus m'endormir: les idées surgissaient en foule; je les sentais comme se heurter, jusqu'à ce que deux d'entre elles s'accrochassent, pour ainsi dire, pour former une combinaison stable." Henri Poincaré, *Science et Méthode* (Paris: Flammarion, 1920), 51.

The French reflexive verb *s'accrocher* ("to fasten together as in crocheting") is a more vivid description than the English verb allows, Halsted mentions. The more frequently cited translation translates Poincaré's word as "collide," as seen here. Poincaré, *The Foundations of Science*, trans. George B. Halsted (New York: The Science Press, 1913), 387. Also see Albert Rothenberg, *The Emerging Goddess: The Creative Process in Art, Science, and Other Fields* (Chicago: University of Chicago Press, 1980), 104–5.

63. Geim, quoted in Geim and Novoselov, Nobel Prize interview with Adam Smith, December 6, 2010.

64. Ibid.

65. Kevin Dunbar, "How Scientists Really Reason: Scientific Reasoning in Real-World Laboratories," in Robert J. Sternberg and Janet E. Davidson, eds., *The Nature of Insight* (Cambridge: MIT Press, 1995), 365–95.

66. Dunbar, interview with Yasmeen Qureshi, research assistant for this manuscript, May 2011. All quotes from Dunbar are from this interview unless otherwise indicated.

67. Ibid.

68. Thomas Lewis, Fari Amini, and Richard Lannon, *A General Theory of Love* (New York: Random House, 2000), 81.

69. Liberty to explore across domains, the hallmark of Friday Night Experiments, is part of what has motivated a movement for "open science," sharing findings using the low-barrier platform of the Internet instead of relying on peer-review journals that can be glacially slow, costly, and exclusive. Now, social networking sites allow for crowdsourcing to solve problems collectively and share the results. Some were even being formed out of discards, such as the no longer extant *Journal of Serendipitous and Unexpected Results (JSUR)*, and *The All Results Journal*, which allows for both positive and negative results in their submissions and is entirely open access. Unlike peer-reviewed science journals, authors can publish at no cost and their articles are available for free to all. See Thomas Lin, "Cracking Open the Scientific Process," *New York Times*, January 17, 2012, D1.

70. Kathryn Schulz, *Being Wrong: Adventures in the Margin of Error* (New York: Ecco, 2010), 21.

71. An extensive 2006 study by the accounting firm Ernst & Young showed higher ratings in year-end performance reviews by 8 percent for every additional ten hours of vacation an employee used. Another study involving NASA scientists showed the same—post-vacation, performance assessment rose. Tony Schwartz, "Relax! You'll Be More Productive," *New York Times*, February 10, 2013, SR1.

72. Sarah Goodyear, " 'Desire Lines' and the Fundamental Failure of Traffic Engineering," *The Atlantic Cities*, December 5, 2012, http://www.the

Notes

atlanticcities.com/commute/2012/12/desire-lines-and-fundamental-failure
-traffic-engineering/4061/. /. This fact about Finland is attributed to a
public planning report, "Earls Court Project Application 1: The 21st
Century High Street," Royal Borough of Kensington and Chelsea, 3.2,
June 2011.

73. Matthew Tiessen, "Accepting Invitations: Desire Lines as Earthly Offer-
ings," *Rhizomes* 15 (Winter 2007), http://www.rhizomes.net/issue15/
tiessen.html. When Dwight D. Eisenhower was president of Columbia
University, he used information from natural desire lines to help determine where to place sidewalks on campus.

74. A variant on this full quote, "The universe is full of magical things
patiently waiting for our wits to grow sharper," is often attributed to
Bertrand Russell or William Butler Yeats, but is in fact by Eden Phillpotts (1862–1960) who stated it in his book, *A Shadow Passes* (1918) in the
following passage: "In the marshes the buckbean has lifted its feathery
mist of flower spikes above the bed of trefoil leaves. The fimbriated flow-
ers are a miracle of workmanship and every blossom exhibits an exquisite
disorder of ragged petals finer than lace. But one needs a lens to judge
their beauty: it lies hidden from the power of our eyes, and menyan-
thes must have bloomed and passed a million times before there came
any to perceive and salute her loveliness. The universe is full of magical
things patiently waiting for our wits to grow sharper." Eden Phillpotts, *A
Shadow Passes* (London: Cecil Palmer & Hayward, 1918), 19.

75. Novoselov, interview with the author, December 20, 2012.

76. Ibid.

77. Thomas West, *A Guide to the Lakes in Cumberland, Westmorland, and
Lancashire*, 4th ed. (London: Printed for W. Richardson, under the Royal
Exchange; J. Robson; Kendal: W. Pennington, 1789).

78. Henry Petroski, *The Pencil: A History of Design and Circumstance* (New
York: Knopf, 1990), 46, 58.

79. Jonathan Otley, *A Concise Description of the English Lakes and Adjacent
Mountains*, 2nd ed. (Keswick: Published by the author; London: John
Richardson; Kirky Lonsdale: Arthur Foster, 1825), 133–38.

The Grit of the Arts

1. Psychologists say we struggle with this because the more we experience
success alone, the less likely we are to seek out information from critics, often resulting in a scenario in which we don't make improvements
because we think that things can't get any better. It also occurs because
there is a high emotional cost for taking risks after success, a cost that can
garrote its continual unfolding.

2. There is England's Dee Bridge in 1847; Scotland's Tay Bridge in 1879;

the Quebec Bridge in 1907; the Tacoma Narrows Bridge in 1940; the bridges built in Milford Haven, Wales, and Melbourne, Australia, in 1970; and London's Millennium Bridge and the Passerelle Solferino footbridge in Paris in 2000. These last two both shut down for excessive swaying in their opening days.

3. Henry Petroski, *To Forgive Design: Understanding Failure* (Cambridge, MA: Belknap Press of Harvard University Press, 2012), 36–7, 344, 339. Also see Henry Petroski, *Success Through Failure: The Paradox of Design* (Princeton: Princeton University Press, 2006), 150–56, 170–72.

4. Angela Lee Duckworth and Patrick D. Quinn, "Development and Validation of the Short Grit Scale (Grit-S)," *Journal of Personality Assessment* 91, no. 2 (February 2009): 166–74.

5. See Paul Tough, *How Children Succeed: Grit, Curiosity, and the Hidden Power of Character* (New York: Houghton Mifflin Harcourt, 2012), 74–75.

6. Angela Duckworth, Research Statement for Angela L. Duckworth, August 9, 2012.

7. Ibid.

8. See Walter Mischel, Yuichi Shoda, and Monica Rodriguez, "Delay of Gratification in Children," *Science* 244, no. 4907 (May 26, 1989): 933–38. Also see Walter Mischel, Ebbe B. Ebbesen, and Antonette R. Zeiss, "Cognitive and attentional mechanisms in delay of gratification," *Journal of Personality and Social Psychology* 21, no. 2 (February 1972): 204–18. Walter Mischel, "Processes in the Delay of Gratification," *Advances in Experimental Social Psychology* 7 (1974): 249–92. Earlier, in his 1968 book, *Personality and Assessment*, Mischel argued that personality was a function not independent of but dependent on context, not an obvious conclusion at a time when Rorschach ink-blot tests were being used to predict one's personality.

9. Duckworth, quoted in Kevin Hartnett, "Character's Content," *The Pennsylvania Gazette* 110, no. 5 (May/June 2012), 61.

10. Duckworth, "The Psychology of Achievement," presentation to the National Association for Gifted Children, May 2012.

11. She found Seligman while researching psychology doctoral programs late one night with her infant daughter on her lap and fired off an e-mail to him. Playing an insomnia-induced game of bridge online, Seligman saw her e-mail and dashed off a reply with an invitation to a research event with his colleagues the following day. By the end of the group session, he was floored by her comments. He lobbied his colleagues to abandon the admissions timeline rules, since it was already July. They gave her an interview and she started the doctoral program a few months later. Martin Seligman, *Flourish: A Visionary New Understanding of Happiness and Well-being* (New York: Free Press, 2011), 133, and Kevin Hart-

nett, "Character's Content," *The Pennsylvania Gazette* 110, no. 5 (May/June 2012), 61.

12. The findings about grit seem to build on work that Stanford psychologist Carol Dweck has long championed about the importance of a growth mind-set. As Dweck's landmark research has found, focusing on praise exclusively and shielding students from feeling as if they made a mistake can result in a fear of failure that inhibits learning and in many cases even results in regression. Instead, encouraging effort in students, and not just praise for grades, led to both thriving after a challenge or failure and markedly higher records of academic achievement. In other words, the wisdom of errorless learning is now under question. See Robert A. Baron, "Negative Effects of Destructive Criticism: Impact on conflict, self-efficacy, and task performance," *Journal of Applied Psychology*, 73, no. 2 (May 1988), 199–207, doi: 10.1037/0021-9010.73.2.199. Pino Audia and Edwin Locke, "Benefiting from Negative Feedback," *Human Resource Management Review* 13 (2003), 633.

13. Hartnett, "Character's Content," 60.

14. Paul Tough, "The Character Test," *New York Times Magazine*, September 18, 2011, 40.

15. Drew Gilpin Faust, conversation with Walter Isaacson, May 2012, New York City.

16. Faust, "By the Book," *New York Time Book Review*, May 24, 2012, BR6.

17. Faust, "Baccalaureate address to Class of 2008" delivered June 3, 2008, in Cambridge, Massachusetts, www.harvard.edu/president/baccalaureate -address-to-class-2008.

18. Christopher Merrill, interview with the author, February 2012.

19. Angela Duckworth, "The Nitty Gritty: Self-Esteem vs. Self-Control," *in character: A Journal of Everyday Virtues*, May 28, 2010, http://incharacter .org/observation/the-nitty-gritty-self-esteem-vs-self-control/.

20. Ibid.

21. See Dr. Tuomas Tepora, " 'Sisu': The Finnish for 'Stiff Upper Lip'?", *The History of Emotions Blog*, October 30, 2012 (last accessed April 1, 2013), http://emotionsblog.history.qmul.ac.uk/?p=1955.

22. Aini Rajanen, *Of Finnish Ways* (Minneapolis: Dillon Press, 1981). Also see "Northern Theatre: Sisu," *Time*, January 8, 1940.

23. Bill Thomas, "The Finnish Line," *Washington Post*, March 26, 2006, http://www.washingtonpost.com/wpdyn/content/article/2006/03/22/ AR2006032201943.html.

24. As Anu Partanen outlines in "What Americans Keep Ignoring About Finland's School Success," *The Atlantic*, December 29, 2011, http:// www.theatlantic.com/national/archive/2011/12/what-americans-keep- ignoring-about-finlands-school-success/250564/. This statistic is due to

the PISA survey that the Organization for Economic Co-operation and Development (OECD) conducts.

25. Partanen, "What Americans Keep Ignoring About Finland's School Success."

26. See Partanen, "What Americans Keep Ignoring." Partanen emphasizes that in Finland, there are also no private schools; even independent schools are publicly funded—a key difference between this Nordic country and the many that are looking to its model to make improvements. Also see Pasi Sahlberg, *Finnish Lessons: What Can the World Learn from Educational Change in Finland?* (New York: Teachers College Press, 2011).

27. See Tom Ashbrook with Pasi Sahlberg, Okhwa Lee, and Marc Tucker, "Education Lessons from Top-Ranked Finland And South Korea," *On Point*, National Public Radio, February 7, 2013, http://onpoint.wbur.org /2013/02/07/finland-south-korea.

28. Will Smith in conversation with Tavis Smiley, *Tavis Smiley*, PBS Video, December 12, 2007, http://video.pbs.org/video/1869183414/.

29. James Watson, interview with the author, July 24, 2012. All quotes are from this interview.

30. Samuel F. B. Morse, May 3, 1815, Letter to his parents Elizabeth Ann Breese Morse and the Reverend Jedidiah Morse, *His Letters and Journals*, vol. 1, ed. Edward Lind Morse (Boston: Houghton Mifflin, 1914), 177.

31. The full quote from Morse's November 20, 1849, letter to James Fenimore Cooper reads as follows: "Painting has been a smiling mistress to many, but she has been a cruel jilt to me." Morse, letter to James Fenimore Cooper, November 20, 1849, in *Correspondence of James Fenimore Cooper*, vol. 2 (New Haven: Yale University Press, 1922), 637.

32. Kenneth Silverman, *Lightning Man: The Accursed Life of Samuel F. B. Morse* (New York: Knopf, 2003), 240. This common nineteenth-century term "to write at a distance" is similar to the language that Karl Marx used to describe the effect of transportation and communications. "The more developed the capital, therefore, the more extensive the market over which it circulates, which forms the spatial orbit of its circulation, the more does it strive simultaneously for an even greater extension of the market and for greater annihilation of space by time." Karl Marx, *Grundrisse: Foundations of the critique of political economy (rough draft)*, trans. Martin Nicolaus (London; New York: Penguin Books, 1993), 539. See James Carey, "Technology and Ideology: The case of the telegraph," in Robert Hassan and Julian Thomas, eds., *The New Media Theory Reader* (Berkshire, UK: Open University Press, 2006), 225–43.

33. Silverman, 240, 242, 422.

34. Silverman, 40–41, 70, 80–81, 177. When Morse consigned his 7 x 11' painting *The House of Representatives* (1822–23)—a scene of the never-

before-depicted congressional chambers while the House was in session—he gave it to agent Curtis Doolittle, a name which gave away what would happen next: nothing. The cost of the tour outstripped the income by nearly two to one. "Grave" comment: see Morse, draft of an article for *New York Observer*, 7 Jan 1851, M14. Also see Silverman, 319.

35. Jean Brockway, "The Artist Who Gave Us the Telegraph," *New York Times*, Feb 14, 1932, SM11. It is hard to date the beginnings of Morse's contraption precisely. As Morse's biographer Silverman mentions, "He had been quietly developing it for five years . . . Through experiment Morse had often changed the design of his telegraph. The apparatus that existed around 1837 remained so crude that he was reluctant to have it seen . . . He built the device from a wooden frame otherwise used for stretching canvas," 148. Also "Of Morse's work on the telegraph between his first inklings on the *Sully* in 1832 and the port-rule/register of 1837, only glimpses remain," 154–55. This is, in part, because the original sketchbook from his trip on the *Sully* is no longer extant. "He was reluctant to have it seen," see Silverman, 148. "So rude," Morse quoted in David McCullough, "Samuel Morse's Reversal of Fortune," *Smithsonian*, September 2011, 80–88.

36. Samuel I. Prime, *The Life of Samuel F. B. Morse L.L.D., inventor of the electro-magnetic recording telegraph* (New York: D. Appleton and Co., 1875).

37. Silverman, 154. Frank Jewett Mather Jr., "S. F. B. Morse and the Telegraph," *The Nation*, August 26, 1915, 255-57.

38. Jackson made an "insane claim" with his unsupported argument that he had first conceptualized the idea on the ship. Mather Jr., "Morse and the Telegraph," 256.

39. Morse omitted the French Romantic works that hung there, such as Théodore Géricault's *Raft of the Medusa* (1818–19).

40. James Fenimore Cooper, who had arrived in France with his family years earlier. In the painting's left-hand corner, Cooper appears with his wife and daughter as gallery visitors. Morse's goal was to support the development of history painting as an American art form as it existed in Europe. Also see Cooper, *Letters and Journals of James Fenimore Cooper*, vol. 2, ed. James Franklin Beard (Cambridge, MA: Belknap Press of Harvard University Press, 1960–68), 239.

41. The full quote is "My profession is that of a *beggar*, it exists on *charity*," (emphasis Silverman's). Morse, quoted in Silverman, 129.

42. Morse's painting was purchased in 1982. In 2005, the purchase of Asher B. Durand's *Kindred Spirits* for more than $35 million broke that record. Carol Vogel, "Wal-Mart Heiress Buys Library's Painting," *New York Times*, May 13, 2005, B4.

43. Brian O'Doherty, "Notes on the Gallery Space," in *Inside the White Cube: The Ideology of the Gallery Space* (Berkeley: University of Califor-

nia Press, 1999), 15. The picture plane, no longer mainly a stage for pictorial illusion, has now been reconsidered as a medium itself. Over a century later in Paris, Yves Klein would make an empty gallery, painted with a lithopone white pigment over the course of two days of meditative painting, the very content of his exhibition at the single-room Iris Clert Gallery titled *Le Vide (The Void)*. The show was so densely packed at the opening that the police had to break up the attendees, who were all drinking cocktails dyed International Klein Blue. New use of gallery space such as this was one that Morse, meticulously painting all that actually still hung on gallery walls, might never have imagined. See Nan Rosenthal, "Assisted Levitation: The Art of Yves Klein," in *Yves Klein, 1928–1962: A Retrospective* (Houston, TX: Institute for the Arts, Rice University; New York: The Arts Publisher, 1982), 118, and Sidra Stitch, *Yves Klein* (Ostfildern: Cantz, 1994), 132–40. Some laughed, one man "trembled and couldn't hold back his tears," and Albert Camus wrote, perhaps sincerely, perhaps in jest, in the guest book "with the void, full powers." See Thomas McEvilley, "Yves Klein: Conquistador of the Void," in *Yves Klein, 1928–1962: A Retrospective* (Houston, TX: Institute for the Arts, Rice University, Houston; New York: The Arts Publisher, 1982), 50.

44. *Samuel F. B. Morse, His Letters and Journals*, vol. 2, ed. Edward Lind Morse (Boston: Houghton Mifflin, 1914), 19.
45. Silverman, 244.
46. Duckworth, interview with the author, June 14, 2012. All quotes by Duckworth are from this interview unless otherwise stated.
47. Morse, letter to parents, August 24, 1811, in *Samuel F. B. Morse: His Letters and Journals*, vol. 1, ed. Edward Lind Morse (Boston: Houghton Mifflin, 1914), 43–44.
48. Morse, quoted in Silverman, 24.
49. Morse, letter to parents, May 25, 1812, in *Samuel F. B. Morse: His Letters and Journals*, vol. 1, 75.
50. Morse, letter to father, March 25, 1812, in *Samuel F. B. Morse: His Letters and Journals*, vol. 1, 69.
51. Silverman, 98.
52. Ibid.
53. Ibid., 71. Also see Morse, letter to wife, December 1824, in *Samuel F. B. Morse: His Letters and Journals*, vol. 1, 258.
54. Morse quoted in "A Samuel Morse Letter Turns Up," *New York Times*, April 25, 1926, 8. Selling photographs must have seemed particularly odd. After visiting Daguerre, another painter turned inventor, in France in 1839, Morse wrote: "I am told every hour, that the two great wonders of Paris just now, about which everyone is conversing, are Daguerre's wonderful results in fixing permanently the image of the camera obscura

and Morse's Electro-Magnetic Telegraph." David McCullough, *The Greater Journey*, 157.

55. Silverman, 216, 218, 326.
56. James Fenimore Cooper Collection, YCAL MSS 415, Box 7, Folder 176, Correspondence with Samuel F. B. Morse, New York, July 21, 1833, Beinecke Rare Book and Manuscript Library, Yale University.
57. Duckworth, "Breakout Session," 16th Annual Women's Leadership Conference, Bay Path College, April 29, 2011.
58. The Torrance Test activities are both written and pictorial, but researcher Kyung-Hee Kim of the School of Education at William & Mary in Virginia focused on the figural part of the study, which asked questions about making a picture out of incomplete figures and objects. This comes from a study by Kyung-Hee Kim not published at the time of the study that made me aware of it. See Po Bronson and Ashley Merryman, "The Creativity Crisis," *Newsweek*, July 2010. Also see Erin Zagursky, "Smart? Yes. Creative? Not so much," *Ideation*, February 3, 2011 (last accessed February 22, 2013), http://www.wm.edu/research/ideation/professions/smart-yes.-creative-not-so-much.5890.php.
59. Dominic Randolph, interview with the author, June 6, 2012. All quotes from Randolph are from this interview unless otherwise indicated.
60. Randolph, quoted in Tough, "The Character Test," *New York Times Magazine*, September 18, 2011, 85.
61. Eli Whitney endorsed this leather piston, and Benjamin Silliman printed images of it in the first issue of his new periodical the *American Journal of Science*, which became one of the country's leading papers for scientific discoveries, as found in Silverman, 45.
62. Henri Focillon, *The Life of Forms in Art*, trans. George Kubler (New York: Zone Books, 1989). A different kind of thinking comes through making art, as curator, artist, and Yale School of Art Dean Robert Storr reminds us. It is the foundation beneath artist Jasper Johns's axiom: "Take an object. Do something to it. Do something else to it." That "doing" is critical. See Storr, "Dear Colleague," in *Art School (Propositions for the 21st Century)*, ed. Steven Henry Madoff (Cambridge, MA: MIT Press, 2009), 64.
63. Lisa Yuskavage, quoted in Jori Finkel, "Tales From the Crit: For Art Students, May Is the Cruelest Month," *New York Times*, April 30, 2006, A34.
64. John Baldessari, quoted in Sarah Thornton, *Seven Days in the Art World* (New York: W. W. Norton & Company, 2008), 52.
65. Finkel, "Tales from the Crit."
66. For more on definitions of *creativity*, see Bronson and Merryman, "The Creativity Crisis."
67. Finkel, "Tales From the Crit," A34.

68. Robert Farris Thompson, *Flash of the Spirit: African & Afro-American Art & Philosophy* (New York: Random House, 1983).

69. Chinua Achebe, "The Art of Fiction No. 139," *The Paris Review*, no. 133 (Winter 1994), 159.

70. George Kubler, *The Shape of Time: Remarks on the History of Things* (New Haven: Yale University Press), 33.

71. Ibid., 33, 39–40.

72. Frank Gehry, "Project: First Drafts," *The Atlantic Monthly* 307, no. 4, (May 2011): 56.

73. Joan Miró, Letter to J. F. Ràfols Montroig, August 21, 1919, in *Joan Miró: Selected Writings and Interviews*, ed. Margit Rowell (New York: Da Capo Press, 1992), 63.

74. Tharp with Mark Reiter, *The Creative Habit*, 133–35.

75. James Watson, interview with the author, July 2012.

76. Comment from the student, see Samuel I. Prime, *The Life of Samuel F. B. Morse, L.L.D.*, 724.

77. Daniel Huntington, quoted in *Samuel F. B. Morse: His Letters and Journals*, vol. 1, 486.

78. C. P. Snow, "The Two Cultures," *Leonardo* 23, no. 2/3, (1990), 169–73. Reprinted from "The Rede Lecture, 1959," in C. P. Snow, *The Two Cultures and a Second Look: An Expanded version of "The Two Cultures and the Scientific Revolution"* (London: Cambridge University Press, 1965): 1–21.

79. Edward O. Wilson, "On the Origins of the Arts: Sociobiologist E. O. Wilson on the evolution of culture," *Harvard Magazine* (May–June 2012): 33–37. Reprinted from Edward O. Wilson, *The Social Conquest of Earth* (New York: W. W. Norton, 2012).

80. Mae Jemison, "Teach arts and sciences together," TED Talk, Monterey, California, February 2002, accessed February 24, 2013, www.ted.com /talks/mae_jemison_on_teaching_arts_and_sciences_together.html. Posted May 2009. She goes on to say, "The difference between arts and sciences is not analytical versus intuitive, right? E=mc squared required an intuitive leap, and then you had to do the analysis afterwards. Einstein said, in fact, 'The most beautiful thing we can experience is the mysterious. It is the source of all true art and science.' "

81. Consider the work of Charles Willson Peale or Alexander von Humboldt, to name two of many examples.

82. Mather Jr., "S. F. B. Morse and the Telegraph," 255.

83. Silverman, 65, 144–45. John Trumbull had begun the work in 1817 with four 12 x 18' canvases. Four other American artists, John Chapman, Robert Weir, John Vanderlyn, and Henry Inman, were commissioned to finish the work in 1837. Morse, despite his petitions, and his position as founder of the National Academy of the Arts and Design, was not. [The

institution was later called the "the National Academy of Design."].
Regarding his rejection, some scholars suspect that Morse's nativist politics might have done him in. Morse's politics were anti-Catholic and nativist. See David McCullough, *The Greater Journey: Americans in Paris* (New York: Simon & Schuster, 2011), 150.

84. Samuel Isham, quoted in *Samuel F. B. Morse: His Letters and Journals*, vol. 1, 437.
85. Silverman, 410.
86. Ibid., 301.
87. Ibid., 319.
88. Karen Armstrong, *A Short History of Myth* (New York: Canongate, 2005), 11.
89. Morse, letter to James Fenimore Cooper, November 20, 1849.
90. Morse, draft of an article for *New York Observer*, Jan. 7, 1851, Samuel F. B. Morse Papers, Library of Congress, microfiche 14.
91. Silverman, 326.
92. Duckworth, quoted in Hartnett, 64.
93. This conversation took place in a special program at the annual meeting of the Association for Psychological Science on Friday, May 27, 2011, at the Washington Hilton in Washington DC. See David Brooks and Walter Mischel, "The News From Psychological Science: A Conversation Between David Brooks and Walter Mischel," *Perspectives on Psychological Science* 6, no. 6 (November 2011): 519.

Epilogue: The Stars

1. Carl Sagan's application to a UC Berkeley graduate fellowship in 1959 leaked these details, which biographer Keay Davidson found. The U.S. Air Force hired scientist and astronomer Sagan during the Cold War to determine if a lunar detonation was mathematically possible, so fixated were they on showing military might to Russia. Project A119, "A Study of Lunar Research Flights," was secret until details of it inadvertently became public in Sagan's biography. The horrifying idea shows us how little we consider what is beyond us, around us, and the intricacy with which it is all tied. (Sagan performed the calculations needed to see just how large the moon's mushroom explosion expansion would be.) See Antony Barnett, "US planned one big nuclear bang for mankind,"*The Observer*, May 14, 2000, 1.
2. Virginia Woolf describing *The Waves*, formerly titled *The Moths*, in *A Writer's Diary*, ed. Leonard Woolf (New York: Harcourt, Brace, 1954), 139–40.
3. Trevor Paglen, *The Last Pictures* (Berkeley and Los Angeles: University of California Press; New York: Creative Time Books, 2012).

3. Trevor Paglen, *The Last Pictures* (Berkeley and Los Angeles: University of California Press; New York: Creative Time Books, 2012).

4. "There's an old saying that victory has 100 fathers and defeat is an orphan." John F. Kennedy News Conference, Apr. 21, 1961, in "The President's News Conference of April 12, 1961," *Public Papers of the Presidents of the United States . . . 1961* (Washington, DC: Government Prining Office, 1962), 312.

INDEX

Page numbers in *italics* refer to illustrations. Page numbers beginning with 203 refer to notes.

Index

Index

Index

Gehry, Frank, 188
Geim, Andre, 141–50, *144,* 153–55,
    160–61, 163, 237–38
Gendler, Tamar, 94
generosity, 95–96
George VI, King of England, 128–29
Gilovich, Thomas, 25
Giovanni da Pistoia, 20, *21,* 206
Glass, Ira, 213
Gombeski, Peter, 72
Good, Ashley, 114
Gore, Al, 29
Gosling, Ryan, 127
Goya, Francisco, 47
Graham, Martha, 38, 41, 45, 54
graphene, 141–50, *142,* 161
graphite, 141, 148–49, 164–65
Greenfield-Sanders, Timothy, 231
Gregory, Pope, 181
grief, 74–75
Grigorieva, Irina, 145
grit, 12, 167–93
Grotto in an iceberg, Antarctica
    (Ponting), *62*
Gustafsson, Veikka, 173
Guston, Philip, 141

Haidt, Jonathan, 95, 221
Hammer, Langdon, 46
Hammonds, Robert, 108, 115
Handel, George Frideric, 53
Hartley, Martin, 67
Harvard, 8–9
Hayes, Terrance, 220
HBO, 27
heart lines, 23–24
"heart stoppers," 26
Hemingway, Ernest, 57
Henson, Jim, 130
heptathlon, 26
Herzog, Werner, 28–29, 196–97
High Line, 107–8, 115–16
Hinduism, 76
Hirsch, Edward, 220

Holdengräber, Paul, 196
Holroyd, Rachel, 232
Home Journal, 179
Homer, 119
Horst, Louis, 41–42, *41,* 54–55
House of Representatives, The (Morse),
    190, *191*
Howard, Ron, 95
"How to Become an Original Writer
    in Three Days" (Börne), 152
Hugo, 95
Huntington, Daniel, 189
Hyde, Lewis, 11
hygge, 111

Igbo, 187
Impossibility of straight lines (Taylor),
    18
improvisation, 50
Industrial Revolution, 238
In Memoriam (Tennyson), 68
innovation, 9, 11, 49, 155, 158–60,
    163, 183
Innovation Work Group, 30
In the Footsteps of Scott (Mear and
    Swan), 84
Ironman, 30–32
Isham, Samuel, 191–92
iVillage, 112

Jack and the Beanstalk (Taylor) 47
Jackie, 137
Jackson, Charles, 177, 181
Jacopo da Pontormo, 52–53
Jamison, Judith, 190
Jarrell, Randall, 81
jazz, 50
Jefferson, Thomas, 89, 221, 224–25
Jemison, Mae, 190
Jobs, Steve, 10, 56
Johnson, Nate, 160
Jones, Bill T., 37
Joyce, James, 119
Joyner-Kersee, Jackie, 26

Index

Index

Index